Sifted Like Wheat

DAN ROBINSON

ISBN 978-1-64468-857-1 (Paperback)
ISBN 978-1-64468-858-8 (Digital)

Covenant Books, Inc.
11661 Hwy 707
Murrells Inlet, SC 29576
www.covenantbooks.com

My heartbeat expressed by a nineteenth century composer:

"They want me to write differently. Certainly, I could, but I must not. God has chosen…and given me, of all people, this talent. It is to Him that I must give account. How then would I stand there before Almighty God, if I followed the others and not Him?"

Anton Bruckner

Contents

Profound Appreciation

*I fought this one for some time, yet God in His grace kept nudging
me personally, while getting directly in my face with the likes of:*

My precious wife, Bonnie, whose persistence and support is legendary.

*International Bible teacher and author, Mike Wells, along
with his wife Betty, for being encouraging voices and
tangible support where the rubber meets the road.*

*Dominic Migliozzi marked Bonnie and I out as Hook
Ministries long before our outreach was ever formalized.*

*Chaplain "Pat" Pattison, my adopted second
father and mentor in prison ministry.*

*Any number of inmates who poured into me as
much, or more, than I ever poured into them.*

*Sheldon Sorge, an upper classman during my time in Bible school
in the early seventies, who four decades later gave me the final kick
in the seat that got me off dead center to sit down and write this.*

*Tom Waller, a brother whose selfless input and understanding
have encouraged me in more ways than I could possibly count.*

Acknowledgements

I cannot recall ever hearing or reading a more moving work, outside of the Scriptures, which held me spellbound. I was gripped and held, as though amid the scenes presented in SIFTED. The "real world" language affords no room for one to escape the thrust of the message.

As I read, I was often in tears as I considered my selfish and wayward ways of misapplying the all-fulfilling gospel of God's love as lived out through our Lord Jesus Christ. His mercy, grace, wisdom and compassion hold me in awe and gratitude toward so great a Savior.

I challenge the reader to consider this work without being drawn closer into the arms and heart of Jesus. I found it to be "meaty" and difficult to lay down. I wish I had written this!

Chaplain Homer "Pat" Pattison

In a time where it seems that all we do is hurry to our next destination, never slowing down to take in the world around us, its truths and where we fit among them, it is refreshing to find a voice that takes us off the interstate. SIFTED LIKE WHEAT was an enjoyable trip on a winding, rural highway of faith that allowed for a deeper, clearer understanding of our fit and intended destination within God's Word.

This is Christian mentorship at its best.

John "Ski" Sledzinski

Dan, your vulnerability throughout has been very loud and very clear. Your book makes me think, so I read and read again. "Sifting is the outworking of Calvary's grace through faith." Amen. I wholeheartedly agree!

Rondale Lockley

Only bread "broken" by the Lord's hands is fit to be food that endures to eternal life. This reading will engage and comfort you intimately and deeply with the lives of Peter, John, the other apostles, and even Dan himself. But really, this is book about God! How He draws us close to Himself; how He molds us into the purpose He's had for us from before the foundations of the earth; how He aligns our wills with His. God's ways are uncanny, counterintuitive, unconventional, yet divine, eternal and higher than ours.

Dan gets real and raw with us concerning the lengths our heavenly Father is willing to go to liberate us from the delusions of the flesh, transforming us into children of God who are led and energized by His Spirit.

Monir Wood

I worked and worshiped with Danny Robinson during his trumpet-playing Bible School days. We bonded both as musicians and would-be disciples of Jesus. Then our pathways diverged. Forty years later God bumped us back into each other, and I was thrilled at the ministry God had given Dan. I discovered that one of the gifts that had emerged over those years was his capacity to write his God-given vision in such a compelling way that it rivets our attention no matter how busy we may be. (Think Habakkuk 2:2.) In SIFTED, Dan beautifully and oh, so vulnerably weaves his story with the biblical story of Peter, thereby inviting—no, compelling—us to lay open our own stories. Honestly. Hopefully. Redemptively. SIFTED dares us to trust that the great Story-maker who persisted with Peter and with Dan, can and will persist also with you and me. Soli Deo Gloria!

Rev. Dr. Sheldon W. Sorge
General Minister
Pittsburgh Presbytery
Presbyterian Church (U.S.A.)

Before We Launch Out

What I've written is extremely personal. Strange, though, it was another man's struggle, an inmate who failed badly on parole that got to me. His soul was trashed.

"You, my friend, need to be sifted like wheat." He didn't see me coming, so I give him a push. "You left prison, thinking like Peter." I smiled, remembering a ragged place my heart called home years earlier.

I wasn't smiling then. God knows my life was in shambles.

But what about Peter? What did a man on his way out of the state penitentiary share with a first-century apostle? And me, for that matter? What was my connection?

Good questions, and we haven't gotten to you yet.

There's common ground, a fertile landscape we as believers share. Call it passion, raw desire. What can I say? Jesus does things to hearts—men, ladies, little people. Kids were forever getting in His snuggle space. Can you blame them?

The Master has, and will continue to ignite fires that have never been lit.

In so doing, He exposes us, our weakness. Color that a good thing. I know this now. What I didn't know or even remotely comprehend was my own impotence. Talk about being in good company!

I've learned alongside Peter and others it's not enough to espouse convictions, to know you've been called and have wind in your sails, not when it's your own. But we're blind and deaf, not seeing or hearing the violent rush of our own wind devoid of real power and substance. Thank God for the love and inimitable grace in the cross that, at times, blindsides with crushing brutality for your good and mine. I say this knowing you might walk out on me. Please don't. As one who's been repeatedly schooled at Calvary's tree, I've come to appreciate God's style, if I can put it that way. His goal, I'm convinced, is to deliver the best and worst of us from doing life, from serving Him, out of our most proficient and determined efforts. It's got to go, friend, the lot of it lock, stock, and barrel.

This simple yet profound reality blindsided me. I in no way anticipated my story should find a place in what I was hoping would prove to be a strategic narrative, quite possibly an unexpected unwinding of one of discipleship's critical pieces.

What began as an honest look at twelve men's self-discovery in the presence of a Nazarene rabbi rapidly morphed into an inter-weaving of situations, people, and a haul of seeming mishaps. The ensuing account is a sincere invitation to track with me into what, at times, may seem disjointed but isn't.

A unified whole is presented by way of Peter and company knit together with my own fallout reconfigured alongside bits and pieces gleaned from brothers doing time in prison.

The common thread in all this is Scripture, a biblical context scanning Old with the New, zooming specifically in on those who got next to Jesus while having their respective worlds upended.

"My ways aren't yours" never proved truer than with the Master.[1]

My heart then is to see these folks as part of an inclusive portrait with the likes of you, me, and a few others interwoven as a telling composite.

The writer of Hebrews pulls it together: Their stories aren't complete without ours.[2] As such, there's room to come with hearts and minds wide open. I've had to.

Calvary remains our magnetic north and integrating point, a place of death to one life and birth to an altogether new one—eternal life that works out as Christ in us.[3] Trust me, this isn't for spectators. Jesus calls us to negotiate a mine field, the safest place in the world when to live is Christ and death is gain.[4]

You'll note the word "radical" comes into play quite frequently, considering the timeless impact of the cross. The word itself meaning "at root," touches heaven's intrinsic heartbeat, the root of all God ever intended for you and me. The root Adam rejected.

So, for a hostile, fallen world to see Jesus as offensive only confirms that they—and at one time we—are grown from an altogether different root. The difference is truly radical! And it means? It means there will be times Jesus throws us radically off balance.

It begs repetition.

The pastoral role I enjoy with so many of our incarcerated brothers hits where the rubber meets the road, and I pray we make a connection with those of you who walk through the next number of pages with us. My approach has been to make the message accessible in bite-size pieces, short chapters with references and descriptive endnotes to document my work. If that seems to fit, I'm hoping you'll zoom in and pan wide with me. Make it personal. Enter in, will you?

Judas, one of the twelve, appeared with a great crowd armed with swords and staves,[1] sent by the chief priests and Jewish elders.

—Matthew 26:47, J. B. Phillips N. T.

At this, Simon Peter, who had a sword, drew it and slashed at the high priest's servant, cutting off his right ear. The servant's name was Malchus.

—John 18:10, J. B. Phillips N. T.

All this time Peter was sitting outside in the courtyard, and a maidservant came up to him and said, "Weren't you too with Jesus, the man from Galilee?" But he denied it before them all, saying, "I don't know what you're talking about." Then when he had gone out into the porch, another maid caught sight of him and said to those who were there, "This man was with Jesus of Nazareth." And again he denied it with an oath—"I don't know the man!" A few minutes later those who were standing about came up to Peter and said to him, "You certainly are one of them, it's obvious from your accent." At that time he began to curse and swear—"I tell you I don't know the man!" Immediately the cock crew, and the words of Jesus came back into Peter's mind—"Before the cock crows you will disown me three times." And he went outside and wept bitterly.

—Matthew 26:69–75, J. B. Phillips N. T.

Peter Was As Unlikely As They Come

If you were asked to lay odds as to which of the twelve Jesus would have chosen to spearhead a toddling church, who would you put your money on? Good question, one the boys tried hammering out among themselves, remember? Over dinner—the last Passover Seder Jesus's disciples shared with the Master—things got a little heated over who carries the real weight in their ranks.[2] Thank God names aren't rehashed or the tense volley of words! Three years and some change invested with Him, and they still don't get it, but we can't throw stones, can we? It spells hope for the likes of us because this wasn't their first go-around.[3]

No wonder Jesus steps in to set the record straight with the whole servant-leader paradigm.[4] Keep in mind, though, He does have a batting order, so again, who would your pick be? My knee-jerk response is John, the disciple Jesus loved.[5] Not that the Master didn't care deeply for the others, but there was a special, if not unique, closeness John experienced firsthand, an intimacy he enjoyed that really touches my heart.

Peter was different. He was a slippery fish—impulsive, not the careful, calculating type given to weighing pros and cons before making his move. Chess definitely wasn't his game. No, baseball was more Pete's style. Swing often; swing hard even if it means striking out. I'm thinking Babe Ruth right now. The Babe struck out more than twice his home run average, but when he connected, the ball went flying! That's Peter. Being first off the line is the impulse of his heart. Jesus affected him that way.

But didn't Peter deny knowing Jesus? Sure he did, but let's get the cart and the horse in the right order. We've first got to ask, "What's really going on here?" Is this some lopsided caricature, an elephant panicking at the sight of a puny mouse? I don't think so. What about Gethsemane where Judas shows up with a makeshift posse armed to the hilt with clubs and swords?[6] Peter's reflexes kick in, and he's ready to take on the whole lot of them. If anyone's going to make a grab for Jesus, they'll have to go through him!

By the time we get to the high priest's courtyard, a veritable lifetime has played out for Peter and company, so think with me, will you? Being with Jesus the last several years has redefined everything for one simple fisherman. *Radical* is the word. For the first time in his sweaty, blue-collar existence, Peter has value. Jesus is life to him, his identity and magnetic north. Jesus connects the dots. The Son of Man spoke and acted like no one else, demonstrating the kind of authority that made the powers of hell quake in their boots! Now they're leading Him off like a common criminal. What do you do with that?

There's no safety net, or so it seems, and your hopes, forget it. They've crashed in flames, but why? Again, it's Jesus, One you've placed the sum of hopeful expectations in; now He's gone. What can I say? A fisherman has lost his anchor and compass. Meaning? Any sense of stability much less direction or purpose is ancient history.

We Forget, Don't We?

Or it could be we never caught the left hook followed by a lethal overhand right that dropped Peter for the count? All right, so maybe boxing isn't your cup of tea, but tell me, do you know what it's like to take a hit you didn't see coming, to be so thoroughly dazed and confused you're not sure where you're at or who you are? Do you know the feeling? I do, and that's him. That's our man. That's Peter in the high priest's courtyard!

How many circuits are tripped when you get blindsided on the highway? The car rolls, and your next point of contact is with the ER physician who tells you your daughter, your precious grins and giggles sitting next to you in the passenger's seat, was...no, she couldn't be DOA! It's her birthday, and the anticipation of sharing special time together left the two of you in giddy hysterics. Now this. *This!* Nothing, absolutely nothing exists but a heart that screams in aching, bottomless torment. That's you for sure, and it's Peter in spades.

Rivers of sweat sting swollen eyes as our chaotic friend struggles in vain to warm thick, calloused hands amid piercing glares of doubtful outsiders. You know the type—morbid curiosity seekers, a would-be lynch mob. "Who are these people," he panics. "What do they want with me?" Peter flails. "What's the matter with you? I don't know the man!" Self-preservation. And against a backdrop of nameless faces, pointing fingers, and unintelligible murmurs, tension mounts like a cresting wave as a nearby rooster crows, and Peter hits rewind.

Luke tells us, "The Lord turned and looked at Peter."[7] Just when our impetuous brother thought he couldn't get any lower and Murphy's Law had seemingly done its worst, Peter finds himself cut deep in places he didn't know existed. "You're going to deny Me three times" severs that soul and spirit, joints and marrow connection as one journeyman angler realizes he can't tread water. Not now.[8] The thoughts and intentions of his heart have been laid bare releasing a wellspring of bitter tears as Peter looks back and remembers. He remembers a lot.

Jesus Changes Everything

Time stands still the day Andrew chases his big brother down. Stubborn insistence, as "We've found the Messiah!"[1] segues to a private place where permanent boundaries are marked off in one Jewish fisherman's heart while doing a serious number on his head. "You shall be called the Rock."[2] It's not in Peter, and he knows it. This is one of those God moments where He speaks what has never been and makes it so. It's not in Peter; it's in Jesus. His presence in this insignificant nobody's life changes him for good and forever.

Along with others numbered among the select elect Jesus apprenticed, Peter was accustomed to setting his alarm with a view toward mapping out the day according to his own scheme of things. The boys were pretty self-reliant where doing life was concerned. Jesus changes that. His presence at the helm kept them off balance, if you hear what I'm saying. They never know what's next. When this unlikely lot clears the cobwebs over their morning cup of Joe,[3] the question, if only to themselves, is "I wonder what Jesus is doing today?"

He reframed their personal borders and set the pace. Think of it as direction and dependence.

> The twelve got used to their lives being ordered, not regimented the way it is in prison with controlled movements and regulated inmate count. He in no way resembled the tyrannical feel of Rome's iron foot or the condescending

glare of the religious elite who fancied the rank and file as lower than dirt. With Jesus, it's different. He didn't need a heavy hand, not when you're right. Jesus was always right, and His disciples…they knew it. They saw. They sampled His rightness firsthand. The Master's words came with genuine humility and no-holds-barred authority. Everything He did had substance, nothing forced. He was the Master of each and every moment. Those who followed Jesus looked to Him as the place where the pieces fit and life came together; though, He often left them scratching their heads.

As it was with our man Peter, there's much to learn in lives where Jesus radically changes everything, a truckload of discoveries concerning Him and us. Think about it. What does it mean to be taken in by love that stands in stark contrast to this world's meager offerings? Love as it comes to us in Jesus is totally other than anything, or anyone, we've ever known or imagined. It's no wonder John was blown away in dumbfounded amazement. "What kind of love is this that claims the likes of us as one of God's own kids?"[4]

The Call to Follow

Now as Jesus was walking by the Sea of Galilee, He saw two brothers, Simon who was called Peter, and Andrew his brother, casting a net into the sea; for they were fishermen. And He said to them, "Follow Me, and I will make you fishers of men." Immediately they left their nets and followed Him.[5]

It's yesterday, right? The call was real and specific. "Why me?" or "Where are we going?" aren't questions you ask when your heart is the target, not at first. Peter had been chosen, and he knew it even if he didn't know the rationale driving it. So, what's the big deal? Lots of young men in the world of that era were invited to participate in some form of hands on apprenticeship. Not by Jesus. His call was unique as He was unique.

Who knew unless you were marked as a target or one of a privileged minority with an inside track to the camel-haired Baptist who identifies an obscure Nazarene carpenter as one whose shoes he couldn't stoop to untie, "the Lamb of God, which taketh away the sin of the world?"[6] The Baptist singles Jesus out in a way that trips a switch in two of his own followers who make a beeline to connect with Him. The story is short yet intriguing. The Master stops and turns with a pointed question: "What do you seek?"

Not *who* but *what*. What are you looking for? For years, I blew past this gem, one I saw as little more than congenial small talk, an icebreaker to get John's apprentices talking. Boy, was I wrong! This was Jesus cutting to the chase and going straight for the jugular. We're talking culture, first century in the near Middle East, where the boys' distinctive responses give the game away: "Teacher, where are you staying?"

I went belly up not having so much as a clue as to what were these two were asking. I heard one pastor liken this to going brain dead in the presence of a celebrity. Years ago, my wife, Bonnie, and I were enjoying a quiet evening in a small supper club where jazz great Dizzy Gillespie was playing. Wouldn't you know he came by our table as a cordial gesture. I went blank. He's a trumpet player, and I played too. God knows the questions I might have asked the man, but no. I zoned and got stupid. The pastor I speak of suggested John's disciples did the same—tripping over themselves with, "So uh...where do you live, teacher?"

Not even close. Unlike contemporary Bible school or seminary students, these disciples wouldn't think of checking Jesus on His theology, zooming in on a statement of faith or denominational alliance. Not a chance! They want to get next to Him, observe the Rabbi in action. "Where are you staying?" means, "Can we hang out with you,

Jesus?" That's where the meat is. Who knows? He might invest in them the way John had.

My point is, Jesus doesn't have a doctrinal position as you and I see such things. He *is* His doctrine, a living statement tried in life's burning crucible. Everything about our Lord proves the efficacy of the Father's presence as it continually pours in, through, and as Him. "If you've seen Me," Jesus assures, "you've seen the Father."[7]

Bottom line? The boys want a taste, something substantive they could sink their teeth into, not a sound bite or bullet points, much less lofty Talmudic musings.[8] Think hungry and teachable. What a lead-in to where Jesus was headed, and Mark's gospel nails it cold! Further on up the road we'll take an even closer look at the way this Nazarene Rabbi pinpoints those He'd chosen that they might be "with Him."[9] I love it, the nearness of Jesus—genuine intimacy. Nothing He would ever say or do had any context outside of the immediacy of His presence. Now fast-forward three years as He trips them up with, "I'm going away, and you can't come with Me."[10] Guess who feels stranded?

That's a good thing. If our Lord accomplished anything with this bunch, it's the personal investment of Himself in the hearts and minds of men who now realize that above all things, they need Jesus. They do, and they want Him. He invaded their space, their world, everything His disciples had ever known or done, and drew them to Himself, into His space, His world. Life as they knew it went up in smoke, and Jesus became life to them! "Come to Me," He says.[11] "I am the way, the truth and the life."[12] Crazy, isn't it? Complete and total madness, but it works. It's the only thing that does. No wonder Peter comes unglued. Arresting Jesus means He's gone.

For years, I poured myself into the pursuit of believing right, as though sound doctrine, in and of itself, was the end-all for truly committed believers. Believe right to do right. Simple? Not really. Dogma based on the so-called "clear teaching of Scripture"[13] draws hard lines in the sand, and on either side, everyday folks and champions alike fall prey to trials and garden variety pitfalls affirming with one voice, "We need Jesus! We need Him here!"

Now before anyone writes me off as edging toward heresy, let me explain. I'm not promoting ignorance, and there's certainly no space, much less justification, for a doctrinal free-for-all. There's plenty of room for Jesus, though—knowing Christ as Savior, Lord, and Life itself.

The song and popular worship chorus, "In Christ Alone," rings true. Our hope as believers is the person of Christ, who Himself, is the dynamic energy and vital substance of this thing we call Christianity. Why? The long and short of it is He, alone, is capable of living such a humanly impossible life. God doesn't dispense light, strength or song, much less love and peace as disposable commodities. Jesus Himself has become to us all we will ever need, everything, as Peter says, "pertaining to life and godliness."[14]

This, friends, is where Jesus is taking His boys. Their falling out and falling away were absolutely necessary to realizing His desired end. We'll talk more on that later. Right now, it's important for you and me to see a group of very real and honestly sincere men whose lives had begun to come together in Jesus, falling apart at the seams without Him and His abiding presence to hold them together. Memories fade to gray at the thought of flying solo as they had done before He stepped into the picture. If anything is sharpening in lost and confused cross hairs, it's the stark realization that life apart from Jesus is a complete wash. Amen, it truly is.

More in the Rearview Mirror

Our friendly fishmonger groans as he docks his craft after a long and lonely night on the water. Peter and his crew got skunked. That's right, they came up empty. And in their business, no fish means no paycheck. It's a sad and sorry tale, but there *is* one consolation. If you can't catch fish, then unplug, call it a day, and catch a few z's.[1] Makes perfect sense to me. The thought of his bed is sounding *so* good, and in one fisherman's longing mind, he's all but laid his weary head down for some well-earned shut-eye. Amen, I'm with him.

Then what's this? No, it can't be Jesus! Of all people, He shows up and parks His backside in Peter's boat. "Hey, I've got an idea," the Master shoots with a knowing smile. "How about we do some fishing today?" Do some fishing, as in launch the boat and *go back out there*? The man's nuts! He's crazy! "We've been on the water all night, Lord," Peter sighs. "It was a complete bust, and I'm so beat I can barely see straight, but if that's what You want [the emphasis being *You*], we'll do it." And you know the story.

The ride out to the fishing grounds was a quiet one marked by rhythmic lapping of water on the boat's sun-bleached hull with Jonah's number one son[2] mumbling under his breath. He wasn't alone. Souls shift gears in light of the previous night's exhausting debacle as muscles tense in the cool morning breeze, pushing tired minds and aching bodies further and further from the solace of a little rest and relaxation. The guys, they were trashed, but their bone-tired hearts said yes to Jesus for one reason. It was Jesus. Had anyone else tried pushing Peter's buttons, I promise you, this wouldn't be happening.

What can I say? Jesus got in on this bunch like nothing and no one. Look at them. Who in their right mind would have called this sorry lot together? Talk about a mixed bag, yet here they were, a zealot alongside a dirt bag tax collector serving with a handful of common fishermen—but that's God, His kingdom—and it's sheer genius! It's the wolf with the lamb, a leopard napping next to a young baby goat, the calf and a lion with a child leading them![3] It goes against the grain, yes, but Jesus's game plan works. It works great!

Hold on the Fish Story a Moment, Will You?

We'll get back to it, I promise, but this is the perfect place to break in.

Distanced by thousands of years, you and I open our Bibles to read, study, discuss, and even memorize, but do we smell? You heard me, and I'm not trying to be cute. What about the poor demonized slob from Gadara? Did he bathe before Jesus shows up?[4] Our time in Scripture is distanced from people and circumstances we read about for one simple reason: We're not physically present to them. Who cringes at a scaly leper or pulls back in disgust from a passing Samaritan or Roman official these days? Don't know any?

The question stands, then, who *are* we present to? The Book, among other things, points us to the stuff of life right under our noses, figuratively, yes, and sometimes literally. All right, so maybe lepers are at a premium. Got any homeless people? How about ex-cons or sex offenders? Growing up with America's civil rights movement on my doorstep, I'd hear neighbors talk about blacks, how strange they looked, their hair and skin color. The big one was how black folks "smelled." Like whites don't stink? I had had a lot to learn.

Stench is about attitude, and with it comes revelation, if we're listening. Our Lord brings it home in ways we'd never imagine. I'm thinking of men I've met over the years who were baptized in the vinegar of hardcore bigotry, some of it "Klan."[5] Racism to the nth degree,[6] so check out the dude who signs on as a white supremacist gangbanger proving he's someone to reckon with. And that means

29

what? In prison, it means putting a lock on your ground. That's your turf! It is until love Himself invades your space. Like I said, Jesus has a way of getting in on folks.

What happens, then, when our kind, compassionate Savior gets next to the man by way of a new cellie,[7] a black one? It happens. And anyone, I mean anyone, who's truly been close to racial prejudice where the roots go deep understands smell, real or imagined. Some call this God's sense of humor. I don't. I call it love, the all-out radical kind that breaks through and trashes hateful, scandalous identities and toxic comfort zones.

Am I talking to someone? This isn't just race; it's a mixed bag of attitudes and convictions you and I hold when we look in the mirror or at the world around us. I'm talking people and circumstances. And whether we've done time or not, what we see and how it makes us feel may, in fact, be the layout of your prison and mine. You heard me. Long before a judge's gavel sounds or sentences are doled out, souls are imprisoned.

Think inheritance, Adam's birthright to you and to me—to every man, every woman, each and every little person—looms the price tag of independence. Adam's choice. And where many see the tree of the knowledge of good and evil as symbolic myth, God says no. It's the critical point of choice over against the tree of life: Trust God and live. Don't and you're on your own. Color that prison, the real kind.[8] And we've called it reality.

Ouch! But if the shoe fits, oh well. Welcome to the mold unbelief squeezes us into. Don't believe God; don't trust Him. Believe what then? A lie. A lie becomes your prison and mine, a lie masquerading as truth. Why not? It seems legit enough. It fits albeit we may feel trapped, suffocated as the world around us affirms its rightness. Love it or hate it, it's got our names on it. How well I remember.

Keeping It Real

I was a puny kid, short and small framed. I hated it. Genetics, right? It is what it is, and size for me played out as a cruel penalty, a handicap at best. I was a midget in a land of giants. I'm talking physically, mentally, emotionally—you name it. I felt like a midget, thought like a midget, and acted like one. There was no escape, no hiding place, no rest whatsoever. I was put on display so everyone could see. That's how it felt.

The worst, it seemed, was physical, sports especially but not exclusively. Where other kids got jazzed at the idea of playing ball, my soul locked down in frantic trepidation, but what do you do when there's nowhere to run? You're in a fishbowl. Funny, it's what they call prison. Everyone sees, everyone knows. Everyone.

All right, so Dad grew up on a nickel-and-dime chicken farm in hicksville West Virginia. What did he know about baseball or football? I often wondered how he'd stack up in a "My dad could beat up your dad" showdown. Not that I ever held that against him. He tried. Dad taught me to draw when other kids were in their backyards learning to swing a bat, play catch, and throw spirals. This was a landscape I had no compass or bearings for, no way to negotiate the path before me. I didn't fit. See it as emotions driven by twisted imaginations.

Prison is a world where heavy-handed feelings and imaginations rule even if you believe you're past such nonsense. You don't feel anything, numb in a netherworld of nothingness. A zero.

It got bad in grade school. Junior high was worse, gym class especially, and recess when everything moved outside. Play ball, guys! Here's where recognized captains squared off to pick up teams. We knew who they were, everyone did—the jocks. Back and forth snatching up heavy hitters and strong runners, guys with arms for throwing and hands for catching—the naturals. After them, the decent and the so-so players, then me. "Hey, you guys get Dan!"

"Aw, not again. We had him last time. Why don't you take him?" Do you feel it? I can't say as I blamed them. I wouldn't want me either.

The batting order never had me at the top. I prayed for lots of action to delay the inevitable, anything to keep me out of play, but the process of elimination claims its losers, and my time at bat always came around. Standing over the plate with a "Louisville Slugger" poised over my shoulder felt wrong and had to look wrong. Watch now as the outfield moves to the infield clapping hands while chanting, "Okay, easy out. Easy out. Let's get this over with!" I understood why. Boy did I ever.

What can I say? I never intentionally struck out. And every once in a while, I'd actually get a piece of the ball, a low pop up the shortstop nailed or a bobbled line drive that was easily scooped up and fired off to the first baseman. Heart pounding, I breathed as tension let up for a moment and a world that had little or no place for a midget continued to turn. Invariably, though, I'd hear it, the epithet that made me a terminally marked man. "Wow, you really stink!" That's me, gang, one of the charges leading to my life sentence.

Back to the Fishing Grounds

Lowering damp drift nets into seemingly lifeless waters adds insult to injury. A joke, right? A bad one at that, rubbing salt— coarse ground—in freshly reopened wounds. The boys go through blind, half-hearted motions, but why do it? For the same reason they launched after last night's bust. Face it. Over against every deter- mined human effort stands Jesus—what He thinks, what He wants, what only He can do. Guess what that means?

If being with Jesus has proven anything, it's that He carries seri- ous weight, the kind they've never seen. His disciples are learning faith, gut-level, feel it or not, one baby step at a time.

"Pull in the nets, guys! Make it quick!" Peter blinks, and you talk about fish? Nets bulging with outsized hauls split under prodi- gious weight. The crew panics, calling out to their boys across the way, "Over here, over here! Hurry!" Every second counts. These guys are seasoned journeymen who've done this in their sleep it seems, but this, *this* is different. They pull together, and before our boys know it, they're over capacity. So many fish in strained hulls has both boats sinking! Think above and beyond, far above and beyond.[1]

Getting back to unload the day's catch is all they can do as a few dots connect for Peter. He sees Jesus; then, he sees himself. It's Isaiah in the presence of God's glory recast.[2] Forget the fish. Forget every- thing. This just got a whole lot bigger than anything this poor man had ever seen or touched. "Keep away from me, Lord. I'm a mess!"[3] Do you see it? Really? Jesus nails His mark. Simon, along with his fishing buddies, has been ambushed by grace! It isn't about Peter, and

33

it isn't about Andrew, James, or John. It's about Jesus, who He is and what He's doing, His call and claim on them—on all they are and ever will be.

> From now on you're going for a different
> catch, boys. You'll be catching men.[4]

And when our friends finally dock, they've got new eyes, not twenty-twenty mind you, but Peter and Zebedee's thunderous sons see exactly what they need to see. Nothing is forced, nothing contrived. No doubt there's a lot this unlikely and often wobbly crew doesn't connect with yet, but everything's as it should be. All they ever knew as life is behind them now. They're following Jesus,[5] and He's their focal point. Jesus is their vision.

Closeness to Jesus

Peter gets pumped; he says and does things. He's a knee-jerk kind of guy. More than once, fragile disciples find themselves in over their heads. Heaven planned it that way. More than once, it involves a boat, lots of water, and a chaotic storm. But Jesus isn't in the boat, not this time.[6] Battering winds and brutal swells all but capsize their crude, utilitarian rig. It's enough to make rugged seamen panic. They do.

Hard driving rain and squinted eyes make for poor visibility, and addled fishermen see…is that something or someone? "It looks like a man, guys. He's walking on top of the water!" That'll drop your teeth, and Jesus's quaking apprentices are convinced it's a ghost—not that disembodied spirits make sense to them—but when a man heel-and-toes it where no one does because they can't, then it's a ghost. It has to be.

Now, hit pause and work through this with me.

What if Jesus *is* present amid the fury of such brutality? (I'm remembering a certain Babylonian furnace at the moment.[7]) Here's where Peter goes for the jugular. "Lord, if it's really You, then tell me to come out to You!" And with no backup, no life vest, the man takes the plunge. And then? Peter walks too! What do you do with that? Don't even try to overspiritualize the moment because it won't hold up. This is real wind here—real wind, real water, real everything—real Peter, and a real Jesus.

Okay, so Pete goes down. What can I say, he messed up? Our friend let gale force winds get to him, not to mention spray from blistering swells and thick, matted hair in his face. Fear put a choke hold on his heart. But guess what? Jesus was there! He pulled our man out of the drink, and Peter didn't drown.

What gives? All right, so one man steps out while the rest play it safe. We know the story. But did you ever stop to consider an overriding possibility, that for one reckless moment wind and water didn't matter to Peter? Crazy, I know. Who downplays potentially life-threatening conditions? True enough, but maybe there's a better, a more pertinent question. What's Jesus doing out there in the first place? Is it to display His primal authority over the elements?[8] Could be, but not in toto.[9] Not by a long shot.

Asking "What kind of man is this?"[10] points us to the "more than" aspect of our Lord. God knows we need it. And in a world where Jesus is reduced to honorable teacher, a moral guru, He assures those who have eyes to see His surreal otherness. This One, who though being fully human, is like no other. Yet there's more. A sometimes-sordid lot is confronted head on with the nearness of Jesus. Period. Their spiritual formation—and ours—is shaped by more than academics. It's vine life, an understanding that begins in places like these.[11]

Bottom line? The nearness of Jesus changes everything. He didn't let Peter sink, did He? And the others? They were deeply and profoundly affected, us too, I hope. The "O thou of little faith"—the line Jesus hit Peter with—was not to condemn but to probe.[12] Peter, for a moment, was oblivious to wind and water. Why? He saw Jesus, only Jesus. Then what? Faith shifts gears where conditions, at times people, take center stage.

Don't I know it? Truth is, I never realized
how self-reliant my faith was. Faith in what?

Faith in whom? When love and acceptance are performance-driven, it's me trusting my efforts to please Jesus, and that's scary. God knows I refused to admit such anxiety-ridden nonsense to anyone—myself included—but that, friends, is where the rubber meets the road, and I had to be broken. It could be why I can relate to these guys. Peter's denial of Jesus came when he felt trapped with no way out. Mine was no way out of, "Wow, you really stink!"

Either way, it's performance gone sour. I'm a hopeless victim, and why? Self-pity. Not measuring up to my, or someone else's, doubtful expectations. It all comes back to choices, which means the lot of us are on the hook. Everyone.

Peter fits here; he loved Jesus. I understand. The Master owned Peter's heart like nothing and no one. Again, I understand. Growing up in a home where acceptance was iffy at best, my first taste of Jesus—His unconditional love—blew me away. My heart was His. For Peter to insist he'd be there when everyone bailed was real for him, but it was Peter and only Peter—Peter's fire and determination.[13] Sorry, my friend, but that isn't enough.

Who knew? Not Peter, certainly not me. When the bottom drops out in the high priest's courtyard, or quitting my freshman year in college, what's left but an emotional free fall? The cock crows, and the total investment of a man's heart vaporizes, and like one devastated fisherman, I feel trapped, imprisoned by runaway thoughts and feelings. The real deal? Pride masquerading as bottomless inferiority. Yet I can't shake the sense that my connection with Jesus is bigger than me, bigger than my best and most determined efforts. I don't know why.

More to Remember

"Who do folks say that I am?"

Now there's a question, and it's an easy, if not entertaining, one. Jesus has a way of stirring imaginations that activate rumor mills and get people talking. They talk a lot. Opinions as to who He might possibly be are legion. "Some say you're the Baptist." "Yeah, well the crowd on the lower east side are convinced you've got to be Elijah." "You hear Elijah, I hear Jeremiah, and Bartholomew says pick a prophet, any prophet. Levi's been hit with so many names he's lost count." And on it goes.

Popular opinion being what it is, Jesus is this, that, or the other deceased somebody who's returned from the grave to make a splash for God, and boy has He ever! Hit pause, and you could hear a pin drop as Jesus opens this slippery can of worms: "And who do *you* say that I am?"

I wasn't there (obviously), so this is 100 percent conjecture on my part. Imagine, if you will, the deafening silence right about now. Taking the chill off dank night air around a yawning fire, men tentatively shuffle back and forth eyeballing each another. Who's going to step out? No one wants to get the pop quiz question wrong. A select band of hungry, yet undeniably green, apprentices find themselves riding the crest of the biggest wave they, or anyone, had ever seen much less heard of. The question stands: *Who is Jesus really?* "You are the Christ," Peter ventures. "The Son of the living God."[1] The hope and expectation of all things Jewish.

Abraham's promised seed and God's pledge to every nation[2] invaded their darkness giving form and substance to the "I Am" of eternity as witnessed in the Law and the prophets.[3] He's right here, guys. Emmanuel, at this moment, is pouring Himself into to a crude bunch of misfits. Yeshua Ha'Mashiach.[4] You'd have to be Jewish to appreciate the impact of the moment. They were. Seeing what these boys had seen, hearing what they'd heard, hones a fine edge to renewed anticipations of what all too often felt like moth-eaten promises.[5] Now here they are, and there He is as time and eternity are permanently bridged.

We get jaded. Many who count themselves members of Christ's body recite verbatim, "I believe in God the Father Almighty, Creator of heaven and earth. I believe in Jesus Christ, His only Son, our Lord,"[6] etc., but what does it mean? What did it mean for those whose dreams and suspicions were confirmed that day? How do you wrap your brain around the fact that you've had a face-to-face encounter with the living God, something Moses and others desired but never got close to? You don't, not at first. You can't possibly. Your heart takes the first hit, and your brain catches up later, sort of.

I go back to Mark Lowry's "Mary Did You Know?"[7] the staggering observations and questions he raises! "Did Mary consider that kissing her precious newborn meant kissing the face of God?" What awestruck wonder and amazement, yet this precious bundle looks like a baby. That's because He is. He's a real baby, a baby boy, but the little guy is so much more. "Do you get it, Mary? Nestled in your arms is the unbeginning God of eternity, the great I Am?" I'm not surprised. I'm not in the least amazed that unbelief rages, "Blasphemy! Crucify him!" while the teachable stand in awe as heaven opens hearts to what they could never know—beginning with Peter.

"Flesh and Blood Has Not Revealed This to You."

That's the blessing, Simon Bar-jona. No man pointed this out, and in no way did your own cognitive processes lead you to such a startling conclusion.[8] No way it can happen! The world as it is cannot and will not come to know God by way of its carnal wisdom and insight.[9] No one fully and intimately knows the Son except the Father, and vice versa.[10] The bottom line? Apart from divine epiphany, us human folk will find ourselves out of the loop entirely, totally clueless. Imagine the wonder in Peter's heart when he knew that he knew.

There's This Thing Called Context

Something in Jesus touches Andrew, so much so he makes a beeline to his brother.

Simon Peter wasn't one of the Baptist's trainees. Fishing's his game, and he was good at it. Andrew gave his sibling a leg up with Peter's trade, but God and His kingdom clearly have first dibs. The raggedy camel-haired prophet and the repentance he preached resonates in deep, previously untilled soil.

It certainly wasn't the cuisine.[1]

But look at John. There's something to be said for a man who abandons this world's offerings to satisfy a deeper hunger, and it's evident he's sated. It draws hungry people in. No wonder Andrew chases hard after Jesus, then Peter.[2] His appetite's whet, and there's more of what captivates him to go around, a lot more.

Then for baby brother to come at Peter with such passionate certainty ("We found the Christ!") tells us his all-too-brief encounter with heaven's Lamb was truly infectious. I'm intrigued, though, that one man sees early on what so many others don't much later. He's only just met Jesus. The words are there, yes, but Andrew's mind, does it grasp so much as a fraction of what stirs his pounding heart? It'll come, just not yet. The road to, "Who do you say that I am?" is fraught with convoluted twists and turns.

Color This Life

We're talking people and circumstances, the dynamic crucible that shapes these folks—how they see themselves and the world around them. Think of it as the place where the boundaries of their unique prisons are framed. And before you write me off as an extremist with some twisted jailhouse motif, I'd like to direct you to a little common ground we share as those born into Adam's fallen race, his prison and ours.

"Through one man," Scripture tells us, this thing called sin entered our cosmos, "and death through sin, and so death spread to all men, because all sinned."[3] One transgression spells death and condemnation for everyone. Guess what that means? In Adam, we see ourselves, every man and every woman. His undoing is ours![4] That's bondage, folks. It's prison, a perverse mold that squeezes you and squeezes me to conform to the lost and fallen world that birthed us. When Jesus declares Himself as One anointed by God Yahweh:

> To bring good news to the afflicted;
> He has sent me to bind up the brokenhearted,
> To proclaim liberty to captives
> And freedom to prisoners;
> To proclaim the favorable year of the LORD[5]

He touches a commonality you and I share with the transcendent hope only grace affords.

Grace comes to us as a person, not a thing. He Himself is the one key capable of unlocking our cells and opening the gate to a supernatural new birth and radical new identity. We're talking Jesus, right? It's in Him or it's nowhere, and *radical* is the word. We don't know how radical until He exposes the empty facade we've built on, a veritable sham. Even our best is likened to filthy menstrual rags,[6] but we haven't seen it. No surprise, it's all you and I have known, yet the lot of it has to go—the cup Jesus drains to its bitter dregs.

There's no other way.

God knows I didn't have a clue. My prison was a given, my sentenced fixed. "Oh well," I assumed. "That's me, and there's no way out." I'm in good company; I realize this. But what about the favored elite, the popular and privileged I so bitterly envied? The naturals. Why couldn't I be strong and attractive, witty, intelligent, a personality-plus type who qualifies without trying as inner-circle material? That's a prison I'd gladly live with, or so I thought. Yet how could I have known that my context, my unique prison was the best, the most ideal construct for Jesus to show and express Himself where I was concerned? I couldn't, could I? Neither can you.

More of My Prison's Architecture

I grew up in a church-going family.

Not believers, mind you, we were programmed. The Robinsons attended Sunday school and church services religiously—Dad the dutiful preacher's kid he was raised to be and Mom, she didn't know anything else. Decent people go to church. Period. And in the black and white "Father Knows Best" suburban fifties and sixties I called home, my siblings and I went because we had to. There was no joy; it was obligation.

Our church was as dead as they come, but people knew when to nod, when to smile and say, "Good sermon, Reverend," shaking the minister's hand while filing out the door like Stepford robots.[7] It all seemed phony, so incredibly empty, especially for Dr. Howe, our senior pastor who didn't believe the Bible and blatantly said so. My folks thought they did, but Mom and Dad unwittingly gave the game away after my alleged confirmation, a rite of passage for a twelve-year-old who reached the infamous "age of accountability."

"Now it all begins," Mom asserts
with unusual solemnity.

Now what begins? Whatever "it" was couldn't be good, and it wasn't. "Starting now," she decreed, "God is going to keep a detailed record of your sins. At the end of your life when you stand before Him, He'll weigh the bad you've done against the good to determine whether you go to heaven or hell." My heart sank. I couldn't put my finger on the why of a very immediate and deeply intuitive awareness that was crystal clear to my naïve, young heart. If the weight of my eternal destiny rests on my shoulders, I'm in serious trouble!

I nailed my father in search of a different spin on things, something my youthful soul could lay hold of that had some semblance of hope attached to it, but no. Mom and Dad read from the same script leaving me in limbo, so why even try? Why shoot for what I was incapable of? It's like I said earlier, I felt like a pint-sized midget in a land of monolithic giants who were more capable than I ever would be.

Send in the clowns, gang,[8] and enter the dark ages, a truly sorrowful season where more than anything I craved acceptance with little to no performance qualifiers. God knows I wouldn't find it at home. It didn't exist there. Dad—I'm not sure who he was at this point in either my life or his—faded to obscure translucence in a world where Mom called the shots in no uncertain terms. I was hopelessly lost and knew it, yet I wondered about heaven. Would it be possible for me to spend eternity as a three-year-old, to never grow up?

Crazy, isn't it? But three seemed safe. Three is a place where rejection and pain are denied admittance on any count. Three means Mom won't read me the riot act for skinning my knee, much less acting out. Three works. Three means I'm not scratch-and-dent sale material, at least I hoped. At three, I felt wanted.

Feeling wanted. At six, my mom faked calling the cops for God knows what I'd done. I remember what she said, though, and the hard as nails tone in her voice. "Police, I have a bad little boy who won't listen to me. I need you to come pick him up." All right, so the whole thing was bogus, a cheap shot aimed at getting me to straighten up and fly right, but to a fragile six-year-old heart, it screams, "You, son, are dirt!" Forget walking on eggshells or even trying to get your act together. Life is set in concrete, and you know it.

Please hear me out, will you, and listen carefully. The whacked-out picture I've just painted can't be seen, much less processed, through eyes where common sense rules with reasoned logic. A six-year-old walked this path. A six-year-old went to prison. To him, it's real. This is life, the raw essence of his formative personhood, and apart from grace that chooses to embrace a little guy's pain by making it His own,[9] he's kicked to the curb over and over. A boy's heart has been trashed, making him an easily disposed commodity while clearing the decks for, "Wow, you really stink!" Make that: "Hey, kid, don't you get it? Nobody wants you!" And it sticks.

I honestly can't believe I'm telling you this, but I know I'm in good company. Gnarled thoughts and feelings we keep locked in private containment make for rancid, festering wounds that are anything but safe. A diseased soul left unchecked finds hurtful expression in despairing minds, deeply impaired emotions, and at some point, vulnerable bodies. It's inevitable. Mine came as I crested life's thirty-year mark with an ulcer and near nervous breakdown. I'm not alone, I know. Countless souls wallow in assorted flavors of self-pity in search of enablers they hope will aid in justifying their misery. I know this too.

I'll admit that what I'm saying may sound more than a little cold or even extreme, but for the lost and misguided, this, friends, is grim wallpaper lining a bleak and desolate world. Sad, isn't it? None who find themselves trapped in such a floundering malaise either sees or knows of a far greater reality: compassion, the kind that has their names on it.[10] It's God-sized, for sure. His invention, not ours.

Little did I know how my own confused insistence kept me from tasting the love and grace I was sure had abandoned me. From where I sat, I'd given Him more than ample reason to kick me to the curb, proving what? Proving I really didn't know His mind or compassionate heart for me. Proving I really didn't know Him.

The David-Mephibosheth Story

Mephibosheth, now there's a name.

If we go by how that rolls off the tongue, we'll miss a priceless gem. This son of Jonathan bore the proud banner, "No more shame!" every time his name was called. How God's people had been humiliated by brazen Philistine arrogance as their loud-mouthed champion stripped Israel naked with flagrant taunts that went unanswered by their king and his cowering, spineless army. So, when Goliath's head came off by David's youthful hand, Israeli hearts shouted in resounding unison. Who's surprised, then, that "No more shame!" should fill the prince's heart in naming his firstborn. In Israel's God, there can be no stigma, no disgrace, no shame.

Too bad, though, Jonathan and his brothers died in battle on Mount Gilboa at the hands of uncircumcised pagans—the price of Saul's unbelief who shamefully took his own life.[1] In fear of reprisal, the child's nurse snatched the unwary five-year-old and ran, tripping over herself while crippling the boy. He was carried to some nowhere town in Gilead—Lo-debar, to the house of one Machir who raised the prince's disabled son.[2]

Fear was his prison. The man lived in hiding. Philistine invaders posed an ongoing threat, and David? The newly crowned king had long been the people's hero, but he was a man grandpa Saul feared would write him and all that was his out of the picture. Okay, so you know, and I know the king's paranoia was demonically driven.[3] David would take any pretended assassin on before he, or anyone, laid a hand on Israel's demented monarch. It's called integrity.

Don't lay so much as a finger on God's anointed.[4] Saul didn't see it, he couldn't. His twisted rantings echoed in the paid help's hearts and minds with mad, corrosive David talk. Constantly.

Mephibosheth heard; he absorbed. With no father to set the record straight, I can see how derogatory thoughts concerning David might steal his peace and rob him of sleep. Mephibosheth doesn't know the love that's there for him. He's oblivious to a covenant sealed in blood binding the king to his deceased father years before his birth.[5] We're talking permanence, a commitment that holds. "I've got your back," love insists. "I'm your shield, your defense and financial cover. Anything that touches you touches me. Your concerns are mine no matter what."

Color that God's heart.

It's with this in mind, friend Jonathan calls his blood brother to commit: "You shall not cut off your lovingkindness from my house forever, not even when the LORD cuts off every one of the enemies of David from the face of the earth."[6]

Amen it stands, and years later when God subdues Israel's enemies, David remembers. "Is anyone left in the house of Saul?"[7] a caring yet a troubled heart wonders. But why? Why the house of Saul? "I want to show them kindness for Jonathan's sake."[8] Feelers go out, and Saul's one-time servant Ziba shows his face. David zooms in. "Come on now, isn't there anyone from Saul's house I can show God's kindness to?"[9] God's kindness? *God's kindness?* After Saul's determined efforts to eliminate this innocent man—to have him murdered—the king's heart is for grace. Whoever it is, regardless of what they've done, there's a greater reality.

A covenant sealed in blood has the last word!

My God the tears! Can you imagine David's heart pounding, his mind racing to learn Jonathan has a son? The boy is crippled, but he's alive! "Where is the young man? We've got to get him. Bring Mephibosheth here. Do it now!" Fast-forward to a shanty in the middle of downtown no town. The sound of horses and chariots jars a sorely broken man. "Come with us, boy. The king wants to see you." Imaginations kick in, and they all end in death—Mephibosheth's. Falling prostrate in fearful obeisance, the man braces himself expecting the worst.

"Mephibosheth."

"I am your servant."

"It's okay, son. I want to restore you. I'm doing this for your father, Jonathan. The land that belonged to your grandfather Saul is all yours. From now on, you'll be eating at my table like one of my boys."

Dead silence.

"I don't get it. I'm nobody, a flea on a dead dog's carcass."

David turns, directing his full attention to Ziba.

"Everything that was Saul's belongs to this man."

"Take care of it and take care of him, but he'll eat with me. Got it?"

"Got it, sir."

All those years locked down in fear and trepidation, and for what? A lie. What seemed so real was an illusion, a fabrication of vivid imaginings—but it looked and felt legitimate. Oh, the shock of actually hearing the truth, the sheer disbelief! It can't be, yet the man is a welcome guest in David's house sitting at the king's table.

He's family now. He always was, but who knew? Not Mephibosheth. He did nothing to endear himself, nothing to reach out. The embrace that accepts and secures him has nothing to do with anything he's done and everything concerning a love bond outside of his actions and attitudes. The same was true for me; although, I didn't know how much until years after I said yes to Jesus. My guess is we both found out at the right time.

Think about it.

8

Dumbfounded Amazement

Timing is critical.

"At the right time," we're told, "Christ died for the ungodly."[1] In the fullness of time, the Father sent Him.[2] However you slice it, timing is everything where God is concerned. He's never early, never late. Never. The word Scripture uses to depict time—the right time, the fullness of time—is priceless. Kairos.[3] We're talking pinpoint precision, but only when all of the right and necessary components have come together.

Think of a woman giving birth. Conception initiates a process so staggering, so downright breathtaking it's hard to imagine. Chemical and physiological changes in an expectant mother's body are nothing short of symphonic artistry in concert with a divine complexity of design we've learned is ever changing, ever developing. A tiny person in formation is being shaped to bear an image and likeness heaven alone can fill. Then at the right time, at the precise moment when it all comes together according to design, a young woman's body unites to liberate itself and this precious new life to a world of never-ending discovery.

That's kairos.

God knows I didn't see it. Apart from the obvious, like when my daughters were born, I've been clueless to either see or appreciate the Master's behind-the-scenes preparation in unwary hearts. You and I catch a glimpse of Andrew chasing Peter down and taking him to Jesus; then, en route to Galilee, our newfound Rabbi calls Philip who fairly jumps at the chance to follow, but why? It was the right time.

Heaven knows the dots God has already connected in a man's heart at the precise moment Jesus steps in. It could have been months, possibly years. We get the birth announcement. At precisely the right time, an unsuspecting Philip is accosted. "Follow Me," may just as likely have been this disciple's "Glad to meet you," as "Leave your country"[4] was for Abraham. Segue to strange things that happen when Nathanael meets Jesus.

In John's gospel chapter one, new kid on the block, Phil, pulls Nate aside with, "Hey, we've found the One Moses and the prophets wrote about.[5] His name is Jesus, and He comes from Nazareth of all places!"

"You're kidding, right?"

"No, why do you say that?"

"Nothing good comes out of Nazareth!"

"Come see for yourself then."

Jesus calls him out with, "You're so genuine, so honest!" Say what? The two never met.

"I don't get it," he stammers. "How in the world do you know me?"

"Oh that…before Philip snagged you, I saw and knew." Jesus wasn't just reading his mail. He tapped in on our unsuspecting friend before creation's dawn and Nate made the connection.[6] Could anyone but God nail him cold like that? Not a chance. "You're the Son of God, Rabbi!"[7] The whole thing seems knee-jerk, but the man sees something. Again, the right time plays out. It's God all the way, but where's He going with this? Keep your seat belts buckled, we're in for a bumpy ride.

To Say the Least

I said yes to Jesus at seventeen. I didn't see it coming. A high school buddy, one of the guys I played in jazz band and orchestra with, exuded something I'd never seen in anyone—a presence—and he carried a Bible. Who takes a Bible to school? I never carried a Bible to church! No one did, not me, not anyone in my family or people we knew. No one. So, I watched, I listened, but I still didn't connect the dots. It was like breathing to him, effortless it seemed.

Then there was Mom, Dad too. They were so burdened, Mom especially. You could feel it. I remember the infamous "Now it all begins" lecture. Mom thought she was doing me a favor, tutoring her naïve, still wet behind the ears firstborn in the grim realities of life. I can't fault her. It's all my mother knew, all she'd ever been told. I get that now. Back then, I asked, "Are you going to heaven?" Hey, why not? If the weight to perform is on us, I needed a sense that someone I knew had a shot at clearing the hurdles—to themselves if no one else.

"I don't know," she said. "No one knows for sure until they stand before God, but I hope so."

I hope so? You're kidding me, right? Don't tell me you're making book on this![8] Who in their right mind would allow their eternal destiny to hang by such a careworn thread? But if it's all you know, all you have to work with, then life—from that vantage point—is a crapshoot. Give it your best shot and cross your fingers.

That's mom.

Okay, so there's no assurance here, and Dad played the same card. Theirs was a strange, even bizarre fit. Mom was quick with her tongue, cutting hard and deep. Maybe I deserved it, but Dad? It didn't make sense. He was a stand-up guy, a straight arrow as I saw him, but Mom was quick to cut the man short. Stinging barbs aimed at my father laid me open like a cold stiff on the coroner's table. I felt emasculated. God knows how my father fared. Dad never talked about such things, at least I never heard him. Firm in his silence, Dad was a man in love, a romantic floundering in hope for a little warmth. I know this. I think everyone did.

Who would have guessed my pint-sized matriarch grew up with a bonehead alcoholic father who brutalized her mother and siblings?

I didn't, not for years. The ripple effect was a killer. She was a powder keg with a short fuse. My guess is Mom never realized how she came off with us, especially Dad. Welcome to my mother's prison, Dad's too. Looking back, I can only imagine the extent of her many festering wounds and how grateful I am for the grace that ultimately sought her out, her and Dad both. He sought all of us, me first.

I honestly can't remember what was going on in my life, much less my heart, when my musician friend showed me Jesus. I recall the awakening, though, a resounding, "Yes!" that witnessed as nothing ever had. "This is it! This is what I've been so hungry for!" It was the right time, my personal kairos. Jesus breathed life into my dead spirit, enfolding my poor, wounded soul with an altogether foreign compassion—love that genuinely wanted me for me. Jesus wanted me! I'd never seen Him in church, but He was here on a school bus, alive in my friend's genuine concern, unconditional love Himself. I'll never forget. I couldn't possibly.

Andrew and Peter Understand

Then there's our good brother John who spoke not only for himself but a slough of others—ladies included—who heard and had seen our Lord, and not at a distance. They touched Him, and He touched them. I'm at a loss, though, to put into words the awe (and did I say significance?) of making tangible contact with a very real Son of humanity who, in and of Himself, is the dynamic, self-sustaining Word of life.[1] Some things you don't forget because you can't. When a man or woman, even a four or five-year-old, who's touched and been touched by Jesus, the imprint sticks. I'm thinking about a lady, several actually, daughters of rejection whose souls were caressed when love Himself reached out to the unreachable, joining their hearts with His.

A quick sidebar...

I find it more than a little curious how we as evangelical believers speak of your "accepting Jesus" or my "receiving Christ" as though you and I are the ones to be congratulated. I say "we" as one who's been there, done that in gross ignorance. Didn't Jesus come looking for us? It all begins with Him, right? "God so loved the world," it says. He takes the initiative, a reality that unexpectedly and sometimes rudely boots us out of guarded and well-conditioned comfort zones. It could mean a trip through Samaria, a

call to the unsuspecting to embrace the unembraceable. Maybe both, I know. The love of God
is scandalous!

The stench factor remember?[2] When a woman of the street
drops sobbing at the Master's feet, self-righteousness takes offense,
and the lady? She finds unfettered freedom through love packaged
as wholehearted acceptance through forgiveness.[3] How about one
the, "Well, I never" crowd has a field day with, a flagrant adulteress
blindsided by grace in the face of stone-cold bitterness and ruthless
accusation. She understands.[4] There's another, isn't there, one whose
prison fence is trimmed with rejection's razor wire.

A smelly foreigner. Respectable Jews have long since written the likes of this lady off, but so have her own people—snooty
Samaritans—women specifically.[5] She's ostracized from their company. And we know this how? Ms. So-And-So comes for water in
the hottest part of the day and travels alone. All right, so that means
what? It means women folk with an ounce of brains and the slightest
modicum of decency come in the morning when it's cooler, and they
come without *her*. It could be she's not welcome in their ranks. Why?

I'm dating myself, but I remember a day when divorce was
hush-hush in "respectable" community. People whispered all day
long behind closed doors while condescending, if not glaring, eyes
spoke volumes in public. Something's wrong. Speculation abounds
where *their kind* are concerned. Just walk around them. Guilt by
association, you know. Five husbands and now a live-in, the woman's
tainted. She's got to be. No one enjoys bearing the scarlet letter[6] or
the shame that goes with it, but the woman has to survive. So, she
does what? She grows a thick layer of skin pretending none of it matters. Who's fooling whom? She's not fooling Jesus.

He goes straight for the heart. "Can you give Me a drink?"
bypasses small talk nailing His mark full force. The Jew-Gentile
thing is a wash with Him, and He's nixed any male-female stumbling
blocks.[7] The real deal is identification. Who are you, the sum of your
performance failures or successes? Is it who people say you are? Not
anymore. A cool drink from an ancient well foreshadows Calvary

where our Lord risks making Himself a scandal. How, you ask? By drinking from the lady's cup, putting His lips where hers touched. He'd be one with her, one with her stench, one with her sin. Exactly. And she'd be one with Him.

"He (the Father) made Him (the Son) who knew no sin to be sin on our behalf, so that we might become the righteousness of God in Him."[8] Here's where, "If you knew the gift of God" comes into play, and not only for the lady. You and I are part of a mix who don't know the gift of God, not really. We've gotten so used to seeing Him and ourselves through filters made up of so many gnarled thoughts and feelings tainted by people and circumstances that unknowingly write God out of the equation, or severely distort His image.

It happens a lot unfortunately.

And the one voted "Most Likely to Succeed" has Charles Manson for a cellie.[9] They both have severely bent and twisted images of God, so the mirror they see themselves in is a gross misrepresentation that goes undetected, especially the so-called success stories. Talk about distortion! But a little spit shine on the ego keeps folks chugging along, be they corporate CEOs or gangbanging shot callers. It's all the same cloth. You'd be amazed at the number of preachers and preachers' kids doing time alongside men and women whose mothers and grandmothers dutifully escorted them to Sunday school as kids. So many churchgoers.

Guess where they were before coming to the department of corrections? Prison, but who knew it? Who had eyes to see? No one. It escapes the lot of us that no man or woman was ever intended to build an identity in themselves. No one. Apart from Him who created us to bear His image and likeness, we're incomplete.

Dare I say less than human?

You weren't told that were you? But we sense it. Jesus connects the dots. He fills in the picture, giving it depth and substance. He makes it complete. It's bigger than you, bigger than me. Our best shot at articulating what's happened to us is a flabbergasted, "I was blind, but I can see now!"[10] Fast-forward to our Samaritan lady friend who finds herself chasing down, not women, but men—leaders in the community—to tell about Jesus. Forget status, or what will they say. She's Andrew, or is it Philip? It could be she's Mary racing in blind hysteria from an empty tomb. Mad hilarity, that's it. I remember. "Joy unspeakable," says Peter.[11] He knows. What he doesn't is the stuff that clouds his vision, the distortions. He will, though, and not just him.

Peter Shuts Down

The big galoot couldn't bear any talk of death, not Jesus's death.

He wasn't alone. It's staggering to imagine that on the heels of the greatest and most incredible unveiling given or received by anyone at any time—the word *outrageous* comes to mind just now—flows the worst news imaginable. How do you come off, "You are the Christ" and all that goes with it, then get slammed with talk of impending rejection, suffering, and death? No way that'll fly! Death spells the end, and Jesus is just getting off the ground. Momentum with the people is building like crazy, and now He's pulling the plug? That's the way things look, and it's definitely what this nightmarish fiasco feels like. What Pete doesn't know, or want to hear, is the kingdom and Calvary's cross go hand in glove.

Get inside friend Peter's head, then feel his heart. How much he heard of Jesus's third day resurrection speech is anyone's guess. What wasn't about to happen was any more talk of pain or executions, not if he has anything to say about it. This is where love steps in and becomes a roadblock. "God forbid, Lord. No way this is going down!"[1] With fire in His eyes, the Master picks His shots with precision.

"Out of My way, Satan!"[2] That stops him cold. Peter must have felt like he just got his head lopped off and handed to him. The last thing he wants to be is a stumbling block, yet in the wake of divine revelation, blessed Simon Bar-jona plays right into the devil's hand.

And in the high priest's courtyard, he does it again.

We talked about it, the feeling of complete and total abandonment with nowhere to go, no one to go to. One fisherman on the skids isn't the first grown-up to feel like a six- or eight-year-old under fire. I've been there. My first-grade teacher dumped the contents of my desk on the floor in front of the class searching for an assignment we'd been working on, then called my mother. How many times over the years I felt naked and ashamed before a laughing world like I did that day? Joe Louis nails it, "You can run but you can't hide," and in a crowd huddled around a fire on a dark and frigid night, Peter stands out. Curious onlookers say so, something about his accent.[3] They press hard, and Peter hits the wall.[4]

The devil understands inertia. Set a ball in motion, and watch it roll. All it takes is a nudge, an occasional push to keep it going. Enter Gethsemane, then Judas et al. on the heels of all the cross talk. So much joy, unbridled anticipation agrees it really is Jesus. He's the One, Lord Messiah, and now this? For all the love, the passion, and genuine concern Andrew's brother thinks he feels for the Master, the last jolt from a neb-nose housekeeper takes Peter down and knocks him cold, thank God. Thank God, you say? What's with that?

Why thank God? I'll tell you why. The last thing you and I need, and the absolute worst that could have happened to Peter, John, or any of the boys, would be for one or more of them to find a shred of confidence to stick it out because—now hear me on this—they had to fall, every last one of them. No exceptions. I realize this goes against the grain of what many of us have been taught, but heaven's wisdom is solid, and it holds.

Satan Gets Downright Insistent

Hours before His arrest, Jesus confronts Peter head-on. "Simon, listen to Me. Satan has demanded permission to sift you like wheat."[5] Now there's a kick in the teeth. With all that was brewing, talk of a new covenant sealed in Jesus's blood over against participation in an eternal kingdom, Diabolos himself decides he wants a piece of the rock, and more.[6] "But I've prayed for you Peter."[7] Prayed? Why didn't

You tell old snake eyes to get lost, to take a flying leap?[8] That's what I'd have done, so it's a good deal none of this was riding on me. Peter didn't get it. If anyone had Jesus's back, he did. Everyone could fall but Peter.

Come dawn, one angler is reduced to ashes, right where the accuser wants him. Funny thing, though, it's where God wants him too. You heard me; now please hear me out. The devil wants to break Peter, to crush him. So does God, but for entirely different reasons. The thief, we know, comes to steal, kill, and destroy.[9] No secrets here. God, on the other hand, is about tearing down all that can't possibly be redeemed. Shake everything that can be shaken.[10] More on that later. For now, let's take a closer look at the slick one, Satan, the particular method to his madness.

Consider our good friend Job. Now here's a man who carried serious weight; God said so.[11] Integrity's the word, fearing God while turning his back on evil and moral corruption. The man utilized wealth he was blessed with to assist the less fortunate and his clout to "break the jaws of the wicked."[12] Color that walk, not just talk. Eden's twisted serpent hates it, and not for Job's sake. It's God. The slippery one wants to get in on Job, no doubt about it, yet his real target is God. Satan hates Him and will take any route, assault anyone to get in on our LORD, be it Job, Peter, or the likes of any one of us. That's old Scratch's bottom line.[13] Always.

All right, so Job was a key player in his day, but no one really knows for sure when that was. Early on is pretty much it; although, *when* isn't nearly as important as *why*. The revelation of God our brother owns at the time the book opens could best be described as limited. Oral tradition probably, but that ain't half bad.[14] The man's knee-jerk response when the bottom drops out is one of worship.[15] That speaks volumes. When all is said and done, Job sees God with new eyes, and the devil has enough rope to hang himself.

Which he does, by the way.

God is good, despite Satan's slickest moves to persuade us He isn't. Where we, with Adam's bent, get wrapped around the axle, along with Job and Peter, is none of us knows just how "me" centered our God connection gets at times. And that means what? It means there's a lot we don't see because we can't, not when your stuck feeler or my twisted rationale locks in as the measure of truth.

If Peter could, he'd have slammed the brakes on Judas and pulled the plug at the cross. His infamous "God forbid" speech and sword wielding in Gethsemane tell the story.[16] Religious leaders who pushed for Jesus's crucifixion were clueless, as was Peter who so wanted to resist. After the fact, our fishing buddy sees, but up front, forget it. This well-intentioned trawler man was as blind as they come. Apart from God, he'll never make the connection that his very best efforts and most productive intentions miss the mark more than a mile.

The same goes for us.

However, we define life; your flesh and mine are skewed toward making messed up assessments. The reason? Our flesh is "me" centered. Everyone's. Peter seems to have qualified success as Jesus moving onward and upward in the eyes of His own Hebrew nation. Surprised? Not hardly. Jesus is on a roll, and the powers that be are green with envy because they're losing their grip.[17] So when the Master fixes determined sights on Calvary, the tension in Peter's spring tightens. The heat dials up, and he folds like a cheap suit. And us? In cringing for Peter, we cringe for ourselves because you, me, we blow it too. We blow it badly.

"If I could only go back," folks say, hit rewind and redo life as though anyone left to themselves would change where it counts. Who are we kidding? Flesh begets flesh. Ask Jesus.[18] If a man could go back, he'd mess up again. Make no mistake; it's still us, so it's still flesh. Unless Peter is broken and yielded to Jesus as a branch to the vine, he'll continue to make boneheaded choices based on what seems and feels right to him. Us too.

I Needed to Feel Right

I needed it badly. Somewhere along the way, I got a new name, "You'll never amount to anything." Again, it was Mom—a fit for both of us—hers for giving, mine for receiving. I heard it often. Watching and listening to guys in prison, you see how repetition factors in. It's part of the mold. Day after day the "greens" go on, standard attire in Colorado's correctional system, green uniforms fitted with nametags and state "offender" ID numbers. As an inmate in the system, you are the offense bearing your conviction, and you wear it.

Green blurs quickly and so does personhood.

Before I take this any further, could we step back to clarify something? My woundedness, in reality, is my unique perception of people and events that have shaped and molded me in some way. Which makes them what? Let's say they're filtered memories of what happened and why. I touched on this earlier, but we'll continue to consider the ramifications from different angles as we kick this around, so bear with me, will you?

The pivotal component here is our discovering how you see, and I perceive, people and events that hurt us in deep places. They pass through distortion lenses. We feel the impact not realizing the hit we take gets filtered. The filters? Lies and more lies, convincing fallacies masquerading as truth. As such, I might possess a reasonably clear audio-video recall while putting a twisted spin on it. Think strongholds.

I say this lest you think I'm "mom bashing." Not even close. There was a time I did, but no more. I can't. The grace that's now my hope and daily sustenance allows for memories to be skewed by any number of feelings. I look back on hurtful things my mother did and said as I envisage her pain, yet I can't. Too many missing pieces. More than thirty years after leaving home, I learned how my inebriated grandfather—who always gave me the creeps—backhanded Mom and pulled a knife on her. Again, I can't imagine, but it explains a lot, more than I could even try to reconfigure. Thank God He heals emotional wounds and badly twisted memories.

So, Where Were We?

I remember.

I needed to feel right. The stigma of "You'll never amount to anything" kept my soul locked down in lonely, inhibiting confinement. A seventh-grade teacher secured what began at home. My response? I closed up and shut down around people with hopes of securing my heart. I thought it worked. What was left to me but the dark side? Hang out with rebel types—smoke cigarettes, try to look hip, and garner a new vocabulary. Cute, huh? Not really. I was a loser there too. Not cool, not tough, definitely not a ladies' man. They laughed at me.

But I got a new trumpet teacher.

My folks started me on music lessons at the ripe young age of ten, and it was all right, I guess, but practice was boring, as in, "Wake me up when I'm finished, will you?" Then everything changed. The man I'd been studying with couldn't teach me any longer, something about a conflict in schedules, so Dad arranged for an assessment of my skills with one of the premier educators in the city who more than held his own both as a player and teacher at a prestigious university. What a commanding presence, what a vice grip he had!

The man's "I love winners and hate losers" philosophy might have squished me like a grape if it weren't for his hopeful assessment of my playing. "I think you've got it, boy!" put wind in sails I never thought existed. In my world, I wasn't much, but in this man's studio, the kid had potential. I was on my way to becoming a winner!

Sounds good, doesn't it? But the squeeze to perform, to be the best in a circle of winners, was nothing short of brutal. Kudos and award medals kept me shooting high even when it got scary. Then reality hit. The fall of my senior year of high school was marked by the toughest, most unforgiving competition ever, first, because of the technical complexity of the audition piece chosen by the judges and, second, my teacher. Nix any margin for error. My teacher's benchmark? "There's only one place for you, boy. It's gotta be first!"

In a world of performance-based acceptance where it's the top rung or nothing, maintaining favor is a slippery slope that makes calling it quits an increasingly attractive option. Not here, though. Not now. I had to play and then critique my audition to Mr. Pasquarelli, my teacher, over the phone. "How'd you do, boy?"

"I thought I did pretty good."

"Pretty good won't get you first. Get first or don't come back!" The grape just got squished. Dropping my trumpet off in the high school's music room Monday morning met with a smile from one of the adjudicators who heard me play.

"Congratulations, Danny, you got first! No one even came close to you."

"You blew them all away."

Really? I should have been flying but no. My teacher's self-congratulatory grin and robust accolades at my trumpet lesson a few days later were little more than pompous fluff, a prelude to future torment. "The higher up the ladder you get means there's more guys below trying to kick you down, boy!" Gee thanks. I could feel it. The kid who would never amount to anything bailed his freshman year of college without looking back. Why prove what I already knew? I was marked for failure. Besides, who would want me on their team?

It amazes me, though, how effortlessly I'd transposed my trumpet guru's "It's number one or nothing!" outlook on God. My guess is "You'll never amount to anything" made for a seamless transition, one that kept the One who would have me know Him as Father on a back burner while I took yet another stab at music in night clubs and college frat parties with a band I helped form.[1] The talent was real, but roads were lined with drugs and morally compromised choices. I was invited to "play gay"[2] part time as a way to get ahead, but the thought dumped me face first in pig slop where a beat-down prodigal began coming to his senses.

Who knew this was an integral part of my discipleship?

Not me. And like a son who found himself knee-deep in crud for a sobering reality check, I needed my own hard, cold slap in the face.[3] Life, across the board, put my perception of God in the toilet, meaning I had to crash and crash hard before I'd come to my senses. Seeing my Father from a loving and strangely hopeful vantage point would require the removal of accumulated layers of dust and gunk from long since faded memories of Jesus. Peace I was sure I'd fabricated awakened an inner awareness…or was it a dream?

Bad Self-Serving Intentions

That's Satan in a nutshell.

The name means "adversary," and it comes through in spades with God as his bull's eye. He spits venom in retaliation to the Almighty's "Have you considered My servant Job?"[1] masquerading as a victim who's been shortchanged. "God, You won't let me get next to him."[2] Poor me, right? But again, God is this fallen angel's target. "Does Job fear God for nothing?" he retaliates with unbridled contempt, as though the man's been bought and paid for to keep up appearances.[3] It's called inference, an attempted stab in the dark based on circumstantial suggestion that God really isn't all that good. Enter Satan's game, and he's good at it.

Toxic is the word. It's lethal where the naïve and unsuspecting take the bait. Job didn't bite; God said so. Eden, now that's another story. Don't jump too quickly, though. It's easy to miss the obvious, so give this a minute.

Scripture tells us God provides abundantly for His own, above and beyond our scope of imagining.[4] "Trust Me," He says. "You've got to choose." Choose what? The obedience of faith,[5] choose life not death. Choose God. Imagery aside, He is the tree of life, a vine who Himself is our functional source and means of all that truly completes and sustains us.[6] Apart from Him, forget it. God alone makes us human! His faithfulness and love, our LORD's immeasurable goodness is more than overwhelming. Creation testifies to Him continually.[7]

A contrary voice infers otherwise. "Did God say?" doesn't challenge what so much as why. Arousing doubtful suspicion concerning the fact of the Creator's directive points to motive. Why in the world would He say such a thing? Why would God restrict you this way? The question is smooth and very seductive.

Does God have ulterior motives?

Watch and listen as the slippery one leads by redirecting their thinking when the subject of death is breached. "That's crazy!" he insists. "You're not going to die!"[8]

Do you see what's going on here? The serpent inserts himself as a caring benefactor by strategically weaving this bold-faced denial of God into the mix. The reason? Eliminate threats of negative consequences should they opt for unbelief and disobedience.

"You'll be like God and He knows it."[9]

Now before you and I go half-cocked, there's a larger, more inclusive context we've got to consider.

The temptation to be "like" God has nothing to do with taking on divine attributes such as omnipotence or omnipresence.[10] Read this as, "You will be like God," in this sense. "You can know good and evil for yourselves."[11] Consider the implications. "Why do you need God doing your thinking for you, telling you what to do? Shouldn't any self-respecting man or intelligent woman be able to decide for themselves what fits and what doesn't, what's good and what's evil? Self-sufficiency is the ticket!" Oops! That doesn't work, does it? Dependence spells life. Independence? Dude, that's death. Trees mark the point of choice.

It all boils down to what do you believe, really?

What will you submit to?

The fruit's poison is its lethal deception, the yin and yang where you and I attempt to achieve harmony and balance in and of ourselves. No God. The mother of all lies writes Him out of the picture at every turn suggesting independence is everyone's best shot.

And where heaven's deposed worship leader[12] would see God's heart reduced to bitterly mangled mulch, he zeros in on Adam. Who's surprised? In this first man and his precious lady stands every man and every woman. Touch them, and stand by for the ripple effect.

Things Aren't Always As They Seem

The times I've pitched a fit over Adam's boneheaded blunder are too many to number. I'm in good company, I know. Truth be told, I blamed God and so have you, so don't get religious on me. We've all asked, if not demanded, a credible explanation for the serpent's presence in Eden's garden paradise as though our concerns and personal sensibilities require satisfaction. Inquiring minds want to know.

I've read articles and books, taken part in discussions ad infinitum, and listened to teachers, preachers, and educators speculate on "What if Adam hadn't sinned?" or "What is God's eternal plan and purpose apart from the Fall?" but why go there? Why travel a road that doesn't exist? God doesn't. Okay, okay, I'm not trying to pick a fight with anyone. Honestly, I'm not. I'm just tired of trying to force square pegs into round holes by asking questions I don't believe our Lord has raised or pointed us to. I could be wrong, but what I see is an utterly profound reality that stands outside of time.

We're talking eternal, from vanishing point to vanishing point, everlasting to everlasting.[13] It's who God is eternally; He's a Lamb slain from before the world's foundation! Revelation 13:8.[14] I'm not suggesting this portrait in particular is the sum total of who God is. That's not possible, yet—now hear me on this—all God is and ever will be in His omniscience, omnipotence, and omnipresence somehow finds expression at this vital junction. Calvary's cross stands before time begins[15] and long after it closes out.

God knows I need to catch my breath here, but I'm thinking 1 Peter 1 right about now and reading from the New American Standard Bible, verses 18 through 21.

Knowing that you were not redeemed with perishable things like gold or silver from your futile way of life inherited from your forefathers, but with precious blood, as of a lamb unblemished and spotless, the blood of Christ. For He was foreknown before the foundation of the world but has appeared in these last times for the sake of you who through Him are believers in God, who raised Him from the dead and gave Him glory, so your faith and hope are in God.

And that means what?

It means Jesus isn't an afterthought.

No patch job here. He's not heaven's last-ditch effort to somehow rectify humanity's disastrous head-on with him whose sole bent is to steal, kill, and destroy.[16] Jesus is the original idea—heaven's eternal paradigm—the image and likeness the Godhead envisions in the decree, "Let Us make man." Before the first word of creation is spoken, Calvary is firmly etched in the Father's heart and precisely fixed in His crosshairs. Think plan A, not B. Everything then, in heaven and on earth, finds its true meaning and precious substance in God by way of the death, burial, and resurrection of Jesus, or it finds it nowhere.[17] Amen, it's true in spades.

How Could Peter Know the Cross Is Primarily for God?

How could anyone?

The devil enjoys presenting God as a self-absorbed tyrannical despot bent on having things His way to our hurt.[1] Talk about twisted! The Book is more than clear: everything starts with Him. "In the beginning God."[2] You, me, the entire cosmos not only begins, it exists expressly for God's will and purposes.[3] That pleases Him. It pleases Him a lot.[4] A self-sustaining Trinity holds everything together and keeps it rolling.[5] Ultimately it all returns to Him lock, stock, and barrel.[6]

Surprised? I was, and I'll tell you what, if life in a fallen world does anything, it puts a proverbial "me" spin on the whole ball of wax, God included. For years, and that's after Bible school, I saw Christ's redemptive work as "my" salvation as though I and other grace recipients were His central focus. Sorry, guys, we're not. This is for Him first and foremost.[7]

Don't get me wrong; all who are "in Christ" benefit in ways that can't be measured. It's that huge. Eternity itself will prove an ongoing disclosure of the Lamb who was slain and what it means to us, but in the first order of things, the saints—you and I in concert with everyone the Lamb's blood has purchased—will bow in wide-eyed amazement to learn even a fraction of what the Lamb means to Him who sits on the throne.

A Heavenly Perspective Gives Us
a Correct Lay of the Land

Forget me and mine. That's not the nucleus, He is, and we who are in Christ have been seated with Him in heavenly places.[8] What a vantage point we have! Instead of the moment-by-moment unfolding of this thing folks call life, a frame-by-frame existence, if you will, the One who chose and called us to Himself has laid out a perspective that makes sorting out the present more of a slam dunk if we'll learn to fix our eyes on Him.

Hey, I'm not trying to be cute or simplistic. God wants us to see Himself alone as our all in all. "Come to Me," Jesus says. "I'll give you rest."[9] Words so dear to me now that for years were a universe removed from any place my heart called home. I couldn't see it, but why? Me and my stuff had a lock on center stage. God's job (I thought) was keeping it all intact; although, I'd never admit to it. I was far too religious, and like Isaiah, I fellowshipped with a host of kindred spirits.[10] A run through the meat grinder is what I needed, sifting like wheat. Again, why? Knowing Christ as our resting place comes together on Golgotha's hill and nowhere else.

From everlasting to everlasting, the cross is central.

After the Fall when first blood was shed—and that by God— He points to Calvary, as with Abraham and Isaac on a mount called Moriah.[11] How about Passover?[12] The list goes on touching men and precious women whose lives and calling paint graphic images they couldn't begin to wrap their brains around.[13] We speak of Abraham, and rightly so, but God only knows what Isaac went through![14] As Peter and the boys are drawn closer to Jesus, they don't see it either, not yet. How could they?

Loving Jesus as His disciples do, this crew is still self-absorbed. They just don't know it. I get that. The Master seems clear when it comes to His disciples carrying their respective crosses, but participation in His? There's no tangible frame of reference for it, or is there? All those years, centuries as a covenant people collectively participating in the blood of the paschal lamb, feeding on Adonai's love gift, a very real exodus from the bitterness of bondage. We're talking death here, complete severance from all Egypt speaks to. He's here now! Christ our Passover has been sacrificed for us, as us.[15] We participate and not positionally. Actually.

Sure, it's scary. Jesus sweats blood in anticipation, and so-called apostles run hard and fast when the cross comes into full view.[16] John alone stands with Jesus's mother watching her firstborn die. I get that because I ran. I ran from everyone and everything I feared, opting for drugs, porn, my job, and ministry. Color me strange, but logic shuts down where the search for significance is scripted by the way life feels one moment to the next. Extreme hours at work coupled with high-end audio promised a way out for me, fishing too. Add SLR photography[17] along with selling hi-fi stereo. I get dizzy thinking about it. And the disciples?

Talk of suffering and death falls on deaf ears.

When the vision planted in your heart crumbles like so much rotten wood under foot, where's the next step? What is brokenness to the hopeless, and surrender? I remember Bible school with its impassioned appeals to "lay it all on the altar." What did it mean? There was no context, not for me, not then. The call to ministry was as real as the grace that reached out and claimed my heart. The outworking? That's another story.

Blindsided Again

Pacing the maroon and black carpet floor in my dorm room, I prayed, "Lord, I want to be part of the answer, not part of the problem," and I meant it. My time on "the holy hill" concluded, and my soul was a mixed bag of thoughts and feelings.[18] Bonnie and I were engaged, but I needed employment before we could get married. Counseled not to pursue full-time ministry just yet, my teacher and mentor spoke from valued experience. "God has something to teach you that you can't get in Bible school or seminary." I found a job in printing.

Good thing. Moving to unknown places had my twenty-one-year-old heart pounding. What can I say? I had to see if there was a place for me in the small inner-city church my mentor pastored, something outside of what I saw as the traditional church box. Folks assured me I was a shoo-in.[19] This lot was real as they were unique.

My toddler years as a believer outlined more than I'd seen before, more than I could ever have imagined. It stopped me cold watching egos spin off axis as families were sacrificed on the altar of ministry. Identity, wouldn't you say? The influx of "wanna be" pastors in search of their own multimedia megachurches were legion. Idols come and go as hearts are tried in fiery crucibles where personalities go up in acrid black smoke while groupies fall by the wayside. So much for romantic illusions where feel-good dreams crash in flames because they have to.

Knowing it's Jesus who calls strikes wonder and amazement coupled with heartfelt nuances we hope will translate into lasting value and genuine substance. With all the ups and downs, you never know. I look back on the bizarre dichotomy shaping a convoluted self-image that forever kept me guessing, "You'll never amount to anything," over against, "It's first place or it's nothing." Cutting through the fog, though, I knew God was fitting me as part of the answer. Little did I realize it would mean a trip to hell and back. It had to.

The same goes for Peter, James, and John.

Their history as run-of-the-mill[20] Jews was converging although not as any Hebrew might anticipate, certainly not as they hoped. One to one is anyone's guess. Fishermen in ministry? Better yet, a tax collector? Paradigm shift hardly nails the twists and turns this crew was immersed in. Jesus goes deep, places where trust and assurance are tried and redefined. I'm talking radical where the bottom drops out and those who abandoned all to follow feel abandoned themselves, but they're not, are they? Jesus takes them to Himself, to places He would shun if He could, yet doesn't.[21] He takes us there too, you and me, by faith.

Brokenness, surrender, death,
burial, and resurrection.

Pull Off the Road a Minute

I wasn't planning on this sidebar, but I'd like to air a concern because I'm scared, and I am not alone. Far too many who identify as Christians don't know why they believe what they say they believe—evangelical, the Church of Rome, orthodox, and Messianic. "It's what I've always been taught," gets old fast while a favored Bible teacher or particular group says so is a bucket that, "I'm sorry, can't hold water." It leaks. It leaks badly.

God knows the untold numbers of young people who get chewed up and spit out on the floors of lecture halls in higher learning institutions over tepid milk toast faith are legion. My freshman year at Bible school included an outreach to a nearby university where the lion's den was ravenous to devour a neophyte who actually believed the Bible! Licking my wounds, I felt the ride back to school was long and painful as I bathed in silent shame over the way I disgraced the name of Jesus, but I needed it. I needed it badly.

It brought me to my knees and back to the Book.

Knowing God is a believer's birthright.[1] It is, yet not in the strict academic sense where knowing about God is an end in itself, a dead end perhaps. No, we're talking relationship as in intimacy, active participation, engaging a Person who takes the initiative, a dance where He leads. But what did I know? The Bible school incident I spoke of messed with me concerning my calling and competence for ministry, or the lack thereof, arousing fearful, intimidating suspicions. Was I a midget in a new land of giants? Thank God for emotional free falls where prayer is radically redefined and He catches us, but we don't always know it at the time.

I didn't; although, I'd given myself to investigating Scripture in conjunction with other reputable sources searching out all I could glean of the "right stuff." You know what I mean: useful and truly relevant material coupled with studied opinions of respected educators—good, if not the best information on tap—the doctrine of God, as they say. Yet it seemed to me as though the Holy One, all too often, was being laid open and dissected as a biology lab project in the interest of constructing an organized theological system that varies from school to school. I understand the rationale why folks give themselves to a disciplined study of God through His Word and the input of others, but I couldn't find a place to hang my own hat.

Luther, Calvin, Wesley, and others seemed to
break down at one point or another.

It's a Matter of Depth

Learning about someone out of history fits if we pursue the likes of Beethoven or Michelangelo through biographical sketches enhanced by a few well-invested evenings at the symphony and unhurried visits to a fine art gallery. Why not do it right and shoot off to Vienna to take in a little of the maestro's old stomping grounds or the Vatican to browse the Sistine Chapel and St. Peter's Basilica? The ambience of it all! Still we never quite make Ludwig van's acquaintance, and no one engages the raging fire of an Italian Renaissance master who considered himself more of a sculptor than a reluctant painter on commission, do we?

"Of course not!" you say, and your point would be well taken. These men are dead, long gone, but God isn't. He's alive, He's well, and He's engaged in His creation. All right, so God has, at times, been accused of hiding Himself.[2] I understand, but the long and short of it is the living God will be known to His people, first and foremost, to the nations as well.[3] Tangible evidence of the Designer's invisible qualities are clearly woven into the fabric of creation for everyone to see while His chosen get an inside look.[4] He who is our hope of salvation and life itself takes us back to square one—time's birthplace—Genesis 1:1.

The source and first order of all things is God, remember?

Understanding given to Moses on the subject of origins, as it pertains to God's unfolding purposes, were initially spoken for the benefit of those who left Egypt for their own encounter with Him who gave form and substance to the heavens and the earth. The God of their fathers rocked their world, and for what? *Freedom* is the buzz-word, but to those who've known only slavery what is that to them—no more brick pits, no stinging bite of a whip? Freedom, in its truest sense, means resting in Him who not only secured their deliverance; He, in fact, *is* their deliverance. In His embrace lays their hope and identity, but no one sees it. How could they?

Fear ruled the day.[5]

Understandable. Sinai never was the intended end, only the means. Stone tablets point to Jesus.[6] He's the energy, the life source of our God connection. And did I say the guarantor of a covenant in His own blood that pulls everything in heaven and earth together in one fixed assurance. All who are purchased of that self-same blood will know Him from rank-and-file nobodies to the heavy hitters among us.[7] It's a level playing field, so whether you push a broom or chair the board meeting, we share the same advantages.

> His divine power has granted to us every-
> thing pertaining to life and godliness. (2 Peter
> 1:3, NASB)

No one's exempt, not if you're in Christ. The beauty of it is we all share the same faith—that is, "the same kind of faith,"[8] "a faith of equal standing with ours."[9] Peter's got no special edge. Neither does Paul or John. In his letters, our beloved fisherman writes to believers who, like himself, are taking some serious heat. They're being sifted, so affirming them in who they are and what they've got is the ongoing constant for the lot of us who share the same Jesus. Every man, every woman in Christ have, without exception, been born again of incorruptible seed that's alive with all Jesus is, the seed being the living Word Himself.[10] Amen, it's true.

Scanning ink on paper or listening to select Biblical passages goes up in smoke apart from His breath that makes it life to us. Knowing this, studying to show ourselves approved[11] has less to do with academics and more with disposition. Our perception of God affects the way we as believers see ourselves and approach Him. Cain won't cut it with his, "Look at me!" antics. "See what I can do."[12]

No performances, please. We're not here to impress God with our best and most determined efforts. Humility is the ticket. Weakness is the key. It's how He made us. Dependent. We come knowing that apart from having our eyes supernaturally cleared, you and I will invariably find ourselves clueless as to who walks the Emmaus road with us. Jesus opens the Scriptures, and we see more than words—we see Him.

Reclining Around the Table

"When the hour had come..."[1]

How common is this thought, targeting the hour, His hour? Prior to Matthew's gospel, any mention of the word "hour" is all but nonexistent—five times, and all in the book of Daniel according to Strong,[2] whereas the New Testament blows up with it! Something about Jesus, the convergence He brings is, in reality, *the convergence He is.* God's purposes—in heaven and on earth for time and eternity—come together in the Son at the right time, His hour. And for all the instances where, "My hour has not yet come," it's here; it's now. It's in Him!

Kairos, remember?[3] Now watch. Observe as heaven and earth meet at this divinely appointed junction. "With longing desire I've anticipated eating this Passover with you before I suffer."[4] Do you hear our, Lord? I can't blow through this timeless encounter for the years it was watered down to me. Look closely and listen as Jesus's heart is laid bare before precious few apostolic appointees remembering a sacred memorial as a here and now reality the Rabbi recasts in His broken body and shed blood—a Lamb without spot or blemish.[5]

The hopes and fears of all the years are met in Thee.[6]

Moses caught a glimpse of holy judgment in the blood and fire of Passover. Judgment, you say? Absolutely. The Paschal lamb is slain, and its blood generously applied to every believing household's doorway—above and along the sides, striking them with hyssop dipped in lamb's blood making each residence an altar of sorts.[7] The lamb itself is "roasted with fire."[8] The wrath of God's judgment fell on Egypt, didn't it? Yet it bypassed those for whom another, in type, bore the inferno of divine retribution atoning *for* the people, *as* the people.

The apostle John, exiled to Patmos,[9] saw in a vision "one like a son of man... His feet were like burnished bronze, when it has been made to glow in a furnace."[10] Do you catch the imagery? Bronze feet cast a penetrating look in the rearview mirror at a bronze altar, clearly reflecting tabernacle or temple sacrifices under an *old covenant* economy. Who's surprised then that our brother should see the Lord Jesus as One who passed through the unbridled fires of judgment as an offering for sin?[11] Passover, with its blood and roasted lamb, pre-figures Calvary as it comes together in a meal where the celebration is more than food.

Longing Desire[12]

Jesus presses and presses hard. There's a vested interest. The word most definitely is *passion*, one that begs intimate participation. It's not their first Passover Seder with the Master, yet this go-around is driven by a distinctive current, if you will, a decidedly different flavor. If the disciples only knew. What they did know, and hopefully see with new eyes, is a cup of wine received in faith is God sealing this improbable lot to Himself.

Let me see if I can explain.

In first century Hebraic culture, a man seeking a bride asks his father to arrange for betrothal by speaking with the father of his cho-sen bride. Her dad's nod of approval secures this most sacred agree-ment as the young man ceremonially offers his intended a cup of wine. "This cup," he pledges, "is my life's blood. Drink, and you'll be mine." Her drinking, as they say, seals the deal, binding them for life. Think covenant here.

Imagine then Jesus's disciples hearing, "This cup is the new cov-enant in My blood." Two ceremonies—one for deliverance, the other for marriage—join in mystical union at our Lord's table[13] as men are confirmed in their chosenness. Love is a poignant draught as they drink in solemn awe and dumbfounded wonder.[14]

Who's surprised then that our Lord anticipates this final Passover with such depths of longing desire? It's not simply the cross as a point of unconscionable suffering; it's what Calvary seals to Him and to us, but there's more. The betrothed couple will not and cannot drink of this cup until they reunite as husband and wife when he gathers his betrothed to himself and takes her home.

Yet again a resonant frequency sounds. "I will not drink of this fruit of the vine from now on until that day when I drink it new with you in My Father's kingdom."[15] Jesus's face is set, His resolve fixed. He drinks purposefully with a view toward brokenness and uncompromised surrender embracing a great deal more than scourging, more than a thorny crown, a hammer and coarse Roman spikes. We're in Philippians two now where attitude is everything, the mindset of faith.[16] Fully God yet fully human.

When You know who You are the issue's settled. Nothing threatens what can't be changed,[17] so releasing Your grip…it's what You do. There's no robbery in being who You are. You're free to lay aside entitlements. Nix reputation. Forget acceptance by deluded pretenders who think they have clout. Let people talk. Your integrity is intact, secure in the Father's hands, so become like one of them choosing what a man must choose, "Not My will, Father, but Yours." See this then as a choice made in eternity and appropriated in time.

"Before I suffer" is the rub. A meal is the touch point where remembering keeps it fresh—Jesus's suffering, His death and our unique participation in it. Convergence, remember? Unbreakable love in His broken body, binding as one in His shed blood. A man trashed humanity.[18] A man must suffer. A real man must die.[19] A new and far better covenant enfolds us, one Sinai could only scan from afar, and that through squinted eyes.[20] As a man, He anticipates in fearful angst that can't be measured. As God, it's a done deal, finished. Gethsemane bridges time and eternity. We eat and remember. The boys don't understand, not now, not yet.

Peter Has to Be Sifted!

Yet the thought of the devil taking Peter apart feels a lot like Jesus bailed.

What if it's us, though? Sometimes it is. If so, it's necessary. A rooster's screech quickly pans to one strung out fisherman who deflates like a wounded blowfish. Our tattered friend looks and feels mentally and emotionally mangled, convinced he's a complete and total wash—a failure, worthless, and incompetent, the world's biggest fool and utter disappointment—to Jesus especially. *Traitor* is the word, a gutless worm. "I tell you tonight, before the cock crows, you will disown me three times," plays and replays.[1] Peter failed miserably! Go ahead; ask him.

We hang so much on Peter, don't we? Knowing the outcome doesn't divorce us from wishful expectations. He's Peter, blessed Simon Bar-Jonah! The man could have done it differently. He should have weathered the storm, we insist, not realizing our good friend had to crash and crash hard. Why? Much of his confidence has Jesus as its source, but a good-sized chunk is still rooted in Peter. What can I say? It is what it is.

God tripped his circuits. He got in on our man and switched up everything. Look at him, a regular guy who once earned his keep by gristle and sweat; now a rooster deflates him. That's Jesus for you, invading a man's turf and upending his world, birthing dreams, stirring the poor slob to repeatedly reach beyond himself, and for what? To give us a taste of reality, that's what. God-sized appointments expose man-sized weaknesses!

"I don't get it," you insist. "Why undress a man that way?" Paul engaged in a similar wrestling match. It took time, but he finally made the connection. "There's nothing good in me!"[2] He's talking flesh here, his own "stuff," and until the light goes on, the likes of Peter, or even Paul, will swing at every ball determined to knock one out of the park. A base hit would have worked for me; not these guys. Do you see where I'm going?

Everyone's stuff is different.

However you slice it, though—good, bad, or all-out ugly— every last one of us is born trying to do life out of our own self-determined efforts, our own perceived self-sufficiency. The only way out then, the only way you, me, or anyone will ever see God as our all-sufficiency is when every confidence in our flesh gets shredded like so many branches in a tree surgeon's wood chipper.[3] Yeah, but when heaven's light goes on, it's rich.

I love how Mike Wells expresses himself in a dedication he wrote:

> To the God who does much with little,
> more with less,
> and everything with nothing.[4]

Tell me then, who in their right mind embraces weakness? Not Peter, not any of the boys. Would you? Gotta be tough to roll with Jesus, right? Wrong. You don't apply for this position. It's a call, and like Abraham, no one sees it coming. "Leave your country," is God's way of introducing Himself to a pagan who prays to the moon.[5]

Leave, if you haven't figured it out, is the call to follow. And that means? It means leaving family. Leave friends and business associates. Leave everything and everyone who ever factored in as any personal sense of identity or security. Leave and don't look back. The reason? We're back to weakness. If the man's going to learn who the God of Abraham is, he's got to be reduced to complete, out-and-out dependence on his newly found God, having nothing and no one to lean on but Him. Amen, it's true.

Things get bumpy, and did I say twisted? It's the only road. Think agony, as in, "Take now your son, your only son."[6] No Sunday school lesson here, no Bible study. All you know is the front end— God's personal claim on the miracle boy Abraham waited a lifetime for, and where our man Abe sits, the last chapter hasn't been written.

He's thinking resurrection, yes, but not before a shepherd's knife threatens to tear Isaac's throat open by his father's own hand.[7] Peter sweats too, as does James and John, but they're determined.

I don't blame them for being rattled. Messiah doesn't die; He conquers. And what do you do with "cursed is everyone who hangs on a tree"?[8] Cursed of God! How could it be? That Jesus would become a curse for us is light-years beyond anyone's frame of reference, Jew or Gentile, but here's where it gets personal. Death by hammer and nails on a Roman gibbet is enough to make anyone's blood run cold, mine included, so when it becomes evident that Calvary won't be denied, Peter isn't the only one moved to die with Jesus.

To a man, all the disciples say they will.[9]

Hearts pound, pledging unfeigned allegiance as brothers who as yet were unaware of the soul and spirit divide of Gethsemane simply want to be with Jesus as He faces the fire. But what do you do when the Master comes unglued? He calls His inner circle aside to wait with Him through this night of horrors, but confusion and fear take its toll, and the land of nod beckons with the promise of relief. "Couldn't you watch with Me for even an hour?" Jesus pleads. "Wake up, will you? Pray like you've never prayed so you don't lose it when temptation blindsides you. The spirit is willing, but the flesh is pathetic. It's so weak!"[10] And weakness predictably falls prey to heavy eyelids.

Who's Surprised?

And therein lies the catch as well as the reason why sifting isn't optional.

Ask any farmer. Sifting is an integral part of the harvesting process. After grain is gathered from the fields and bundled into sheaves,
it's taken to a hilltop or another open-air threshing floor made of
stone or hardened earth where oxen repeatedly trample the wheat
while nickel and dime operations find themselves having to beat it
over and over as part of a long, tedious process using heavy sticks to
break heads from the stalks.

Large wooden pitchforks—winnowing forks as they're called—
are then used to toss broken wheat in the late afternoon breeze. Wind
catches lighter chaff (shell-like husks covering each tender kernel)
along with shorter pieces of straw, blowing it to one side as the grain
drops and gathers into piles where the ladies carefully sort rocks and
rubble from the good stuff. Bugs too. Grain is then taken for grind-
ing with a millstone to make flour. That, guys, is the short version of
what they call sifting.

The Baptist, you remember, spoke of Jesus as having His own
winnowing fork poised for action. "He will thoroughly purge His
threshing floor; and gather His wheat into the barn; but He will
burn up the chaff with unquenchable fire."[11] So is Jesus a farmer?
Obviously yes, but what kind, and how does He go about His business? We need to consider the context. Have you ever thought of
listening to the prophet's heartbeat? I'm serious. There's urgency in
his call to repentance, a sense of immediacy.

> Whatever he may be expecting, John
> is willing to hold his breath.

It's going to happen soon. Our Baptist's words paint an image
Jesus affirms. "The kingdom," He says, "is at hand."[12] So don't put
Him off. Repent, will you? Change your mind now. This is more
than end of the age imagery.[13] There's a duel application, I believe.
Unbelievers are typically portrayed as chaff, gone with the wind and
consumed in the burning fire of God's judgment.[14] Individually,
though—and I'm targeting believers here—we each have our personal chaff that's got to go, but I don't want to get ahead of myself.

Let's go back to the threshing floor, shall we, where wheat is prone to having debris get in the mix, and since no one wants rocky bread, it all needs sifted to separate grain from sticks, stones, and pesky crawly critters. Large wood-framed sieves made of string or reed mesh were typically a four-hand operation; although, one-man versions fit the bill in small-scale mom and pop settings. Whatever it takes. Just get the job done.

Chaff, Stones, and Yucky Stuff

Chaff conveys an image of the unwanted part of grain.

You can't make bread with it; although, cattle don't mind if a little chaff gets thrown in their feed. It's nature's filler, routinely plowed with broken bits of straw into soil for enrichment. In Scripture, chaff speaks almost exclusively to useless trash worthy only of heaven's judgment. This is particularly significant as it deals with us as believers, what drives every man or woman "under the sun,"[1] especially life on my terms—the good and not so good.

I'm not kidding! We see it clearly in Peter. As long as he's on board with the Master, our friend is all in, but the moment Jesus makes a move that doesn't look or feel right, the brakes go on. Us too. We do it a lot, actually. Meet Mr. Control, the illusion that I can keep people, life, or even God in check. So, who's eating from the wrong tree again? Flesh kicks into control mode as knee-jerk thoughts and feelings become your plumb line and my magnetic north, driven by rationale that seems to make sense. That's Peter!

It's true, and thanks to Adam, what we call love and acceptance are pretty much earned commodities. Do what pleases me. Bring something of value to the table, and I'll pay you off with love. I'll validate you with acceptance. Cute, huh? No, but this is life as we know it, what you and I have been weaned on. The late Anabel Gillham, cofounder of Lifetime Guarantee Ministries with her husband, Bill, nails her mark:

> A child interprets the behavior of the
> important others around him from his totally

self-centered view, so if they are workaholic per-
fectionists, he concludes: "Aha! If I want them to
love me, I've got to do what they do."[2]

Color it as you will, we do whatever it takes. Fold if you roll
snake eyes.[3] And whether the target is perfectionism, fitting with the
right group, a promotion maybe, if we're shooting for acceptance,
it's all the same cloth. I've spoken with men who've invested themselves in gay relationships. They hate the sex but crave affirmation.
How about the ladies? I've seen grown women trash their virtue for
the promise of love or status. I smoked dope for the first time (and
many thereafter) in hopes of acceptance and validation from a jazz
musician who carried serious weight in an elite community I sought
entrance to. Choose your poison.

It's rampant in the church.

Where love hunger craves affirmation, leaving no stone
unturned, the church has more than its share of refugees—the
world's offscourings—outcasts and all-out success stories. Hey, now
there's an unlikely, and should I say unexpected crew, an odd couple if ever there was one—rascals and VIPs? Appetites represented
by such a mixed bag are beyond counting, knowing no bounds or
exclusions, and the church is where they show in spades. Why not?
Jesus stands with outstretched arms to the unlikely and unthinkable.
"Come to Me," He beckons, "all who labor and are weary, everyone
who's crushed and weighed down," promising Himself.[4]

Oh, the many who need to be needed, affirmation junkies whose
soulful indigence keeps them wondering if they'll ever arrive. I know.
What about those unfortunates who crash hard and burn on the altar
of ministry sacrificing family and integrity? Heart-wrenching for
sure. Enter the elitists for whom sound doctrine is identity driven,
broad phylacteries and artistically lengthened tassels included.[5] Chaff
has a flavor for every palette.

Prior to Eden's couple acting out in unbelief, love has no strings
attached, no conditions to satisfy, just a liberating invite to dis-

cover man's chief end.[6] God's all-encompassing love was theirs to be enjoyed and freely shared with one another. It's the air our first parents breathed, the embrace they were nurtured in, but the man and his woman walked away taking the rest of humanity with them. And that leaves us where? We've got to convince folks, give them credible reasons to get next to us. And God? Do you and I have to qualify with Him?

What if we can't? What if God looks at everything you call life, your best efforts and all that I value so dearly, and condemns it as being only worthy of judgment and death? What if it's all chaff?

God knows I'm not trying to be callous or even remotely insensitive.

Peter's no pathetic "Pick me!" or prideful snob. Jesus called things out in the man that didn't exist, but Peter is no good to Jesus. He isn't, and Peter's no good to himself either. The man is no good to anyone as long as he's giving it his best shot or committed to trying harder. We're talking truth here. Our best and most noble intentions are but lost memories of Eden gone sour, filthy rags as our good friend Isaiah has it.[7] Do you see? Everything we were created for is given over to striving after the wind in search of self-sufficiency, but no, we don't see it. Reaching yet never grasping, learning and never coming to grips with truth.[8]

What gets me is this: Our fleshly chaff—your bent toward independent thoughts, feelings, and appetites coupled with my self-efforts—is with us from the get-go, from the moment the doctor slaps our naked bottoms and we wail like sirens. It's so much a part of us we're convinced that it truly is the sum and substance of our personhood. Why not? In Adam, it's all we've got, all we can draw from in our attempts to make life work, but it doesn't.

Left to ourselves, we're hopelessly broken cisterns.[9]

Don't like hearing that? Me neither. I thought for sure that I, in myself, needed to be a complete package, a self-contained repository of sorts—something, anything that could be construed as having value. A nod my direction topped off my tank just as Jesus's smile was all Peter needed. It's more than either of us could have hoped for, so loyalty for one simple fisherman was more than big; it was huge.

Me too. I'd go to the mats for the man or woman whole believed in me. What about you? Can you quantify gratitude? I think not, which means Elder Pete was committed to the hilt, but that still falls short for, well, for all of us.[10]

"But," someone asks, "aren't we to love God with all we've got, all of our heart, soul, and mind, all of our strength?"[11] Nice shot! It's what we were created for, but again, thanks to Adam, your best and mine falls short, way short of the intended goal, and besides, it's tainted.[12] Sin, right? Yep, that's pretty much it. You, me, the lot of us were made for more than sin, more than doing life on our own, yet we'll never know anything beyond where we've been apart from a God-sized revelation of our own bankruptcy.

> In myself I may want to do the right thing,
> but I can't.[13]
> There's nothing good in me, in my flesh,
> that is.[14]

My own personal chaff.

> But I need something more. For I know the law but still can't keep it, and if the power of sin within me keeps sabotaging my best intentions, I obviously need help! I realize I don't have what it takes. I can will it, but I can't do it... Something has gone wrong deep within me and gets the better of me every time. (Romans 7:17–18, The Message)

And the Point With All of This Is What?

There's chaff, yes, but the real Peter is made of wheat!

For some, this is a no-brainer. Not for Peter. How could it? His heart is trashed and his head putty. Jesus didn't close up shop and run for cover, Peter did. And for someone who'd been given every advantage, every opportunity, for him to tuck tail and run is...it's unthinkable. Flaky groupies abound, yes, but the real stuff will be tried. Always. The reason? To prove that it's real. Enter the servant girl who does her number on Peter the way she does it to us. I know, we're talking different players at a different time in a different setting. No matter how you slice it, though, it's the same outcome. Left to himself, Peter comes up short. Stunted.

Okay, so what? Is Peter the measure of his performance failures? Is that who he is? Ask him as he trudges in numb disbelief from the high priest's courtyard. He's running on empty, but that's a fisherman's "stuck feeler" talking.[1] This, friends, is a man who's jammed to the hilt! Who wouldn't be? A smug and haughty accuser rubs Peter's face in the acrid stench of bold-faced promises that sour by the minute.[2] "Don't worry, I've got your back, Jesus! I'm here for You, even if no one else is!" From where Peter sits, there's much he regrets, but does his repeated denial of the Master disqualify him? Does Jesus kick him to the curb?[3]

You and I both understand the story doesn't end here, but does Peter know it? Not now, not at this juncture. Hours earlier, Jesus assures His unraveling apprentice he'll come back around, that he needs to be there for the others who are in this with him. Does he remember that now? Not hardly. All Peter hears is a rooster. All he sees are Jesus's eyes. Nothing and no one else exists, absolutely nothing.

But there's a greater reality to this gnarly milieu no one sees. Jesus prayed. No wishful thinking, no hoping against hope. "For the gifts and calling of God are irrevocable."[4] Our Lord intercedes knowing the grizzly ordeal awaiting His boy. The man's heart and head are about to be run through a meat grinder, yet there's hope, a rock-solid assurance concerning Peter that Jesus lays hold of. Hit pause and rewind back to a night of prayer where Father and Son sort twelve for apostolic appointees from a truckload of others.[5] Peter's a marked man, and Jesus knows. He, in agreement with the Father, tags him. The tag holds.

What can I say? There's more to the man than he realizes, a lot more than himself. Imagine Jesus stepping into the picture three years earlier with His humble yet commanding presence engaging unwary hearts. For twelve, their participation in Jesus is larger than all they could have asked for, much less imagined. Guess what that means when the Master is cuffed and hauled off to court? You got it. The boys come apart.

They had to.

Their value and substance, their identity is in Jesus—not themselves, not what they do. It's not in Peter or James, not in John, not in Bartholomew, Philip, or Thomas. Apart from Jesus, there's nothing left to this befuddled lot, and that's a good thing! If three years under the Master's tutelage have yielded anything of value, it's this: Jesus's presence is everything to them, and not passively. He's not Buddha or Mohammed, nothing like Confucius, dispensing wisdom and knowledge, then turning them loose. What Jesus teaches demands His active involvement.[6] So when his flesh—Peter's strength, his know-how and determination—go belly up, a man-sized flounder checks out in shame. Jesus was right in saying Peter would bail. He did.

Anyone who finds him or herself alongside our crushed and confused brother—thinking similar thoughts, getting a taste of what he's feeling—is in for an emotional free fall. Having nothing and no one to hold onto is beyond scary. God may be there and very much part of the equation, but it feels like He's nowhere![7] We need to go through this, though. Desperately. Death to our flesh on Calvary's hell-tree makes no allowances for shortcuts. And Peter thought only Jesus was dying. Little did he know that union with Jesus means participation in His death. More on that later; for now, take two or three steps back and remember with me.

Peter has been called.

Think chosen. "You did not choose Me but I chose you."[8]

I know we've already mentioned this, so please bear with me a moment. When the bottom drops out, you've got to double back. Why? You've got to know, and I've got to know who we are; make our calling and election sure.[9] Peter said that. He said it to affirm believers, others who had received the same kind of faith that kept him afloat [10] (We did talk about this, didn't we?) because they had the same Jesus—the One who ever lives to make intercession for us.[11] "I have prayed for you," Jesus assures Peter. "I have prayed that your faith won't fail."[12] The faith Peter received was effectual because the One who planted it is *faithful.* Peter sees that now.

But Whatever Can Be Shaken Will Be

Understand that where God builds, He shakes, and He sifts.

We've also seen how He sometimes uses Beelzebub and his minions. Some time back I heard a Bible teacher suggest that even though Satan's and his fallen angels' position have changed, their job description hasn't. I like that. God created angels, fallen or not, to serve Him and His purposes. Guess what they're doing? The devil doesn't see it. He's too self-absorbed, so in seducing Adam, the serpent gets his own head crushed.[13] While getting his pound of Job's tormented flesh, the accuser is silenced by the man's humility in worship.[14] God truly is good, and the presence of Jesus in a simple fisherman's life makes him a force to be reckoned with.

Peter is crazy, crazy enough to trust Jesus.

His madness needs to be checked. He's got to be crushed and humiliated, rendered null and void. That's the devil's take on things. God, on the other hand, is bent on death to the natural man who can't wrap his brain around all God has for him.[15] He's got to shatter every ounce, every smidge of confidence Peter has in Peter, in his ability to follow Jesus, his commitment to the Master. Like the apostle from Tarsus, Peter needs a good, hard look at his flesh, his "stuff," as we've said—Peter's strength, Peter's rationale, Peter's limited, if not twisted, and very human understanding, Peter's efforts. Trash the lot of it; there's nothing good.[16] Apart from Jesus, everything our brother puts on the line, even with the best of intentions, is a complete and total wash.

It belongs in the toilet.[17]

> That which is born of the flesh is flesh, and that which is born of the Spirit is spirit. (John 3:6, NKJV)
> Flesh and blood cannot inherit the kingdom of God. (1 Corinthians 15:50, NKJV)

Now get this straight. You and I are not about to beat up on friend Peter for his flesh. It's just not happening, and here's why. Until Jesus invades his space, flesh is all the man's got to work with. Us too, for that matter. We understand only too well then that Peter isn't hearing any talk of death and Roman crosses. I'm on board. Apart from our having walked Calvary's road ourselves, no one realizes how desperately we need this personal touch point. The cross marks boundaries, that which is born of the flesh and that which is born of the Spirit.

An intimate discovery of "not I, but Christ."[18]

The kingdoms of this world are built on men and women trying to make life come together in the strength of their own resources, their determined efforts independent of God. Color that sin,[19] and it's not what we were created for. The cross renders a much-needed death blow to you, and I giving it our best shot because our best won't cut it. Our flesh falls short, as we've seen, decidedly short of the original design and God's ultimate intention.[20]

> We were created to bask in and to radiate
> the glory of God.
> Christ in us is the hope of that glory.[21]

The cross is the means to that end. This, friends, is for Peter, and right now one fisherman isn't making the connection. Imagine that. Truth be told, in sparing Jesus, Peter hopes to save his own neck. I would have attempted the same mindless lunacy. So would you. Reality, though, tells a different story. "Whoever finds his life," Jesus categorically affirms, "will lose it, and whoever loses his life for my sake will find it."[22]

The cross is God's sieve, so when Jesus calls Peter aside with, "Simon, Simon," He speaks directly to what needs sifting—Peter's "Simon life," his "old man" along with his "flesh,"[23] the house Peter built and the mold a rebellious and unbelieving world would squeeze this man into. A radical new creation is at hand, which means the old (without exception) has got to go. Why? "Unless the LORD builds the house," Scripture tells us, "they labor in vain who build it."[24] What He builds stands, what He doesn't falls.[25] It's got to.

> He shakes what can be shaken, putting it to
> death and thereby separating wheat from chaff,
> sifting the stuff of earth from heaven's new life.

What Is God's Best?

It breaks our hearts when folks trip over themselves by going back to fleshly quicksand. How is it, a dog returning to its own vomit?[1] That's beyond sorry, or even sad, it's sick! The real madness is the attraction that looks and (gag!) smells good. To them, it does. And whether that spells a return to DOC or life going belly up, we're talking the same old song.[2] Hit rewind and play. What's scary is where the return seems to smell of success. There's favor on the job and a good flow of cash in hand, yet where's God? People choke on the good life and don't have a clue.

We want to see them succeed, move forward to discover God's best. That's the catch, though, isn't it? God's best. What is God's best, exactly? What does it look like? Any individual who's been put in our path—and we in theirs—is God's personal workmanship from start to finish.[3] And whether it's me or another Hook Ministries volunteer, we're privileged to be even a small part of their particular journey, their process.

Therein lies the key. Connecting with God's best is a process, a discovery process. And God's best for any man, His very best for a woman, can't possibly be seen on the front end, but why? Bottom line? We don't know where He's taking them, or us, for that matter. Steps for each are as unique as they themselves are. To define success, then, strictly in terms of structured appearances is to miss the mark by a mile, maybe two.[4]

I'm thinking right now of a statement Hook Ministries puts in a letter of acceptance, our commitment to men we as a ministry agree to come alongside upon their release from prison:

> We're committed to invest ourselves in getting to know you, your strengths and weaknesses as well as your needs and desires as a person of inestimable value—discovering how and where we fit into the equation. Hook Ministries isn't a large, well-oiled machine with lots of people and resources like an overflowing bank account, but we're willing to give what we have, which is ourselves. We want to see you grow in the discovery of who you are in Christ.

Process and discovery travel hand in glove. They've got to. So much is pent up in a man's soul, things he doesn't understand, much less know they exist, that blow like a volcano or shuts him out when he doesn't see it coming! How much is invested in survival, a strange and fearful proposition as he steps onto a prison yard, or off the school bus as a little guy in a new neighborhood. You get tried, beat down. It could be Dad with a section of garden hose who's bent on reshaping your attitude or a bulldog in the housing unit. Meet your new cellie![5] "Where do I fit?" begs "Is there a place?" where comfort zones come as prime real estate.

I'm still learning. Process, then, is the path where learning quite often comes by sifting. I'm serious. Discovery is a point when knowing rings true for the sifted as "complete in Him."[6] It's the light going on that says, "That's me! That really is me!" with conviction and full assurance. "I'm not a dirt bag anymore."

Knee jerk carries a lot of weight when a soul's locked down. Most don't get it; although, some do. Jerry took a walk with me after church service one Sunday. He'd been out of prison two weeks, or so. The man was quiet—collecting his thoughts, not sure how to say what seemed irrational but felt real. "I feel like..." he hesitates. "I feel like I'm wearing a sign."

"A sign, really?" I probe. "So, talk to me."

"You'll think I'm off, like I'm crazy," the brother stalls, feeling me out. Did I care, did I genuinely want to want to hear his heart?

"Come on, man. Talk to me. What sign?"

Slow, sheepish eyes own the truth: "A sign on my back that says *ex-convict*, and everyone sees it."

"Everyone?"

"Yeah, everyone. I feel it." So many agree.

Paranoia is one of shame's traveling companions

Feel Rules the Day

Feel fueled by imagination. I understand. Thirty-some years ago on the verge of a nervous breakdown, I worked hard on an ulcer, and I'm not being cute. Eighty hours a week, around-the-clock some days, on what I believed was a promising job opportunity. Think I'm kidding? Ask my wife. She's the one who drove me to the ER at godforsaken hours when my stomach was tortured by what felt like a red-hot iron. Amphetamines fueled a tired and seemingly mindless zombie's body that didn't know if it was coming or going—my season in hell, the price of identity and security, I thought.

What was left to me? A career in music was in the toilet while ministry seemed more than questionable. God's refinery in the so-called secular world proved itself an education I would never have received in a ministerial setting, but I was failing the course! Again, it felt that way. A full-on investment as a graphic arts cameraman was at least questionable despite my scaling the industry ladder while making something of a name for myself locally. I felt like a failure, justifying whatever I needed to ease an ocean of shameful pain.

Feel became the measure of truth.

So, can I relate to those who choose to bail? In spades. And like them, what I couldn't see, or wrap my brain around, was the possibility that God could be at work in me. The fog in my soul felt impenetrable, but God was engaged, and my fervent prayer for Him to make me part of the answer, and not part of the problem, was being answered. Yet it felt like God, my Savior, washed His hands of me. Had He? Nope. Not even close.

Peter gets it. My sifting, and his, heightens where the accuser insists we "cough up" a few good reasons for God to keep misfits like us as part of the mix.[7] Okay, gang, pop quiz time: Did Jesus choose Peter believing he was such a prize catch or me for being a guy showing signs of promise? Nix on both counts. The reason for our calling and election isn't found in us; it's in Him. His love gives us value, and we're sifted for the precious wheat it breeds—born again from incorruptible seed says Peter.[8] God's love initiates. We benefit.

The Gift of God

Apart from a biblical comprehension of grace, this often gets twisted.

Understand please, good news for the poor or release to captives doesn't always feel good, not at first, not ever for some. I'm thinking right now of a young up-and-coming professional who didn't know his soul was imprisoned.[1] Imagine that he should be drawn to Jesus. The sad truth concerning those who are drawn, many pull back. Incredible, I know, and in this instance, the key that would have unlocked this man's cell was refused. Why would he, or anyone, deny their own freedom? Easy. See Jesus as loss instead of gain.

It happens all the time. Guys who get released romanticize memories of prison the way folks we know did over Egypt's leeks, onions, and garlic.[2] "Hey, man! I had three hots and a cot!"[3] Really? *Really?* All the comforts of home, right? No. Comfort for the confused is predictable, knowing what to expect and when to expect it, versus the uncertainties of life on the street that call them to accountability. And for a young professional with position and clout, it's the uncertainties of following Jesus—selling all and selling out. He's a camel, as it were, who's got to squeeze through a needle's impossible eye. So, for him, it's not happening.[4]

Icing on the cake for the self-indulgent in self-pity's stagnant mire will only add fuel to their fires. Boy, do I know! Grace begins with seeing and knowing the gift of God.[5] A man of means doesn't see treasure in Jesus.[6] He can't. A dignitary on his order is way too fixated, too self-absorbed. For him, Jesus is an attraction, an embellishment, not the whole package. Any joy associated with liquidating family assets to aid the destitute is nowhere, and for what, to follow some luminary, an esoteric Rabbi? It's religious extremism with too high a price tag.

But not for those who have eyes to see

Good news for a confirmed adulteress comes at the cost of her life. Nearly. Behind closed doors, God alone sees the lady's heart. Is this a one-time fling or a way of life? No one denies the lopsided conspiracy she was dragged into.[7] The real target is Jesus, but she feels the heat, and why not? Soap opera aside, the verdict is guilty, and that's God talking through Moses by way of stone tablets and papyrus.[8] Consider then, apart from direct confrontation, would there be change, any shame, or remorse on the lady's part for her actions? I don't think so. She'd continue to furnish her ho-hum world the same way, for the same self-serving reasons.

The Law, however, exposes choices for what they are, and the lady condemns herself, with or without would-be executioners chomping at the bit. She stands guilty as charged, but there's a far greater reality. God is up to something that blindsides everyone. (Process and discovery, don't forget.) Note then sinful passions aroused by the Law[9] are put on the street for everyone to see—nowhere to run, nowhere to hide—and that's not just good. It's necessary. The grace that makes faith possible doesn't dodge, or in some way nullify, the Law. No, it affirms calling a spade a spade allowing sin no wiggle room whatsoever.[10]

The Law doles out a justifiable sentence: death.

She earned it. Not to be crass or cold, but twenty-first century minds have all but divorced themselves from any framework for morality beyond their own sensibilities, a plumb line on a sliding scale. I want life on my terms where change, quite often, is the ongoing constant. Never has there been such an open depiction of all Adam opted for. "Have it your way." The serpent smiles knowing the harvest is greater than the seed. And if your way takes you down roads where sexuality and personal entitlements are more fluid than fixed, then confusion reigns. It's a bad day for those who would consider darkness light and vice versa.[11]

And that leaves us where? It confirms a simple maxim: people change, God doesn't.[12] Yahweh is His own point of reference, His own magnetic north, and that works for one outstanding reason. He's right. He's always right. And despite the serpent's lie, you and I can serve as independent contractors with one major caveat. We're not right, ever. Which is why God invented this thing called Law. He cares enough to show the likes of us how ugly things get when they're not right because they don't plumb. There are consequences.

Not terribly tolerant, is it?

Old snake eyes forgot to touch on that one. I wonder why. But love, I'm talking real love whatever the cost, sets us straight even if the truth hurts, and hurts badly. It squares with reality, and if that's how this thing actually works, the lady getting caught with her knickers down is God's love and compassion bold-faced. The "I don't get it crowd" mixed in with you, me, or anyone anywhere can't possibly comprehend, much less enter into a meaningful appreciation of how heinous and downright repulsive sin is to One who knows only the beauty and splendor of holiness or how lethal it is to those God created to bear His image and likeness![13]

That's right, lethal. "For in the day that thou eatest thereof thou shalt surely die."[14] No threat, it is what it is—sin's malignant fallout—Adam's choice, not God's. Get this then, as abhorrent as sin is to God and its toxicity to us, a fallen race continues to make going our own way its preference, cursing and denying God, cancer of the soul that invariably finds us out.[15] Remember: God didn't choose death; man did. And the open shame that dresses it keeps us scrambling for fig leaves, a wardrobe we've settled into, our personal prison greens.[16]

The kick in all of this is staggering, actually. Are you ready? For all our excuses and insistence to wallow in sin's yuck and mud, we were created for holiness. Folks, I'm serious. The image and likeness of God is all about being naked and unashamed, which tells on us big time. Sin isn't natural to us. It truly isn't. But please, before you write me off as having lost touch with reality, I have a question:

What sin of choice—pick a sin, any sin—
improves and makes you a better person?

Can't think of one, can you? Me neither. Need an escape? Sin's
your man.[17] Seduce, cover up, power up, but improve and make
either of us better? It's not happening; not now, not ever. The thief,
as we know, comes only to steal, kill, and destroy.[18] The power of sin
is a ruthless taskmaster demanding his pound of flesh. "Everyone
who commits sin becomes its slave."[19] Ask the meth or sex addict. A
lie may get us out of a jam or help close a deal while binding us to
the father of lies.[20] Not good. Truth is. No matter how promising,
how sweet the savor, sin metastasizes, and death is its seal, making sin
altogether unnatural to our humanity.

Strange though, for the death and corruption sin yields, the
ugliness it breeds, God uses sin. He absolutely does. His Law arouses
and exposes sin for what it is,[21] unmasking sham and pretense in
ways that uncovers our sordid nakedness allowing no retreat, not that
we don't try. Adam again, huh? Frail, nasty fig leaves. Sure, but here's
a woman who can't run or even try to cover up. She's painted into a
corner where the same Law that rendered a guilty verdict brings her
a gift she so desperately needs.[22] You know what I mean, the gift who
claims her as His own. Jesus makes her stench His and His righteousness hers while disarming all accusers.

And that does what for you?

Sin is high treason; no pretense, no exaggeration. So, for David
to lure another man's wife into his bed, get the lady pregnant, then
have her mister eliminated, a brother who claims to know God seems
to have jumped ship with capital offenses to face. But can the man
live with himself? Nope. Sin weighs David down, wasting his soul,[23]
especially in the stillness of those long, quiet hours "when our hearts
are most unedited and vulnerable."[24] Our king can't pretend any
more. Excuses he's tried to hide behind won't wash. Surrender to
heaven's penetrating scrutiny hurts like crazy, but what else is there?
And did I say it's necessary?[25]

Identity is tied into our God connection, a connection that either is or it isn't. "In Christ" is a reality David looked to from a distance in hope. Slam dunk! This brother was created for more than indulging vulgar fleshly lusts, and he knows it. David is a man who's seen too much. He's tasted.[26] Nathan's "Thou art the man!" cuts hard and fast through so much fog to get to the real man.[27] His flesh is yuck but go deeper. Don't stay in the shallows. Being found out takes David, it takes you, and it takes me to where we can no longer tread water.[28]

It exposes our God connection; it either is or it isn't.

"Thanks!" you say. "I need encouragement, and you just took what little wind I had out of my sails." Adrift on the sea, are you? That's the look-and-feel department. Try it this way: Your fault and my sorry blunder expose the depths of our need, cutting through so much fog while probing a truly born-again believer's deepest yearning for God Himself. You and I may never face Goliath or stare down a hungry lion, but Bathsheba? She's another story, an increasingly common one. And for the shame triggered when the unwitting surrender to desire's seductive prelude, we learn something of God. You and I, we can't touch bottom![29]

Our lady friend in John chapter 8 is shocked to discover an invite to a God connection she never dreamed could have her name on it. Talk about an unexpected gift! I said earlier grace begins with knowing the gift of God. Not quite. Grace begins with discovering the gift of God, allowing Him to take us to deep places in even deeper waters where only He can keep us afloat. And we learn this how? By sinking, possibly starting to. Thank God Jesus is there. Ask Peter.[30] "In all probability there are more people who are helped by the fact that Peter denied our Lord, than by the fact that Peter walked on the water."[31] Marinate in that a while.

You, Me, and Our Estranged Hearts

Love calls for confrontation at times. Getting in a man or woman's face over costly choices they've made isn't fun by any means, but it is so needed. The intent is to draw them out, to connect and not superficially. Easier said than done, right? Sometimes, and that's often because people are bent on shielding themselves—shielding from others, shielding from God. How about shielding themselves from themselves? Imagine that. If you've been mentally or emotionally assaulted, you know the feeling. Forget easy. It's not happening.

Shielding oneself may seem to create a safety zone, of sorts, but messes with you big time. Trust me. You might be a closed-up kind of guy who's numb more often than not, an emotional flat line, or a frazzled basket case who collapses into a bundle of raw nerves if someone even looks at you the wrong way. Could be you live on the edge and your one-inch fuse has everyone in the vicinity walking on eggshells hoping you won't blow. Find a shoe that fits? There are others. Whatever size or style that's yours there's a good chance you really don't know yourself. You heard me.

You and your heart aren't all that well acquainted.

Whoa, now there's a can of worms! It's true though. And for all our insistence that we know what's best for us, friends, you and I may have to at least be willing to own our ignorance—of God, yes, but ourselves as well. All right, well now that I've dropped a bomb on you, let's see if we can stop and pick up a few pieces. I say this knowing the hope that's ours as a covenant community built on the finished work of the cross. If God can recreate folks from the inside out, Christ in us sifts and shakes, so only what He builds is left standing.[1] By faith, you and I are privileged participants; we enter in as He engages our hearts. It's called learning.

Shame's Oft Tangled Web

Confront someone you care about for the purpose of helping them get to hidden thoughts, fractured motives leading to bonehead blunders, and more often than not, eye contact is broken. Who's surprised? It's easier to stare at the floor or turn nervously to one side when your soul does flip-flops. Anybody been there? Asking a man, "What happened?" doesn't get to the real story, the way "Why'd you do it?" barely scratches the surface.

Please don't get me wrong; they're both good and necessary questions. But we need to see them as launchpads to the likes of "I messed up," short answers to what could possibly be extremely complex. Rejection rides in the top ten, as do unbelief and shame. My all-time favorite, "There was this woman," puts a fresh spin on Adam's age-old cop-out that makes God the bad guy.[2] Cute, huh? Not really. However you slice it, they're only symptoms, not root issues—presenting problems, as they say.[3] Try this one on for size:

"When did you start feeling like things were coming apart on you?"

"Months ago, I guess."

Months? Sometimes weeks, could be days. Whatever it is, time is a man or woman's undoing, not their ally—time that's lapsed, precious, invaluable time that can't be turned back, time that could be all the difference in the world. "So why didn't you call somebody when you were feeling the heat? Why didn't you reach out?" In that split-second, you might catch a glimpse of telltale eyes. Talk of jobs, drugs, and relationships draws them closer to the surface, but when, "Why didn't you call?" hits the front burner, eyes drop, and the air goes cold.

"I was ashamed."

That's it! Something about being brought into the open that takes every last one of us back to Eden as God invades what you and I naively see as personal space, our turf. "Where are you?" He calls, and we cringe in paralysis. Paradise lost is a cold black hole, an empty, bottomless pit with nothing and no one to hold onto.

What do you say, what can you possibly do when there's nowhere to run, nowhere to hide and all eyes are on you? They see what you've done, the choices you made. Was there ever a safe and secure place where "naked and unashamed" spoke your name?[4] Are you the prodigal whose heart has no resting place? Now pigs mock your nakedness. You can't go back, can you? What will they do if you dare show your face? What will they say, Dad especially? There's no rewind button to hit, no pause, only shame and a runaway imagination.

Imaginations kick in, and David understands. "Taking counsel in my soul," he calls it.[5] Fueled by shame, things get more than crazy as scenarios take shape where me, myself, and I write scripts looking forward and back. Forward imagining, "What if this or that happens?" back as we gaze in the rearview mirror mourning, "If only I hadn't, things would be different."

A brother finishes two decades in prison, and like Rip Van Winkle, the world he left has radically changed.[6] Intimidating, to say the least. Finding a place to fellowship, a genuine family connection in the body of Christ, only makes sense, wouldn't you say? Where to look, though? No clue here. I don't live in his neck of the woods or know anyone who does. Count that a God-sized problem. And since we or no one else can be there to come alongside him, our brother flies solo, as blind as a bat. Alone feels so incredibly lonely.

"I'd see myself walking into a church on a Sunday morning feeling like I don't belong there." Anticipating rejection, is he? Imagine that. All eyes are on you. They're reading your sign. "That's nuts," you say, but is it? Where feel calls the shots, it sticks. It sticks big time.

"Hi!" someone smiles. "You must be new here."

"First time."

"So where are you from?"

"Here originally. Been away for a while."

"Really, where?"

"Uh…" long, hesitant pause. "I just got out of prison."

"Prison, how long?"

"Twenty years."

Uneasiness abounds on both sides.

"That's tough. Hope things work out. See you around then, okay?"

He knows it won't happen; they both do. Church member: "I met a guy this morning. Strange, he just got out of prison. I wonder what crime he committed," and on it goes. Imaginations. That's looking forward. Our brother could just as easily have looked back. He probably did. Now there's a road paved with regret, the land of "If only," I call it. "If only I hadn't been such a bonehead, I wouldn't have gotten myself locked up. If only this or that," on and on—the song that never ends. Go forward; go back. It doesn't matter. To this day, I've not met anyone who returns from either of those places encouraged. I never was; I still don't.

Do you know why God never goes there? He can't. The answer's simple, really. I Am is about truth, isn't He? The land of "What if?" and the land of "If only" don't exist! They're not real. As convincing as our active and creative imaginations get at times, the whole thing's an illusion—lies that run us in never-ending circles—lies masquerading as truth. We can choose to reject lies. Believe it's truth, though, and the lie owns us!

It Happens a Lot

Colorful and textured images woven into the pages of Scripture show us the connection between sin and shame. I'm thinking appearances, circumstantial evidence like Potiphar's wife with Joseph's cloak in her clenched, shaking fist, yet he was innocent. She's the culprit. Achan's another story,[1] as is Judah, caught with his hand in the cookie jar, so to speak, after a little extracurricular activity with a disguised daughter-in-law who exposes him for all the right reasons.[2] Saul was found out when his unbelief and arrogance come full harvest in flagrant disobedience to God's instructions and so forfeits his throne.[3] Then there's Samson.[4]

But there's another tack we need to consider.

Gregory Boyle, who authors a gut-level look at the heart by way of ministry among Los Angeles's Hispanic gangbangers, quotes American educator and counselor John Bradshaw, who dares suggest that shame is the root of all addictions.[5] Curious, isn't it? Boyle takes what he postulates beyond the usual scope of substance abuse and the more widely recognized lifestyle and identity addictions to that of "gang addiction." I hadn't considered such a possibility, but the man's got a point. Talk significance and security to those who, in a dark and fearful demonic world, have no place to hang their hat may find themselves painted in gang colors.

On the street or behind the walls, hear the man's heart as he calls out excruciating shame others frequently use to control and manipulate folks by way of their feelings.[6]

The image is one of tangible disgrace that to many 'homies' feels like a lifeline.[7] Gang or no gang, there's no shortage of folks who view street runners and inmates through jaded lenses, and the shame it projects is truly addicting. An inmate with a young family cringes when I ask if they visit him. "I don't want them to," he snaps.

"Why not?" I wonder aloud.

"My boy can't see me here. It's not how I want him to know his dad." Oh, the tangled web we weave,[8] and to what end? The man finished his stint and inside a year "catches"[9] a new case, another fourteen years, I hear. More to his shame, I'm afraid.

Then there's the "me only" crowd, as in: "Leave me alone. I don't need anyone else's drama!" Really? Self-imposed isolation? "Hey, I'm just here to do my time!" (A friend once told us she'd prefer a neighborhood without neighbors within eye or earshot of her!) It's easy to see why folks get insistent. People violate our space when their felt needs attaches your name, or mine, to it. Call it the pressure of expectation and the weight it piles on shoulders that barely manage the bitterness of their own shame.

Yes, but there are times when misery truly does love company.

Those who've tasted life's rancid fallout, or found themselves snagged in the undertow of desperation, realize this sad lot doesn't enjoy the pain they call home. So, what's the draw? Why latch onto it so tenaciously? That's easy. They've gathered a cheering section who will link arms, empathize with them to hopefully justify their right to wallow in the misery of pain and shame while feeding the flame of one another's fire![10]

Think "victim." If there's no way out, if life has confirmed "You'll never amount to anything,"[11] that it's set in concrete, then shame energized by fear will sabotage a multitude of thoughts and choices. I'll facilitate my own demise convinced, "It's who I am." Then what? I'll seek to surround myself with those who keep wind in my sails with, "Wow, you didn't get a fair shake. They just don't understand you." And I'm the one feeding it.

The Last Word?

Actions leading to shame can be costly, to say the least.

Ask our first parents as they viewed Eden in the rearview mirror. Lot's wife can't talk much now, so why go to her?[1] What about Ananias and Sapphira?[2] Joseph's brothers felt the squeeze when the fruit of their jealousy came back to bite them years later. Shame comes as the agonizing spinoff of someone who's been shamefully violated. I'm remembering David's son, Amnon, who forces himself on half-sister, Tamar.[3] A reoccurring theme sounds when a king gets his clock cleaned in battle or a fool goes public.[4] Friends, the shoe fits in any number of scenarios, and it hits like a pile driver, but there's more, a lot more to Peter's story.

It doesn't end with shame.

The man's had his issues, and lots of egg on his face, but when the cock crows the impetus that uncorks a flood of bitter tears isn't just shame, there's remorse. Shame spills out in disgrace that accompanies public humiliation when a man or woman is hung out to dry with their dirty laundry where everyone can see it—which I'm convinced is King Saul's undoing when a teenage David returns to Jerusalem with Goliath's head in hand—shame with jealousy following hot and heavy on its heels.[5] Not so with Peter, not even close.

Of course, there are people in the courtyard, a mixed bag of them, but what goes down when the rooster crows is personal. This is between Peter and Jesus. Shame writes the last chapter only when pride is wounded, and you can't bear up under ridicule from those whose acceptance and affirmation have kept you afloat. Remorse, on the other hand, makes it hard for you to live in your own skin before the God who's enfolded you in so much love, so much favor, so much of Himself. Shame, and shame alone, is Esau caught in self-pity's relentless stranglehold,[6] while remorse is David before Nathan— remorse and repentance.[7]

No more running, no more hiding.

Shame and remorse frequently show up at the same table, and maybe this is my thing, but humor me. David was known for humbling himself at covenant love's throne with, "Let me not be ashamed, O LORD," and why? The king is on the firing line. He's got enemies who would love to take him out if for no reason other than he's the man, he's David, so the king fervently prays that God shield him— keep him from humiliation by ambush or defeat in battle.[8] Should that happen David's undoing is the people's undoing, his shame is their shame. That's a different flavor from what we're used to, isn't it? You know it is.

The shame we see most often in our ministry is wounded pride.

"I thought I was beyond that."

"I can't believe I did what I did!"

"Why didn't I see it coming?"

"I didn't want to admit I still had a problem."

That's What I'm Talking About

Whatever a man's "stuff" looks like, however a woman's fleshly sensibilities feel, the lot of it has to go. Think "chaff." It's all got to be sifted, reckoned at the cross where Jesus took the whole mess to Himself. His choice. "I gave My back to those who struck Me," He confesses. "And My cheeks to those who plucked out the beard."[9]

Now stop right there. With Middle Eastern and certain Asiatic men, a beard affirms masculinity. It spells dignity. "Removing a man's beard by force is to inflict unthinkable shame and open contempt." (2 Samuel 10:4–5).[10]

Sure, and Jesus willingly gave Himself over to such humiliating disgrace, this flagrant, wide-open shame. He took our shame and made it His own. "I did not hide My face from shame and spitting."[11]

A beard was also shaved or plucked out while in mourning. Shame and mourning, it fits. Magnify the cross, look closely, and see a Man who bears in His body and soul the full allotment of sorrow and grief of a fallen race, an impossible burden that can't be weighed or measured. Stand in awe. Stand in dumbfounded amazement, for it was our grief He bore. Ours. Jesus carried our shame and sickness, our sorrow, our pain.[12]

> He was wounded for our transgressions; he was crushed for our iniquities; upon him was the chastisement that brought us peace, and with his stripes we are healed.[13]

Do you hear it?

Do you see it?

The story doesn't end with shame and mourning. It doesn't end with unchecked sobs in a flood of bitter tears. Tears may be a necessary part of the equation, part of brokenness, part of the sifting process, but—now get this—it ends in wholeness. It ends with life and bona fide hope. Let's go back to Isaiah 50 where we were reading about Jesus's beard being plucked out, about shame and spitting and move on to the next verse (verse 7) where He speaks with rock-solid assurance:

> But the Lord God helps Me; therefore I have not been disgraced; therefore I have set My face like a flint, and I know that I shall not be put to shame.[14]

Embracing the vile stench of our corruption, our boneheaded choices and consequential shame isn't the last word. It was a vital means to a necessary end, but it's all paid up. Jesus said so.[15] Regardless of what anyone thinks and no matter what they say, the books have been cleared. The "certificate of debt consisting of decrees against us"—violations committed in thought, word, and deed—have been thrown out of court. Why? It was nailed to the cross, which means the devil has nothing on which to make his case concerning us; no leg to stand on![16] Jesus took our disgrace and shame that we might become the righteousness of God in Him.[17]

No shame here, not even a little.

The Next Time We See Peter...

He and John are racing to a vacant hole in the rock where Jesus was laid to rest. Rumor has it He's alive. Forget the past. Forget failure and shame. The fisherman's heart explodes at the thought that he might actually see something, anything to relieve his tormented heart. It's too fantastic, but Jesus is all that matters. John outruns his friend and stops short of entering the grave. Numb and afraid, he hesitates while Peter shudders with deliberate steps, moving in close. He's got to see. No surprises here either, that's Peter. The linen wrappings are there, His shroud and face cloth, but no body. Then John steps forward.

The apostle sees the empty tomb, and the light goes on; he believes.

> At this point, John's gospel strategically inserts, "They still didn't understand the Scripture, that He must rise from the dead." (John 20:9 NASB)
>
> Curious, isn't it? For all the time our friends invested in Jesus, or should I say the investment of Himself in them, revelation still hadn't come their way. Not here. Eyes opened to see Jesus as the Christ, the Son of the living God, yet nix on His release from death's icy grip. Imagine that. Those who dug unwilling heels in resisting anything to do with rejection, suffering and death

should be slow on the pickup where His resurrection was concerned. I'd be with them. You would too.

There's a principle here, one we'd do well to lock in on. Check me on this. It's one thing to have an awareness of Scripture, to recognize and recite the message verbatim, and another to have seeing eyes to actually hear in a way that penetrates the heart and understanding what the Spirit is saying to His church.

Jesus, if you recall, had a head-on collision with know-it-alls who were convinced they had the Nazarene backed into a corner on resurrection talk, of all things (Matthew 22:23–32). For them the issue was settled until Jesus called them out. "You don't get it, guys. Your problem is none of you knows the Scriptures, and the power of God."

But you don't see this, do you?

There's more to Scripture than academic awareness, more than repeated exposure or scholarly apprehension. If we only knew. Sadducees, Pharisees, and temple scribes had it down cold, and for what? For the blind to continue leading more blind folks? Not good, not good at all. Wrong perceptions rooted in an ignorance of God leads to dogmatic convictions benefiting no one. Both fall headlong into the proverbial pit.

So what then? Are we to find fault with Jesus's followers for not understanding the Scriptures? Not hardly. It's one thing to be bogged down with willful ignorance and another for the time not to be right. (Kairos, remember?) The revelation of the Lord Jesus as Christ came at the right place, at precisely the right time. Having the puzzle pieces fit regarding His death, burial, and resurrection happen when He chooses, when He alone opens their minds to comprehend the Scriptures. (Luke 24:45)

It's the power of God, the awesome power of God.

What now? The boys pack it in to head home. Where they find themselves seems surreal, like a dream really. Others jump in as madness crescendos to all-out crazy.[1] Women insist they've seen and spoken to the Master. Can you believe them? Can you afford not to? Brothers with dust from the Emmaus road still on their feet claim to have spent the afternoon in His presence, and did I mention sitting down to eat with Him? Thomas is a mess. Feeling like an outsider, he's desperately trying to make sense of it all. A ragtag bunch, for sure, and they're beside themselves. Can you blame them?

Everyone has something to say. Everyone wants to be heard, grabbing Andrew by the shoulders, James by his sun-bleached cloak,[2] talking over top of one another in joyous yet fearful madness! Then Jesus appears. He's there, standing shoulder to shoulder with those who knew Him intimately, infusing them with new life while opening the Scriptures and pointing them to the Father's promise of the Holy Spirit.[3] That's a lot for one day, isn't it, more than a truckload.

Can We Return to Sifting Briefly?

Satan demands permission to get in on Peter to sift him like wheat, correct?[1]

Just Peter? At first glance, it seems so, but we need to stop to consider another possibility. The slick, slippery one might have his sights on a bigger piece of the pie. Oh, he wants our fisherman, but there's more, a lot more when you consider the gems God is shaping. Think with me. Derailing Jesus, since that's his target, isn't simply Judas, who finds his fit in the "predetermined plan and foreknowledge of God"—not that the devil knew or especially cared.[2] He's got his own determination. The adversary has his crosshairs set on everyone in the top twelve. Take them all out! Eliminate Jesus; then, flatline His boys. That should do it, straight up the middle.

Look, I'm not trying to mess with anyone. I locked in on Peter at the beginning to get a sense of his thoughts and feelings, one player who's a key component. Now I'm panning wide for a larger lay of the land. We need both. "God so loved the world," or so the Book says, and we as believers long to bask in the warmth of such a staggering platform together.[3] Yet the love of God gets specific. My heart and mind find an anchor in the sure knowledge of One who "loved me and gave Himself for me."[4] Make sense?

Okay, let's get back to Peter and company.

Satan's interests outside of Peter seem obscure where the water runs muddy. It's the English language. We use broad, all-purpose terms that get fuzzy at times. In this instance, the word *you* ("Satan wants to sift *you*") can be either singular or plural depending on context, even body language, but neither one of us were there to see or hear this, were we? Not to worry. The New Testament was written in koine, or common Greek, and the word for *you* in Luke 22:31 is plural both times in the same verse making the major thrust of Jesus's injunction: "Satan has demanded to have all of you, to sift every last one!" speaking of the twelve.

Pastor J. B. Phillips, who began translating the New Testament Greek text for the youth in his church in a bombed-out, panic-stricken WWII London, renders this: "Oh, Simon, Simon, do you know that Satan has asked to have all of you to sift like wheat?"[5] The Amplified comes at it: "Simon, Simon (Peter), listen! Satan has asked excessively that [all of] you be given up to him [out of the power and keeping of God], that he might sift [all of] you like grain."[6] Someone hailing from the deep south might equally do this justice:

"Simon, Satan wants a shot at all y'all!"

So why tell Peter and not the rest? I think He did. For the longest time, I saw this exchange as a private tête-à-tête between Teacher and pupil, but it's not.[7] They were all in. See this as one of those group sessions where the Lord turns to lock in on Jonah's oldest boy.[8] Not that Peter's better than the rest, but he does hold a position. The brother is a leader among leaders. Jesus did that, and for this very reason, He lays out a picture with specifics intended for Peter they all need to be in on, and why? *They're all getting sifted.*

It's clear, and again, very strategic that the devil should use Peter's passion for Jesus against him, possibly one other. Could be John. His gospel speaks of yet "another disciple" who with Peter followed Jesus after His arrest. John was able to gain access to the high priest's courtyard since they must have known each other.[9] It was this connection that got both he and Peter in. Once inside, the lion pounces. "You're not one of His boys, are you?" Divide and conquer. God only knows where John was, but Peter was indelibly marked, easy pickins as they say.

The rest of the crew? They bolt from Gethsemane for places unknown and go into hiding.[10] There's a "certain young man" who in wrenching free of a soldier's iron fisted grip abandons the linen sheet he'd been wearing as he runs into the night as naked as the day he was born![11] The others? Not so much as a peep, not yet.

Consider these snippets, microscopic bits and disjointed pieces of winnowing and sifting no one saw coming. The Baptist delivered what God gave him, yet the dots didn't connect. Rain fire and brimstone on Rome. Cut Caesar and pretending hypocrites off at the knees, but this? *This?* The prophet sees none of his holy edicts realized, certainly not as he hoped. Sitting in a dank prison cell makes sense when the pieces fit. When they don't, you pray, yes, as thoughts and emotions collide in fractured discord.

"Are You the One, or do we look for someone else?"[12]

What to do when life takes an unexpected nosedive? A man finds himself locked up, and for what, holding a twisted tyrant accountable? But John is a strange one. *Eccentric's* the word. Who's surprised? Circumstances surrounding his birth had folks mumbling to themselves. "What will this child be?"[13] Decreed as "prophet of the Most High," one who would "prepare His ways,"[14] our friend's work was clearly mapped out, and he follows it to a tee. When expectations are skewed, and skewed badly, our camel-haired servant is left holding the bag, scratching his head.[15] "Did I miss something?" he wonders. Can't say as I blame him.

Jesus Does Such Things to People

Nothing about the Nazarene fits the mold. Ever. Jesus's birth isn't a king's, His youth is nondescript, and showing up on Jordan's muddy banks, it wasn't expected. Ask John. "Shouldn't You be baptizing me?" yet who notices but the Baptist?[1] He did, though, while directing two of his apprentices to move in and get close to heaven's paschal Lamb. They do, only to discover Jesus offends people—know-it-alls mostly, the self-righteous—and He rubs elbows with low-life sinners, hookers, tax collectors, and such. They're the worst.

John checked out early, didn't he, and not by choice. If we see this as God's doing, the prophet's work must have concluded. Our friend was obviously finished but in no way resolved, not to him. How could it? Paving the way for the Father's "hatchet man" comes with expectations, and given the fire in his prophetic rantings, a little smoke was in order, but no. There were no head-on collisions with Rome, no knockdown drag outs with a hypocritical religious and political order. That comes later. Lord Messiah seems bent on touching the bereft and destitute, drawing the poor in spirit to a place of restful hope.

We should expect this. Heaven's heights and the stuff of earth are immeasurably distanced from each other. Jesus alone bridges such gaps, and He does it with Himself. "Come to Me," He says. "I am the bread of life. Come to Me and drink. I'll give you rest"[2]

"True enough." You nod, and I wholeheartedly agree. "So, when the bottom drops out, we do what?" The thought of missing God is more than sufficient to hamstring any man or woman who sticks their neck out in His name. We've all latched onto hungry expectations gone awry.

I've been there repeatedly.

I don't blame the Baptist for what I personally consider questions asked in earnest. Neither does Jesus. Those impassioned with zeal become absorbed to a fault, I'm afraid, in dire need of a reality check. It's being self-absorbed that puts us in hock, sold out to sin. John's assumptions found their roots in a message God burned deep in a willing heart. It wasn't about him, so when Jesus fills in with the rest of the gospel, John, I'm sure, breathes much easier.[3] He sees Jesus through a refreshed set of eyes. He otherwise dies alone and confused.

Questions are good; they're necessary. When a man finds his movement severely restricted by high walls and razor wire frames a woman's world, questions abound, questions they might never have considered. Good. Excellent. For others like myself, restrictions held me captive apart from physical boundaries, an imprisoned soul. Lies walled me in, fortified strongholds. The enemy's most strategic weapon, then, walls or no walls, are lies seductively disguised as truth. Such soulish infrastructure, often in the name of Jesus, binds you; it ties me up as no prison ever could. So, when He doesn't deliver per our expectations, what happens?

"Blessed," asserts Jesus, "is he who isn't offended by Me!"[4]

Offended by Jesus? God knows the number of folks who've turned to our Lord on a provisional basis, using Him for personal satisfaction then bailing if He doesn't deliver in ways that keep them smiling.[5] Those who would use Him are legion.[6] Jesus offends by refusing to bend to others' opinions, popular or not. He's not running for office, so forget political tolerance![7] His lineage is anything but acceptable, having a hooker and pagan idolatress in the mix, speaking more to grace and less to propriety.[8] That's Jesus and that's heaven.

There are some things folks never warm up to.

Welcome to a fallen earth with fallen people, so who's surprised? Grace will forever be an offensive stench in the nostrils of the self-righteous, and the cross will never fit where morality runs loose and "it's all good."[9] Talk of sin is offensive. The popular Jesus folks applaud has morphed into a smiling Santa[10] who wants people to coexist in tolerant bliss apart from real love and grace that's greater than the worst of our dirt.

Any mention of repentance, the kind John and Jesus preached, is strictly taboo.[11] Funny. This is who John paved the way for, a Jesus whose love is offensive. Why? He calls the self-centered to self-denial, not self-aggrandizement.[12] And it's not as though Jesus lays the burden of expectations on our shoulders. He lays it on His. "Take My yoke upon you," He beckons.[13] Easy and light, Jesus says, extending Himself to those whom life and religion had effectively crushed, frustrated, and thoroughly discouraged.

Radical change calls for a radical choice. Choose a Person, *the* Person, not Christian morals and principles. Opinions abound as voices cry out in the fog: "If we could only return to Christian values!" Really? *Really?* Can I ask you a question, a vital question? What power is there in Christian morality and personal values apart from the Christ who gives them life? We're going for the jugular here. Christian teaching with its related values have no capacity whatsoever when they're left in our hands to carry out in our own determined efforts.

Doing life from me and my stuff is all we've known, for the most part. Grace comes knocking, and Jesus arrests us. We're doing life in His name now. Amen. You and I are too much like Peter at times—a truckload of desire and completely impotent—yet who sees it, who knows? We desperately need sifting, friends, to be crushed and broken, then fitted with a radical reorientation. Only Jesus can live the life we read about.

We'll talk more.

I'm Not Sure I Hear You

Again, I risk being branded a heretic.

Talk of America's founding fathers in wistful tones is passé as the moral and political climate these days is beyond anything anyone could have imagined. Prophetic voices call this country to a sobering accountability, and I couldn't agree more. A lax society asleep at the wheel has been nodding for decades as termites weaken structural integrity while new foundations are laid. "How'd this happen?" groggy bystanders wonder. "How could it get this far?" Easy. Minimize God. Reduce Jesus to superstar status or an ornament on a chain.

A suburban neighborhood not far from where I was raised was affectionately coined "the city of churches," a monument to architecture and religious culture long deceased. It's where my family "went to church," a body that was socially active and devoid of life. Driving through the area after my mother's recent passing, I sensed a profound biblical tie I won't soon forget, the valley of dry bones. And they were very dry. Christian values marked their credo in spades, good will toward men, yet one thing they lacked. Jesus.

I go through this a lot with folks. Walk with me a moment through the pantheon of religious and philosophical thought, so many voices, so much to choose from. Each has its uniquely geographic and cultural origins shaping practices, lifestyles, and deeply rooted identities framed by as many alleged underpinnings of "truth."

Who's surprised when a doubting Pilate counters Jesus?[1] "What is truth?" he sneers. Are you kidding? The Greco-Roman world overflowed with skeptics and dogmatism,[2] truth here, truth there, every color, shape, and size imaginable put on the block for endless discussion and debate, and they loved it![3]

Not so much these days. Freedom of speech is pretty well obsolete for political "snowflakes."[4] The "coexist"[5] Jesus is part of an ecumenically benign mix alongside Buddha and Mohammed with a host of other founders and philosophies. Truth has more or less been rendered a subjective reality until recently. It's generally been held if something works for you, then amen; we'll call it a day. Enter a new breed of intolerant enforcers, stomping out infidels or parading so-called hate criminals for public crucifixion. We're not going for ice cream any more. There's no allowing folks their flavor of choice if they don't agree with yours.

Where truth is no longer subjective, tempers flare.

Jesus isn't political, so He isn't a flavor. Guess what that means? He's not in the lineup. How can He? The living Word who crafted the cosmos, upholding it by the word of His power, couldn't possibly be squeezed in with the well-intentioned but confused.[6] They can't stand shoulder to shoulder, not in His company.

All that is, seen and unseen for time and eternity, comes together and ultimately finds meaning and purpose in Jesus, or it finds it nowhere.[7] He, in fact, is "the Way, the Truth and the Life."[8] It's who Jesus is in essence and substance. He doesn't point the Way; *He is it*, the living embodiment of Truth who in His person is the source of all Life—physical and eternal—so forget the dead-end pursuit of Christian values. Others strive to attain; whereas, the Word incarnate grows into who He already is in wisdom and stature.[9]

Our Lord, as we just observed, doesn't give instructions in the traditional sense. He is His instruction, the dynamic embodiment and functional means of everything He calls us to. The best Mohammed can hope for is to leave what He claims as Allah's directives in the Qur'an along with personal "hadiths"[10] as a map and compass to Muslims as they give it their best shot. Ditto Gautama Buddha with his teachings minus God,[11] and Tao's Lao Tzu, if he even existed.[12] And did we mention Krishna?[13] All try-hard religious systems.

> Christian values apart from Jesus Himself are so much wishful thinking, if not an embarrassment.[14]

Sound extreme? I understand completely, especially if you happen to be one of many who believe Jesus came to start a new religion. He didn't, you know. Religions are a dime a dozen, laying down precepts while enlisting followers in search of another flavor. Distractions really. Artificial flavors. Substitutes. No, Jesus didn't come to start a new religion. He came to start a new race, a new humanity infused with His life. Adam is marked by sin and the death it breeds. Jesus is marked with Himself, all that He is.

And that means? It means only two races exist, only two—Adam and Jesus.

Adam's own require nothing apart from self-effort to keep death's cycle in motion. Don't get me wrong, Adam aims for the sky. He tries to at times. His fallenness shoots high—an inner sense he can't shake—but falls short of created design, and not marginally. We were made for so much more.

I'm talking fullness of life Jesus describes in terms of abundance,[15] outrageously inconceivable abundance, life rooted and birthed out of love humanly unattainable.[16] Sound radical? It is, and that's because it takes God to make it happen. He alone is its source and necessary means. Jesus breathes life, His life, into His new creation birthed in the Holy Spirit. Vine life. We're talking about a vital, living connection making His thoughts and words, Christ's very life, real to us. Think of it as a reality received and entered into by faith alone. Vine-branch life.[17]

"Lord of the Dance," a song I heard Steven Curtis Chapman do some years ago, scores with spot on imagery. A heart is little more than a lifeless chunk of meat apart from a heartbeat, as are eyes without sight. What then are you and I without One who, in Himself, is life and hope? Jesus is more than animation to earthly bodies. He's divine energy, heaven's own life source, engaging all who've been reborn with new spirits fused with His. (See Ezekiel 36:25–27.)[18]

Apart from such intimacy, Jesus's words and values are worthless, if not frustrating. "Apart from Me," He insists, "you can do nothing."[19] Not "apart from My words or valued precepts," but "apart from Me, apart from My immediate and active presence." Apart from My participation, My life as your functional source, your determined efforts are a complete and total wash. Useless. "Christ in you" is the key.[20] Literally. Functionally. Not conceptually, ideologically or "in spirit."[21] Christian values are meaningless; they're lifeless apart from the here and now Christ who Himself animates and gives them substance. Our hope lies in brokenness leading to surrender.

A radical change of mind concerning Jesus and the necessity of sifting. Twelve minus one were radical where it came to Jesus, not realizing how deep the waters got, or how hard and fast the current ran. Jesus carried them though it looked and felt like abandonment. Confusion reigned as fear gives way to unchecked panic. Gethsemane was pivotal in their sifting, yet who knew? Who wanted it? Fearful men slept as Jesus chooses, "Not My will, Father, but Yours." In the face of unimaginable torment, He remains intentional planting precious seed through His being crushed and broken for His own, as His own.[22]

Not a Place to Try Harder or Pretend

Read through Jesus's sermon on the mount.[1]

How does it leave you, dumbfounded, awestruck? Take your breath away? Tick you off at times? One thing's certain: you can't shift into neutral. Jesus doesn't leave us that option. "Blessed are the poor in spirit," He says.[2] How does it strike you as an invocation?[3] Blessing, He offers, is the gifted domain of those who willingly embrace weakness, their own inert spiritual deficiency.[4] Small wonder this should be the launchpad to so much that comes back on Him because it has to. Who but Jesus has, or possibly could pull this off?[5]

Humbling Himself, God the Son lays down all rights and personal privileges of Deity.[6] Consider a man who started the way we all do, as a helpless baby, who grew in total dependence trusting His Father to be everything to Him—in Him and as Him.[7] In that sense, "the man who did everything did nothing," in and of Himself, that is.[8] It was a Father, in a willing and yielded Son. "The Father abiding in Me does His works."[9] There it is, dependence through total surrender and not just Gethsemane; day in, day out as a way of life. Color this rest.

Two thousand years plus, and nothing's changed.

Think "abiding" as a relational proposition, the call to stay and make this your residence, which for the Son is the Father's heart. A boy growing in wisdom and stature finds His heart resonating with an awareness of Abba's connection with the temple where everything comes together for a beloved covenant people. Imagine then a twelve-year-old drawn to make Himself at home there. "Didn't you know I have to be in My Father's house?" as in His humanness eternal realities merge, "the glory I shared with You before the world began."[10]

The Son's oneness with the Father lays claim to those who sense a draw to discover the intimacy of abiding.[11] Only a Son can do that, implanting Himself, His heart in ours sounding indeterminate depths, crying, "Abba! Abba!" A place? No, a Person our hearts now call home.[12] Jesus beckons, "Come. Abide in Me and I in you."[13] Stay, will you? Make yourself at home. A branch is incapable of bearing fruit apart from the vine, a reality in the Holy Spirit we reckon on and draw from by faith intentionally. This, friends, is rest, the real deal.

Have you been to a vineyard?

Ever see a vine sweat? No? Me neither. Row after row, miles of vines span multiple acres. Come early fall branches heavy with bunches of lush fruit fills the air with the fragrant aroma of concord grapes. I remember. The drive to Bible school Labor Day weekend was already pregnant with anxious anticipation for the new school year. Winding through Erie, Pennsylvania, wine country piqued freshly honed senses. It was so good!

But why is it vinedressers never place signs among the many rows of intertwined branches to encourage growth and production? "Think Grapes" might provide a strategic nudge, you know, a morale boost to try harder. All right, so I'm a wise guy, but there's a reason. Branches on a vine don't break a sweat, do they? Connected to the vine, theirs is always and forever a no-sweat proposition, no "Gotta do grapes or I might get cut."

The no-sweat arrangement branches enjoy with a vine is really quite simple. They're connected, vitally so. The vine (can you imagine?) is everything to a branch. Separate the two, and you've got firewood. Marry them, and you're in business! Life from the vine flows through the branch and grapes just happen. Connected to the vine fruit comes as the natural byproduct of their vital union—a restful, no-sweat byproduct of abiding. Detach them, and no amount of sweat or positive thinking can possibly make fruit happen, not now, not ever.

The problem is you and I were made for grapes. We all were. See this then as a key part of bearing God's image and likeness. It's a tree thing, the tree of life. That's Jesus; He's a vine. "I am the vine," remember?[14] A supernatural work of grace binds us spirit to Spirit—ours with His—creating a viable spirit union. "But he who is joined to the Lord becomes one spirit with him."[15] Yes, but get this: He doesn't become us, and we don't become Him. Our oneness is a vine-branch connection in the Holy Spirit, which makes abiding a faith choice. We must choose to rest in and draw on that union. Forget grapes. They won't happen, not on our watch, not by your best shot or mine. Never.

Fruit of the Spirit, Paul says, not fruit of our determined efforts, or what I call "plastic fruit"—a work that begins and ends with us.[16] Some years back, our family was invited to the home of newly discovered friends. Dinner wasn't quite ready, and my fourteen-year-old was beyond famished. "Daddy," she pushes, and pushes hard, "there's fruit on the table. Do you think they'd mind if I took a piece? I'm really hungry!"

"No, I don't think so." I smile.

"Are you sure?"

"Go ahead. It's all right." Now before anyone has me arrested for child abuse, hold a minute.

Shannon inches forward, turning to look back. "Are you *sure* it's okay?"

"Of course I am, kiddo. Go for it." My baby gets to the table; she tentatively reaches, then snaps hard my direction.

"You *knew* it wasn't real, didn't you?" I stifle a laugh.

"Yeah, I did." Plastic fruit. It looks real from a distance. Convincing. In the church and on the street, it's the best we, or anyone, can do if Jesus isn't the source—not His words or fundamental principles, not even His ethics. It has to be Jesus, His life, His energy, His active presence as believers look to Him in the obedience of faith by this thing called abiding. Vine life.

> Abide in Me, and I in you. As the branch cannot bear fruit of itself unless it abides in the vine, so neither can you unless you abide in Me. (John 15:4, NASB)

Foreign turf, no? Yet it's what we're made for, God's design, a perfect fit and radical paradigm shift all in the same breath. Think "human" in the truest sense, dependent in a healthy, restful way. Necessary, not optional. Ask Major Ian Thomas. He's with Jesus now, but as a young man with eyes fixed on foreign missions, he burned out thinking grapes. Do you know what it feels like to be so completely tapped, so spiritually exhausted you don't know which end is up and which end is down? I do, in spades, and so did the Major until he felt as though there was no justifiable reason to continue.[17] I know the feeling. The cross means more than forgiveness of sin and hope awaiting us on the other side. We need deliverance from our deeply ingrained bent toward trying harder, deliverance from plastic fruit!

Is God a Smooth, Underhanded Salesman?

"I think You pull a bait and switch on people!"

I was frustrated, no ticked. Days…weeks of working long, unpredictable shifts, then collapsing on the couch. I was terrified of crawling into bed for fear of not being able to drag my sorry carcass back to the job in another three, maybe four hours. Two months without so much as a day off would pay dividends, I was told, if I didn't die first. Check with my wife; she'll tell you. The kicker is I asked for this, a job opportunity where I was esteemed for a unique skill set that set me apart. Other endeavors I laid my hand to crashed hard as, "You'll never amount to anything," morphed into prophetic reality again, again and again, or so it seemed.

Crazy, isn't it? I could work my tail off, sixteen maybe eighteen hours at a pop, with a twenty-eight here or there, and still get lost in porn afterward. Drugs kept me going, even took the edge off, or so I thought, while girlie magazines provided value. You don't get it, do you? It's easy, really. In a world where affirmation was "iffy"[1] at best, a fantasy world awaited where satisfaction was a sure thing because I wrote the script. I ruled this elite, private domain. I determined the outcome, affirmation guaranteed, and sex was the payoff.

What lunacy! I handpicked ladies, foldouts and full color exposés, on a head stupid with pot, burned out on amphetamines.[2] I called it survival, but it doesn't work. "Loser!" crashes even the best parties, inviting "fear of failure" along for a strained and mostly sleepless ride, leaving knotted stomachs and overanxious imaginings in a tense, wrung out body I'd haul to church come Sunday—well maybe if I had the day off. Sometimes.

What to do then?

"You should pray more, Dan."[3] Yeah, right. The guilt trip I was on came packaged with frequent flier miles. Did I mention there were layovers shared with shame and condemnation? The big one, no doubt, was fear; fear of rejection, fear of failure. God terrified me. I failed Him, didn't I, so prayer? I was torn. I'd seen too much. Memories of love, God's unconditional embrace—the only truly safe place I'd ever known—haunted me, a little boy's longing. I felt small. Insignificant yet frustrated. I wanted Him, but I was angry and scared.

So, here's a question for you: Does God ever take unfair advantage of us?

What I mean is, does He intentionally play games with our heads to frustrate our hearts? Is He in the habit of pushing buttons to goad and try our patience, your understanding and my sense of who He is and who we are? What do you think? Does the Omnipotent, Eternal One bait with enticing promises, then switch the game up, promising one thing and delivering another? That's how it felt. Days on end, sleepless nights isolated in total darkness in what seemed a thankless job striving for validation via never-ending performance expectations.[4]

Was this what God had for me?

Talk about a twisted mess, but who's surprised? Life measured on human terms, shaped by limited, if not confused, concepts of things beyond us are bound to blend truths, half-truths and all-out untruths, as questionable images with limited depth of field; some focused and partially discernable, most of it blurred and not clearly defined. Sow to the flesh, and the road gets bumpy.[5] Don't I know it? Yet here it is, in the midst of hellish confusion as gunk and ugliness surfaces where crude oxen feet trample harvested heads of precious grain that's alive with Jesus. Is this what God had for me? Yes, and amen, most definitely.

Breaking the chaff-wheat connection means crushing, death by crucifixion to perverse images of God and twisted self-styled underpinnings built on lies. Do you hear me? I'm talking stronghold here, an intimidating and impregnable barrier to intimacy with Him, or anyone else. Scripture speaks of God in ways that get filtered through a mental and emotional grid that for me is my black-and-white, cut, and dried mother beside a trumpet teacher who loved winners and hated losers, the easy out of an unwanted player.

Coming Unglued

Layers, I'm talking years of fearful denial crumble like Jericho's walls—my best shot at engineering an impregnable fortress constructed for the express purpose of keeping malicious and hurtful intruders at bay—and there I stood, a confirmed loser. Is this a joke? I'm vulnerable, completely naked and shamefully exposed where any mention of life "more abundantly" feels like salt in open, festering soul wounds.[6] I'll be the first to admit it's an inside job. I'm the saboteur who couldn't measure up, and I admit it, so forget "laying it all on the altar." I've so thoroughly disqualified myself, maggots gag as I voice blown out frustrations.[7]

What's God going to do, take me out? I might find relief. No pretense here. I don't live near Job.[8] The man had lots to learn, but he never accused heaven. The devil did, and I played right into his hand. "How," I wondered, "could God promise life in abundance, an easy yoke, or a light burden?"[9] Easy? Light? Are you kidding me? Crushed is more like it, ground into the pavement. Devastated. I'd given God ample reason to kick me to the curb, lots of them actually, and for the next hour, or so, I was on a roll. No looking back.

What I didn't sense was God's deeper reach.

It happens quite a bit. Getting to the root often begins with letting overheated radiators blow; pressing thoughts and feelings linked with people, circumstances, and God Himself. David cries, "I don't get it, LORD; what gives? How long before You answer? Have You forgotten, or just written me off?"[10] The king knows better, but again, it's raw feel surfacing, a parched deer panting for cool, running water.[11] *Intense* is the word, and calling it *real* means "right here, right now this is all there is." I knew better, sort of, yet life filtered through self-serving pain gave birth to distortions that had to surface before God could strip me of chaff to get to the wheat.

"Have you considered that it's not been My yoke…"

God spoke, not audibly, a recognizable and poignant awareness in my heart I couldn't begin to shake or even try to deny. "My sheep hear My voice."[12] I heard. I knew, and I am not given to subjective impressions; trust me. I've seen too much carnage in the wake of charismatic chaos, and I'm not a cessationist.[13] What I am, and what I was in this dry, barren season, is a soul thirsty for God, for the living God.[14] For Him to functionally suggest that I'd been "slipped a Mickey" dropped me cold.[15] Had I considered the possibility that my own legalistic reasoning became "death in the pot"[16] of a self-brewed concoction intended for life and sustenance?

The long and short of it? I had God all wrong. I blamed Him for my misconstruing Jesus. The yoke and burden I embraced were my own vain imaginings of One who loved winners and hated losers. It was killing me. What I hadn't anticipated was freedom, unbounded relief that came with even considering such an amazing possibility. "It's not been My yoke." We're talking death as in release, release in the deepest sense, genuine release from lies and impossible expectations as an unbearable load lifts from my frayed and sorely fatigued soul, and with it, a series of startling realizations:

> Lord, if the yoke and burden I had taken up were mine and not Yours, I really don't know You, do I? And if I don't know You, I can't possibly know who I am. It stands to reason then if I don't know You and I don't know myself, I don't know anyone, not nearly as I should.
>
> Terrifying but true.

Our Bankrupt Self-Sufficiency

For all I set out to do *for* God, wanting so desperately to finally stand in the winner's circle only to crash in flames, crushed under the prodigious weight of my own commitment, it had to happen. Alan Redpath scores with, "When God wants to do an impossible task, He takes an impossible man and crushes him."[1] I know I'm in good company, Paul for starters. His "wretched man that I am" monologue speaks not to our brother's essential personhood.[2] Au contraire, it directs our attention to the profound revelation concerning his best and most determined efforts to please God in his own inherent fragility, the weakness of his Pharisee flesh.[3]

John Bunyan, author of *The Pilgrim's Progress*, frustrated himself in repeated efforts to cleanse his mouth of fetid profanity. Oswald Chambers was all but ready to throw in the towel on a Christianity he suspected was fraudulent, either that or "I have not got hold of the right end of the stick."[4] John Hyde, and others, found barrenness on India's mission field unacceptable while Andrew Murray struggled in South Africa.[5] D. L. Moody cried incessantly for the infilling of God's Spirit. He, like many, shares one common denominator:

A substantial crisis of faith

Distinctives vary, but one shared commonality seems to be the discovery of just how bankrupt our most committed efforts truly are. What can I say? Bait our first parents hit on proved bogus. They became like God all right,[6] but who'd have guessed that even their best and most noble attempts as self-contained packages fell short of hopeful expectations. No way this duplicitous charade can be called life. It's death, the branch trying to do grapes with no vine to draw from. The vine is self-sustaining. The branch? No way. And for the believer who hasn't come to terms with vine life as a much-needed resting place, forget it.

Confronted with major confusion concerning God, I realized I didn't know myself. Talk about intimidating, yet what a relief— tentative, hopeful relief. Convinced as I was concerning the man I saw in a performance-driven mirror, I stood dumbfounded, shocked senseless really! What if my true self was a man I'd never met, that I wasn't cut from cloth locking me into permanent nothingness? I doubted my own sanity. So, could you to step back with me to consider where this took root, and not just for me? You too.

Eden's tragedy plays out as a loss of life; we know that doctrinally, but guess what follows hand in glove? Humanity took an equally disastrous, if not cataclysmic, heart and soul hit in the tragic loss of love. No exaggeration. Our shared need for significance and security is most deeply satisfied in love that knows only God as its source, love Adam walked out on—love this first man and his woman could only retain as a vague memory, a distant and desperate longing. God's image, His likeness in you, me, in everyone who's ever walked the planet craves His love. No substitutes, please. The embrace that cradles a fragile newborn gives shape to his tender heart, her formative mind. It's a mixed bag and always has been, but one way or another, the craving begins.

I Knew Intuitively But Didn't Understand

I couldn't, you couldn't either. Eternal life, Christ's life, comes by intimacy with the Father through the Son.[7] "Abba, Father."[8] It's easy to talk about, to study and debate. The heart needs more. Mine did. Jesus offers rest, and what did I do? Pile on Sinai's unbearable weight and then some. That's me, at least it was. Aim high, hit low. I assumed as much. "Blessed are those who expect nothing; they shall not be disappointed,"[9] or so I was told, but I was. Disappointment hunted and haunted me. I desired something more. I wanted a Father.

It's a strange, no bizarre, dichotomy that we can be born of the Spirit yet oblivious to a precious Father-son or Father-daughter touch point that's legitimately ours in Jesus. I sensed it for a minute, a brief yet very real season after my first grace awakening in coming to Christ, then in clear, strategic intervals thereafter. I knew His call, His divine appointment that would forever change my life, then *poof,* up in smoke. I had a Father but couldn't draw close to Him, or anyone, the loser who had to be on top. Value, right?

Looking for love in all the wrong places, and the faces?[10] How can you believe them or their promises? Family, friends, pastors, and coworkers seem lost in their own space, seeing but not hearing, not getting close enough for authentic vulnerability. It's too risky. Nakedness apart from trust is a terrifying proposition. Who wants to expose thoughts and fearful anticipations when you're sure you have a fix on how they'll look at you? Imagination then is a filter we believe is critical to survival. I was convinced, and I'm not alone.

Love, where God sits, is a faith commodity meaning you, me, His kids, we can trust Him implicitly. "Faithful is He who calls you, who surely will do it."[11] Easy for Paul to say, or so I've insisted, but what if this is intended to be part and parcel of the easy yoke—the exceptionally light burden Jesus spoke of? I never saw it that way. It makes sense, though, in the exclusive context of His love commitment that comes to us *as* Jesus.

He is the Father's love to us.

Think about it. "You are My beloved Son," is a Father's affirmation sounding depths angels can't begin to fathom.[12] Was an angel ever so intimately engaged?[13] "You are My Son" is bottomless, immeasurable on any level but God's. Yes, and in Christ it's ours; restoration of Adam's mournful loss and humanity's most treasured status.[14] Sonship, beloved daughters. The Father loves the Son why? Don't hurt yourself pressing beyond the obvious. It's not performance-driven, so please don't take it there.[15] The Father loves the

Son for one simple and incredibly profound reason: He's His Son, a status that is because it's who Jesus is.

When my daughters were born, love for them wasn't forced or contrived because my wife and I were told we "ought" or "had" to love them. That's nuts, no insane. They're ours. It pleased us to love them, no arm-twisting required. From the get-go, our hearts were united in the desire that Shannon and Meleasa should be anchored and unconditionally affirmed in the assurance, "You're our girls." Our hope as parents, our ongoing prayer, was to see the love God poured into us penetrate and touch deep places in them that could never be shaken even when our precious ones needed sometimes painful correcting.

"You are My beloved Son," spells hope to us. "How's that?" you ask. Great question. Emerging from Jordan's waters filled with the Spirit isn't the total picture for Him who, in eternity, chose to lay aside the privileges of Deity. Taking on life as a man, a real man with all the inherent weakness and limitations apart from fallenness in sin,[16] requires a Father's stamp of approval. "My boy!" secures a Son's heart as He runs the gauntlet, negotiating a dark and lost world's minefield. It secures hearts in Christ with hope to take the next step.

To even risk moving forward.

What's a safety net to a trapeze artist? "My beloved Son" opens the way to "My Father and your Father."[17] That's more than a safety net. Love for the Son is now the love securing God's own, His adopted kids.[18] What kind of love is this that would grow us in trust for the simplicity of love's rationale: We're His, bottom line, the rock solid, unshakeable foundation for all who are in Christ. I never knew that, not for myself. Not really.

Who and What Do I Know?

Not knowing God, or myself, I was clueless to truly know anyone—close or distant, lost or saved—and I'm in excellent company. "A puzzlement," Yul Brynner might say as Siam's pompous tyrant.[1] Indeed, and to those who fancy themselves good judges of character, please step back and reconsider. Lost or saved, they're a complex mix of genius and ignorance, artistry and incompetence, compassion and cruelty, the refined and crude all bent on doing life à la Frank Sinatra whether they realize it, or not.[2] "My way" is Adam's path, like it or not.[3] See it as the blind leading the blind, so there's nothing new here, nothing new ever. Ask Solomon.[4]

I thought I knew them; people, that is, giants mostly. They seemed bigger, badder, more attractive, more proficient, and considerably more exceptional than my unseemly ilk. Midgets. Imagine the feelings. My first day in Bible school, a freshman awed by the wonder of full-time investment pouring into the Scriptures and for what? I'd hoped it was to discover my fit and unique ministerial calling, but no. I felt shut down before getting off the ground. Can you imagine why? It was my personal library, the meager assortment of books I brought with me.

What? I was green, a young believer with lots to learn and not much to work with. That's how I saw it, an illusion readily confirmed by measuring myself over against another freshman whose outsized bookcase was filled before purchasing any of the required texts we'd be using. Me? I had one *Webster's* dictionary, a Strong's concordance, a new three-volume commentary, and two Bibles—the required

King Jimmy and a recently purchased New American Standard. I was starting in the hole, but catchup's my game even when I'm leading the pack!

It's true, and I'm not alone.

I've spoken with many whose performance ranks highly among peers and a cadre of willing followers while fancying themselves less than, if not complete and total washouts. Hello, that's me, at least it was. "If you knew what I know, you wouldn't think I was such hot stuff." Things I can't admit to anyone, not to you or myself, much less to God. Enter Job's opinionated "homeboys,"[5] so-called friends who fancy themselves a cut above their unfortunate man. I need to be clear, though. It's more than possible, if not probable, to fancy oneself a loser yet present as an equal in good standing. Elitist maybe? Survival is what we're talking about, survival and identity.

The key lies in understanding this thing Scripture calls our flesh.[6] It's not physical necessarily, but human it is, as in fallen humanity, so guess what? Left to ourselves "me and my stuff" is all we have. I'm referring to my perceived strengths and weaknesses coupled with your chosen means for gratifying desires and making life work. And we do this how? Think of it as programming, understandings, and techniques the likes of us have developed that squares with the way we see God, ourselves, and a world as it begins and ends with me.

That's the problem, and we don't see it! A frame of reference where everyone and everything aligns on my terms, according to my particular sensibilities, means I stand as the measure of all things. What a twisted mess! Who's surprised then when I don't get God or anything right? Me obviously, and my twisted thinking still gets in the way at times. Wherever confusion and my stuck feeler lead the way, I'm sure to trip over my own two feet.

What's All This Talk About a New Creation?

New heavens and a new earth are God's long-standing promise.[1]

Radical undertaking. It stands to reason, then, for I Am to realize His eternal purpose requires a great deal more than a superficial makeover, more than a facelift. *Radical* is the word, a complete takedown of sin's damnable corruption with its minions. Paul prophetically addresses the creation's futile slavery to corruption, the impact of diseased souls infecting our planet and temporary home.[2] Adam chose death not realizing the pervasive impact of unbelief and the rebellion it breeds. It's a whole lot more than sweat and weeds.[3]

Liberal teachers and critics who insist on undermining the Genesis creation invalidate the entire Book, to their detriment and others.[4] Take it up with Jesus, why don't you?[5] Paul called it: "We can do nothing against the truth, only for it."[6] So when God purposes to make all things new, it's going to happen as surely as, "Let there be" made all that was good and right in the cosmos' beginning, naysayers notwithstanding.[7] Long time adage, "out with the old, in with the new" is more than a New Year's toast. The cross is where it happens.

Watch carefully, and listen as Jesus willingly embraces all that is old, everything corrupt and cursed. He takes it to Himself in unconscionable suffering to death and the grave. Day number three, Jesus raises up a new humanity—an altogether new race, a new creation alive with His eternal life. Prefigured many times over, Calvary breathes fresh hope and understanding as you and I face caustic uncertainties in the here and now.

Mel Gibson's *Passion of the Christ* zooms in for a strategic close-up as a brutally scourged Savior collapses beneath a cumbersome Roman cross. "See," He grimaces to His devastated mother, "I make all things new." There's no recovering what cannot be restored. It's too far gone. A car that's been totaled goes to the scrapyard, not the repair shop, while a house riddled with termites is leveled. No facelift here! Jesus went to the cross for a corrupt humanity, as a corrupt humanity, to rise as a new humanity. Death and burial are the order of the day—out of death resurrection—a new creation in Jesus! He's it.

Reality from the inside out: an internal cleansing complete with a heart transplant, a new spirit joined to His resulting in new desires and new means from a new and altogether different Life Source.[8] New birth He calls it,[9] the outworking of an outrageously new and far better covenant founded on promises superior to those ratified at Sinai.[10] It's a new day indeed when you and I are no longer bound like woeful captives by fleshly limitations, twisted instincts, and unwanted mental and emotional baggage.

New Is the Operative

"From now on," Paul insists, "we've got to see ourselves, and other Christians, through new eyes. Believers need to lay aside our many feelings-based distortions, fueled by unwarranted perceptions and the illusion of outward appearances the way we have in the past" (my amplified paraphrase of 2 Corinthians 5:16a).

Make sense? The church in Corinth was more than a little confused concerning their own inconsistencies. Such as? Such as behaviors that don't square with the truth of whom they are in Christ. Such as badly skewed perceptions of one another.[11] This, I believe, is what our apostolic mentor drives at with so much talk of not "sizing up"[12] our brothers and sisters in Christ, "after the flesh."[13] You know, from a "worldly viewpoint."[14] "A [purely] human point of view,"[15] moves a little closer, sort of. It's how folks look and feel to me.

The problem is I didn't realize how dense I was concerning my own twisted people filter, and I know I'm in good company. How often have you and I been in the habit of sizing folks up out of feelings generated by someone's presence, or the sound of their voice. How about the mention of their name? Good, bad, it makes no difference. It's a flesh thing, our assessment based on race, associations, social standing, performance, attitude, and body language coupled with physical appearance, the way they sound, smell, or look at us.

And in the church?

Now there's a can of worms beginning with where you attend and whom you hang with. Let's not forget especially favored schools of doctrine or teachers subscribed to. Move over, Corinth, it's getting deep![16] Tensions that take root in such places scream, "It's time to grow up, gang!"[17] Don't get me wrong. I'm by no means advocating anything goes, not even close. Schisms have a way of ferreting out noxious pretenders from genuine articles, thank God.[18] What I'm concerned for are toxic attitudes leaving members who feel inferior, disqualifying themselves while elitists look down long snooty noses while playing, "Can you top this?"[19]

Okay, hit pause. We're back to where we started at the beginning of our study, the last Passover where again Jesus's boys try sorting out the batting order. Who are the heavy hitters among them, and how is that determined? Flesh is flesh, and every last one of them has "baggage" that's got to go, much that's seen as having considerable value. They've all got to taste the bitter shame and remorse that invariably follows when what Peter and the rest saw as commitment is rendered null and void; what they were sure was strength is exposed for the weakness it is.

And why is that?

The call to follow is God-sized, and if these men are to realize the hope of their calling, to lay hold of that for which Christ Jesus laid hold of them,[20] then every confidence and every hope they've ever had in their own abilities and determined efforts has got to be smashed and destroyed where He was crushed on Calvary's hill.

In other words, Jesus's death, burial, and resurrection has got to be personally appropriated and entered into by faith.

And so, we've all got to be sifted, broken, and surrendered with a view toward Christ alone.

"Our wills must be broken to His will."[21] In Eden, a man exchanged the truth of God for a lie transposing life in the key of Him, who is the Source and Center of all things, to death in the key of me. In Gethsemane, another Man, the last Adam, chose brokenness and obedience over self-indulgence to save His own human neck. "Not My will but Yours." That's our hope! Whereas the first man's choice locked a fallen humanity in blind futility, the Lord Jesus standing for and as us chose complete dependence through total surrender.

Brokenness is what it's called.

Shattered dreams are what it feels like.

In his priceless volume by the same title—*Shattered Dreams*—Dr. Larry Crabb lays out the sifting process in a gut-level depiction of places God has got to navigate for us if you and I are ever going to walk as real people manifesting genuine peace and power, not to mention God-sized joy (Isaiah 51:11) regardless of the stuff life throws at us. Only then will we grow into a viable body of those who are joyfully broken whose lives bear testimony to a simple, yet profound reality—the gospel is legit and it works![22] The problem, as Peter and company came to see, is that our fondest dreams for this life, the hopes and dreams we believe are so essential to our happiness, must be fully and completely abandoned if we're ever really going to know God intimately. "But we cannot abandon them without help."[23] Amen. That's why there's sifting.

New creation, or no, isn't the question, not if you're asking it.

All Jesus secured at the cross is just that; finished, a done deal. You and I who've been born of the Spirit, we're complete in Him.[24] "With Paul, being a new creature in Christ was more than a doctrinal position; it was an actual experience which became real by revelation."[25] You've heard, no doubt, of justification by faith? How about sanctification by faith? Not so much? Understandable but not a problem. Everything pertaining to life and Godliness is ours in Christ, yet apart from our participation by faith in the fullness of union with Christ—in His death, burial, and resurrection—our knowledge of God, ourselves, and others will remain twisted.

"When You Have Come to Yourself and Turned Back, Strengthen Your Brothers"

In Jesus's mind, it's not a question of "if" Peter will come back around, but "when."[1]

He knew. As surely as space was intentionally given for satanic powers to maneuver,[2] light would dominate—the lesser giving way to the greater—no exceptions. Out of death comes resurrection including one deeply disoriented fisherman. The issue isn't Peter's tenacity or any man's staying power, rather the predetermined plan and foreknowledge of God[3] for Jesus to be nailed to a cross for Peter, as Peter. Peter only? Not hardly. God in His grace includes a group of unsuspecting brothers in desperate need of strength and encouragement. Jesus would rise, and Peter would turn. The Book bears this out.

An unwary prodigal had to fall in with a lot of foul-smelling swine, so Peter needs the air let out of his tires. He needs the cross. Apart from his own brokenness and death on Golgotha's tree, he'll never know the power of Christ's resurrection. Peter can't and won't make the connection, what it means to live and move and have his being infused with Jesus Himself, to be alive with His resurrection life! A wise father allows his fledgling son to crash and burn out of love in hopes he'd eventually come to his senses. Peter may not have chased the high life the way the kid did, but he's got to hit the wall before our man will ever come to himself.[4]

That which is born of the flesh is impotent.

So much for our brother's own understanding. For all Peter has seen and experienced, for all he thinks he knows of Jesus, there's a lot our impetuous friend has yet to learn. His take on the Master is still quite fleshly.[5] That's about to change. Peter wants to know Jesus, to come to terms with himself, but passion derails the man where flesh and Spirit are polar opposites.[6] It's time to wake up. "I don't know the man," leaves him floundering to stay afloat where stability slips between inept fingers. A new revelation is needed, fresh insight.

Let Me See If I Can Explain

"No one has actually seen God at any time."[7]

The Old Testament Scriptures, the Tanakh if you're Hebrew, speak clearly about Jesus.[8] How Genesis 1 fits with the opening verses of John's gospel is nothing short of staggering. Psalms 22 and Isaiah 53 point decisively to Calvary while barely making a dent in the prophetic calendar with sometimes graphic and insightful imagery that paint a descriptive portrait of the divine presence. There are visuals, preincarnate touch points where Jesus puts in critical appearances, "Christophanies" as the Angel of the LORD,[9] the LORD,[10] and a "son of the gods."[11] So we're off the ground and headed for "good news of great joy."[12]

A babe wrapped in swaddling cloths dovetails with Gethsemane in speaking to One who emptied Himself that we might touch and be touched by the heart of God. Before the cross another surrender comes into play. Incarnation. Both are "not as I will but You."[13] Both are the Son's willful obedience.[14] In it, we see God as a real man, yet who knew? Opinions varied.[15] That's flesh for you. Twelve were drawn in to hear, see, and touch,[16] to get first dibs on realities prophets and kings craved but never got close to.[17] But it's not all proximity.

You can hear, see, and touch and
still not connect the dots.[18]

"You are the Christ," chimes Peter, and he's dead-on. Not everyone gets it, though. Many nod in pretended approval, but the Watchtower Christ is miles removed from the LDS spirit brother of Lucifer,[19] Islam's Isa,[20] the spirit guide of mystics, and moral henchman of liberals, yet none of them make the connection. No one comes to Jesus, no one sees who He truly is apart from the Father—His nudge and uniquely divine unveiling.[21] "I praise You, Father, Lord of heaven and earth, that You have hidden these things from smug know-it-alls who think they have You figured out and revealed it to the weak and helpless."[22]

Twelve were given an inside look at the Master, and they left scratching their heads more often than not.[23] Eyes that see and hearing ears are packaged with a truckload of questions. What can I say? That's how it is when information and necessary insight come on a need-to-know basis. It's called *following*, so who's surprised when the boys come unglued as the One they've so completely given themselves to follow is taken away? He told them it would happen, that it would be to their advantage.[24] Okay, so Jesus's words don't always click, not at the moment, and His absence leaves them sinking in a soulish quagmire of raw emotion.

Imagine that.

Lives given to follow are invested. Think gambler. They're "all in" with no back door.[25] "We left everything to follow You!" Peter gasps, and so they have.[26] It's the cost of discipleship, a price joyfully paid by those with eyes for real treasure.[27] No arm-twisting required, not when a man sees or a woman legitimately discovers the gift of God. Matthew ditches his high-profile position fronting for Rome as one-time cohorts pile in to check Jesus out for themselves, not unlike a few Samaritans we've met along the way.[28] Us too, hopefully.

It's called dependence. We talked about it early on. To follow means adherence to Jesus, an exclusive attachment that spells death to all other attachments.[29] That such an offer should even be extended is nothing short of grace. German pastor and theologian Dietrich Bonhoeffer nails it cold.

What our brother coins "an abstract Christology," some call "head knowledge," is a purely academic framework for grace or forgiveness that waters down what it means to fully engage biblical discipleship, and in many ways, opposes following Christ.[30]

So, when Jesus goes missing, the bottom drops out.

John remembers Golgotha; he was there. The others? Who knows? Gethsemane was mayhem. "I will strike the shepherd," God purposes, "and the sheep will scatter."[31] Guess what happened? Eleven bolt like so many cockroaches.[32] Peter, you recall, makes his way with John to the high priest's residence where he loses it. Were any of the boys interwoven among a demanding crowd gathered before Pilate's judgment seat? Hard to say. John, as we noted, stood in support of our Lord's sobbing mother as she watches her son die alongside a small handful of committed lady friends. Joseph of Arimathea? Probably. Nicodemus too, I think.

A Walk Down the Emmaus Road

"Why do you seek the living among the dead?"[1]

Women on a mission find an empty tomb. They'd done this before. Think custom. Spices were prepped and mixed. Ladies knew the drill, unaware, I'm sure, of what Joseph and Nicodemus were able to accomplish with the rapid onset of Shabbat.[2] Finishing touches were in order. The point here is one of permanence, as in Jesus is dead. Get it? The service and compassion offered this early dawn is the period at the end of a bleak and mournful sentence making the angels' unexpected presence an immediate call for smelling salts.

"Remember how He spoke to you in Galilee recently?"[3] He said lots of things, most of which no one wanted any parts of, talk of rejection and death. And resurrection? Well, yes, but who heard it? No one really. The ensuing litany bears this out, friends and the apostles themselves rejecting the witness of an empty tomb as explained to the women by heavenly emissaries. "Nonsense," they insisted.[4] A conversation bears this out.

Two began making their way on a seven-mile jaunt from Jerusalem to Emmaus batting sorrow and despair back and forth, going deeper and deeper into a hopeless abyss. They're not the first, gamblers whose heart investment went bust. Our friends were mentally and emotionally bankrupt. What to do? Here's where skeptics and naysayers miss the boat, and not by a little. This isn't time to regroup, pick up the pieces, and move on. No way are they about to take up where the Master left off. Keep the Jesus thing moving, everything He started.

It can't, and I'm sorry, but it won't happen.

Not with Jesus. "And why not?" you ask. Others pulled it off. When the Buddha died, his followers didn't close up shop, Mohammed either. Islam is big stuff these days, growing well beyond Middle Eastern borders, and Buddhism's gone global, albeit not nearly as much. What is it with Jesus? We learn a lot by the conspicuous absence of His followers as He hung suspended between heaven and earth on Calvary's cursed and forsaken cross. They were scared, yes. Identification with one Nazarene rabbi could be costly, but that's not the whole story.

We've got to move in for a close-up.

Jesus did. They didn't know it was Him, but that's genius spot-on. It's the Master's way of drawing His lost boys out for a little openness and honesty. "What are you talking about that has you two so wrapped in confusion and sadness?" Cleopas stops cold.[5] "You're kidding me, right? Is it possible that you've come from Jerusalem and don't know what happened over the last several days?" Color him incredulous, both for sure.

All right, so we've been jaded.

How many times do believers truly enter into the gospel rendering of Passover, this Passover? A crowd in near hysterics hails a small-town prophet as the hope of all things Jewish. "Hosanna!" they cry. "LORD save us!" We don't get it though, the passion, their passion. Try changing places. The stench and grit of Rome's foot rides hard and heavy on chafing necks, yours included. And Jerusalem? There's no frame of reference for the uninitiated to appreciate the significance of this one place where Abraham's hopeful sons and daughters come to celebrate their Jewishness in the God of their fathers, Himself alone being their true identity.

Imagine then the promise of David's son, the sovereign King of kings who would crush His enemies. Now here He is, riding in triumphal procession to establish the supremacy of Zion's rule, or so an expectant people yearned with longing, hopeful eyes—and not just the people. Disciples too. Why else would men Jesus called and poured Himself into be jockeying for position among themselves? "Thy kingdom come!" It's how He taught them to pray, isn't it? Look to His kingdom, His coming in glory. Could this be His time, His kairos? Is it now? Not when a rooster crows and the governor washes politically stained hands. Not when Yeshua dies.

"What things are you talking about?"

What things indeed. It's not Peter this time. Cleopas uncorks his own fleshly bent as the Master probes with surgical precision. "We have known Christ according to the flesh,"[6] Paul inserts, that is, seeing and understanding Jesus on strictly human terms. Plug that into memories that now rub salt into raw, gaping wounds for two who are thrown off balance by one stranger's nebbiness. "Jesus!" Cleo mourns, "was a prophet from Nazareth who did and said unbelievably powerful things before God and the people, yet our priests and leaders handed Him over to be crucified. Can you believe it? I can't. None of us can." No surprises here, not for the stunned and stupefied.

"But we *were* hoping," and there's the rub. Past tense. We were hoping. Israel's redemption is on the line. Centuries, no millennia of expectations suddenly fade, and for what? "Jesus was our hope." Underscore was and with good reason. "It's been three days." One day, maybe two, we can still hold our breath. Three? Forget it. Jesus really is dead. Mourning lasts seven, but three makes it official. He's gone, kaput, finished.

If Jesus Is Dead and Gone, That Means What for His Followers?

It means it's over.

What are they, what are we left with? Let's put it this way: If Jesus is dead, as in gone and not coming back, both they and we are left drained and empty. There's no meaning, no substance, no life, not in a memory. Unlike the founders of other philosophies and religious systems whose fundamental principles and teachings hold as a cohesive unity, of sorts, Jesus doesn't. If He dies, it all dies with Him. Everything. There's no thought of forming a committee to collect broken bits and pieces—the best of Jesus—to teach and begin spreading the good news. It won't fly since Jesus Himself is the good news, a Person, not a theological ideology or structured moral values.

God knows He never intended to start what many see as a new religion. Jesus stands as the fulfillment, the consummation of what it means to be Jewish! "The Scriptures bear witness of Me,"[1] meaning the Old Testament in toto. From "In the beginning God" to Malachi's pronouncement of hearts being turned.[2] It all points to Jesus, everything the Father has done from eternity and continues to do through the Son. *Continuance* is the word, a Messiah who reigns over an eternal kingdom. There's no place, no frame of reference for a king who dies.

The words of Jesus demand His presence.

He's got to be actively engaged, which means Jesus has to be alive to give His words life. Really? The call to discipleship isn't following a regimen of spiritual disciplines laid down by Lord Messiah, giving it our best shot. Whether we're talking Peter, James, and John or the likes of us, the call is, and always has been, to follow in the life and energy of a Person not merely His words. The disciples tasted firsthand. From day one, Jesus began laying a foundation for dependence, the no holds barred kind. The investment of Himself over time proved to a select handful one fundamental reality. Doing life apart from Jesus was no longer an option. They couldn't.

> Groupies come and go. Here one day shouting, "Hosanna!" the next "Crucify Him!" We're talking people, and where personal interests and sensibilities write the script, folks who've been offended won't stay for the encore. "Eat My flesh and drink My blood" doesn't exactly generate warm fuzzies. Then there's the "Take up your cross" talk.

> Amid Jesus's many hard sayings and impossible, if not stress-ridden encounters, twelve—Judas notwithstanding—stuck it out. Why? In a word, it was Jesus, Jesus Himself. No one spoke like Him; it's true. Such wisdom laced with compassion and authority penetrates the impenetrable. But it wasn't the words He spoke, per se, that they were undeniably brilliant or conceptually sound. No, it was Him, the logos incarnate (John 1:1).

> Jesus was to these men, to all who come "poor in spirit," the substance aching hearts crave. He didn't bring hope; *the Master was living hope in Himself*, their vital connection to the Father. When it's time for Jesus to leave, as in "where I'm going you can't follow," the boys come unglued.

"You can't go, Jesus," is their silent heart cry. "You just can't!!"

Talk about necessary, that they should be reduced to an awareness of their own pathetic impotence, of complete nothingness. Again, we ask, why? It's more than "we like having You around." No, the light goes on. "We need you, Jesus. We can't do life without You." Amen.

Whether it's loving God with all your heart or "doing unto others,"[3] everything comes back to Jesus. If He's dead, nothing works. The reason? You and I need substance beyond our weak human frame. We're not self-contained packages, remember? It's the vine-branch connection.[4] Left to ourselves, you and I are incomplete. We're less than human. I know, that flies in the face of so much humanistic dogma, but it takes us back to Eden, the declaration of independence that so completely trashed humanity. Jesus flips it around, proving the difference His presence makes in the lives of those He targets and calls to Himself "that they might be with Him."[5]

"Come to Me" is the call and, following an intimate proposition, not merely some abstract doctrinal theorem. "If any man thirsts, let him come to Me and drink."[6] Do you hear this? The draw is to "Me," a living Somebody who alone quenches thirsty souls. Words left to themselves—even Jesus's words—remain hollow, broken cisterns. Jesus alone gives them vitality and substance that penetrates and touches in deep places because He does the touching. This isn't just metaphor. "I am the bread of life" is gut-level soul food because He really satisfies. "Come to Me," beckons the weary and heavy laden to a rest only He can provide, to the rest He is.[7]

If Jesus is dead…

Nothing happens. His words leave the most committed disciples empty and frustrated, embarrassed even. I understand then if any one of them might want to forget what, in their minds, could never be restored. It hurts too much, penetrates too deeply. Apart from a Jesus who's both alive and intentionally holding it all together,[8] there's no God connection—not for them, not for us, not for anyone.[9] There's no hope if, in fact, Jesus alone is the way, meaning the *only* way, therefore the *only* truth, the *only* viable life. Imagine trusting such transcendent realities only to have it all go up in smoke, or so it seems.

Not one of us sees, much less enters, the kingdom apart from a supernatural work of grace.[10] And the Scriptures? The individual hasn't been born who connects the dots apart from God's Spirit.[11] "Eye hasn't seen, nor ear heard."[12] No one's even tried to imagine. It's too fantastic and way too painful. Who's surprised as women bearing reports of a resurrected Jesus are seen as delusional?[13] Can you blame them? Followers had been told what to expect on multiple occasions, but did they hear? Does anyone?

Things That Haven't Entered
the Heart of Man

"O foolish men!"[1]

It's inevitable when or wherever you and I place the weight of our trust in the limited know-how and typically convoluted understanding we generate. Which one of Jesus's most committed followers had so much as a clue regarding the magnitude of shame and rejection Jesus would bear as a prelude to His gruesome death and what seemed a pointless finality of burial? "I am the resurrection," factors in, but only if the Master Himself is present to call the shots as the grave's stone is removed.[2] When He's in the tomb, all bets are off. "Laying My life down" is one thing.[3] Taking it up again is another. Think: "slow of heart to believe."[4]

Believe what? "All that the prophets have spoken."[5] With Christ's resurrection, the Law, as well as the prophets, are solidified, made even more certain—not that there was ever a threat.[6] When God speaks, "Let there be" stands solid. It's good. If Jonah only knew his three-day getaway was but the tip of the iceberg, he might have dressed differently for his soiree in Nineveh.[7] Maybe not. However you shake it, God snagged one reluctant servant taking him into death, burial, and resurrection in order to paint a graphic portrait skeptics have decried for centuries, and in one fell swoop etched in granite the certainty of Jesus's resurrection.

"Was it not necessary?" the stranger
pushes and pushes hard.[8]

155

Mourning tends to blind folks.

I understand. Releasing our most deeply valued treasures—loved ones whose presence decorate and complete life as we've come to know it—is enough to try even the most Spartan constitution. "I'm so sorry for your loss," we fumble, groping blindly to bridge a bottomless gorge. I get this too. What do you say when there aren't words, no assuaging magic, but maybe that's it? Maybe we need to hurt—you, a pitiful me—allowing ourselves to sink into depths where there's no touching bottom and no treading water. "Blessed are those who mourn" when you don't feel all that blessed. You feel empty, lost, and irretrievable.

"Was it not necessary?" suggests something more than my loss. Maybe then, just maybe it's not about me. Ultimately. Things we hadn't considered. Obviously, our friends hadn't. "We were hoping," speaks to profound ignorance, pain beyond theirs and more going on than anyone dared to consider. How could they? With no touchstone, no anchor beyond themselves, a resurrected Jesus opens eternal realities in the here and now—things that haven't entered the heart of any man or woman—things prepared by God, and God alone.[9]

"Who has believed our report?"[10]

Great question! And what does God's strength look like, His incomparable power? The savage pain of loss? If believers are willing to step back and consider possibilities beyond our own means or ends, the way we've always understood life and God, new road is paved. "Was it not necessary for the Christ to suffer these things?"[11] Necessary suffering. Now there's a twist, a far cry, as we see it, from breaking enemies with an iron rod.[12] Beat down is more like it, open humiliation, His beard brutally plucked out by mocking accusers who cursed while spitting in our Savior's face.[13] I can't fathom such crude, barbaric slander, such vulgar disdain.

Jesus suffered for us, yes. He suffered as us, yet it wasn't about us. It wasn't, and it isn't. It's about God, always has been. "For from Him and through Him and to Him are all things."[14] Crazy, isn't it? All the pain, the grotesque and tortured contortions Jesus endured is birthed out of God's eternal love for a world He created to what end? What could possibly be God's rationale? None of the folks our Lord most intimately invested Himself in either wanted or understood His death, much less the inhumane brutality of it. But apart from a radical paradigm shift, folks will continue to pour life into an old wineskin, still trying to make Sinai work.

The age old, "Why would God?" question goes belly up when I'm the bottom line, and *me* becomes *we*, as in "we had hoped."[15] They took a hit, the total investment of deeply committed hearts, but now hear me on this, *it was necessary*. Jesus said so.[16] "It pleased the LORD," Scripture tells us, "to crush Him," putting the Lord Jesus to unconscionable grief.[17] Why? Does God take sadistic pleasure in human suffering, Jesus specifically? The devil would like us to believe such madness, but no. The Father, above all, was pleased with the Son's choice to offer Himself on behalf of a corrupt, sinful humanity.[18] It was necessary for God, making it necessary for a mournful group of crushed and bewildered disciples who were being sifted like so much wheat.

Think "Co-Crucifixion"

Talk about things that haven't entered the heart of man!

Our Emmaus road travel companions are a fair approximation of the others in their collective doubts and fears. Words of Jesus haunt mournful, nagging consciences, but what can this sad lot do? I'm thinking, "If any man would come after Me,"[19] now stands as a monument to regret for the compromised. Ouch! That really hurts, but I'm not throwing stones. Peter and company vowed to lay down their lives without exception, minus Judas. If the Master was sentenced, they would follow suit. The "me too" thing was contagious, and it was real. So much for self-imposed sincerity. The lion roars, and we tuck tail and run. Truth is it had to happen.

We've alluded to this, and it holds. Every confidence true followers of Jesus have in their own resolve and commitment has to go, all of it. That which is born of the flesh is undeniably flesh, and it can't possibly change, so Jesus does the only thing that can be done. He takes them to Himself in His death. You bet He does. In their running from death, Jesus not only dies for them. He dies as them, which means Jesus's disciples died with Him, and not figuratively.

They just don't know or see it, not yet.

The boys will get their shot at a martyr's witness to the Truth, but there's another death that's got to come first—their old man.[20] All right, so I'm messing with someone's head, possibly their heart. I understand, so please hear me out. Everything I've said so far— the whole sifted like wheat thing—has been building to this. The devil is fixated on taking Jesus out and His disciples with Him. So is God, but with a completely different end in mind. We've hit this from a number of angles, but straight on, death to the old creation is Calvary. At the cross, Jesus renders Adam null and void for all who believe and receive.

The power of sin is broken through death, and that, my good friends, spells freedom. Those who've participated in twelve-step recovery programs know what it means to own an addiction, a fear-based identity that can only be broken by death. God agrees. Sin is addictive, a brutal if not relentless taskmaster. Death alone releases us from his tenacious clutches. Knowing this, God secures our death, and He does it in Christ. The Son is our freedom; the cross is His means.[21] His death is our death. Paul clearly affirms:

The one who has died is liberated, set free from the power of sin.[22]

And that means what? It means the Lord Jesus purchases our forgiveness while paving the way for every believer's deliverance from sin's exhausted claim by taking us to the cross with Him. We need forgiveness, and the blood of Jesus effectually settles all accounts, while thoroughly cleansing those who've said yes to grace from all unrighteousness. White as snow He makes us, but does your need or my twisted complications end there?[23] Not even close. Forgiveness addresses my offenses, crimes I've committed in thought, word, or deed, but the root goes deeper. We need deliverance from an identity binding us to an impossible tyrant.

Can we honestly blame Matthew, or point an accusing finger at Andrew, for seeing Jesus's rejection and death as personal loss? What about the "we had hoped" crowd? Do we criticize them for not seeing the Paschal Lamb and their participation in Him? Not hardly. We've done the same, and not one of us considers the gift of death as God's necessary precursor to the gift of life that's ours in Christ. You can't have one without the other. The Son's blood satisfies a holy Father while cleansing us. Our death with Christ spells freedom.

Peter Starts Coming Around

Impossibly far-fetched reports provoke more than idle curiosity. Peter and John, remember? A heart-pounding race against all odds. How could they not? It's Jesus, which means these boys have seen too much. Multitudes came and went, fickle groupies with personal agendas who never really tasted, yet those with God-given eyes for treasure locked in. "Where, and to whom shall we go, Lord? You (alone) have the words of eternal life."[1] Menu reading won't get it. They've both seen and tasted.[2]

I have an illustration I'd like to share, one I'm sure isn't original on my end, but humor me, for a moment. Imagine, if you will, a friend offering to treat you to an evening out, a five-star restaurant is the venue, and it's their nickel. Anticipation is everything from the invite to walking in the door. The maître d' escorts you to a private dining room and a table dressed for royalty. Ambience abounds. Sights, sounds, and wafting aromas are to die for! The waitstaff attends to your every comfort as the menu is presented—appetizers, entrées, and oh, so much more, with descriptive artistry such that one item sounds better and more intriguing than another.

"I'll have one of each," you fancy.

What can I say? It looks and sounds sumptuous, so incredibly appetizing until your friend speaks. "Come on, we've got to leave now. I've got an early morning." Say what? All the promise and build up, now he, or she, is pulling the plug?

"No way!" you say. "You're kidding me, right?"

"No, I'm serious. We've got to leave."

What's the problem? You don't like the picture I painted? Why? We do it all the time. We do it in church! Think I'm kidding? Church is where we're constantly pulling out the menu, pointing folks to its books, chapters, and many verses, proof text after proof text. We teach them the menu, then discuss it. The committed memorize while scholars systematize and categorize the blessed thing, preaching if not burdening souls with expectations we've drawn from its pages—everything but ordering a meal and sitting down to eat! And we wonder why people struggle where it comes to doing Christianity, ourselves included!

Look, I'm not throwing stones. I see how "believe right to do right" falls short, where "sound doctrine" is an end in itself and academic correctness the last word in authentic orthodoxy. What can I say? As a nineteen-year-old heading off to Bible school, my expectation was to line up with others who dotted i's and crossed t's the same way as part of a neat package. Imagine my surprise in learning the staff itself was a mixed bag of denominations and evangelical free agents alongside Episcopalians and one-time Roman Catholics. Talk about a can of worms! But it took me back to the Book considering the scope of reformed and deformed theology.

They fall apart at some point, all of them.

Doctrine Has Got to Be a Person

First and foremost.

The Word became flesh, didn't He? Given that, do you remember Andrew's first glimpse of Jesus? The Baptist singles out a Nazarene carpenter as the unique Lamb of God, and two of his closest protégées move in for a closer look.[3] John's press release arouses awestruck wonder where reading the menu won't begin to suffice. Hungry men want their own taste. Secondhand doesn't cut it. Therein lies the key, and Jesus is the Master at whetting gnawing appetites. He alone quenches thirst.[4]

My first trip behind prison walls left me expecting the worst. Imaginations in overdrive. I felt Paul's pounding heart, a man whose knees were knocking at the thought of mingling with the vile and fearful immorality of a place like Corinth.[5] No lie. Reports from a brother who'd done time in a Texas prison made my blood run cold. Hollywood didn't help as I mentally revisited *Brubaker* and *The Shawshank Redemption*.[6] I saw myself as cheap entertainment for kicked back thugs looking to break the monotony of prison life with a game of, "Let's mess with the new ministry." You know, marksmen taking potshots at the neophyte who couldn't find his butt with both hands. Not here.

That's what it felt like, and I fought God hard.

You know how it is, though, when He has His mind made up. The chaplain introduces me, and I find myself surveying a blurred sea of green—the color inmates dress in—men with arms crossed and X-ray vision fully engaged. They didn't know me from Adam. "Listen, guys," I said. "I'm not even going to try to pretend I understand the world you live in because I've never been there. But I am crazy enough to believe my being here is God's idea, that He's given me something for you. I also believe He's given you something for me." Hit pause and hold. "So, if we can move on with I've got something for you, and you've got something for me, we all might connect with God this weekend." Dead silence. Arms uncross, and hungry men lean forward.

Hungry didn't quite fit the mold, not mine by a long shot. It wasn't what I anticipated, genuine desire in the most unlikely of audiences. What can I say? Jesus has a way of whetting a man's appetite, awakening a parched woman's thirst. "As the deer pants for the water brooks, so pants my soul for You, O God."[7] Hunger and thirst, really? For what? For Himself, "for You, O God."[8] Nothing and no one else satisfies, not ever.

Hungry folks abound, yet most are clueless as to what they truly crave. Eden's crash severed the link for love and acceptance from the only Source that most deeply sates hungry souls. Apart from Him, life frequently remains the never-ending quest. Yes, but when you've tasted as Peter has, it's a slam dunk. "Lord, where would we go? Who else could we possibly go to?"[9] Who indeed. Our fisherman has seen too much. Blunders and all, he can never go back, can he? Amen, it's so very true.

Ask Thomas. For all the bad press this man has received for doubting, the hungry get it. Our brother has a palette only Jesus satisfies, which means when others report His resurrection, the man stakes a personal claim for his own taste. Not to justify anyone's unbelief, but three years up close with the Master is enough to ruin a man for all other offerings knowing this was but a prelude to a promise hungry hearts clutch with tenacity.

It turns Peter around.

I'm convinced. Jesus laid claim to this fisherman's heart, giving form and substance to an understanding that's being sifted—a soul in transition who's been confronted with truth. Someone, not something is the difference.

Shalom, the Gift That Is Uniquely God

"Peace be with you."[1]

Evening resurrection day, but who knew? A few women, yes, yet who actually heard their implausible report of an empty tomb and a risen Christ? No one. A fragmented lot, they wrote the ladies off. Jesus, you remember, ambushed two on the Emmaus road, and somewhere along the way, He got to Peter.[2] The rest? The Master popped in on them, literally, out of nowhere. Not that walking through the door would have had any less shock value. Either way, the boys would have dropped their teeth considering their penchant for ghosts and such. It wouldn't be the first time the Lord was mistaken by His crew for a disembodied spirit.[3]

What's not to be rattled?

Resurrected dead folks are all the rage, aren't they? All right, so I'm being facetious, but I need you to track with me. The head and heart tsunami this unsuspecting lot had recently been pounded with was prefaced by wave after wave of the unexpected—shaking all that can and will be shaken—sifting if you haven't figured it out.[4] I'm talking again about making short work of every last vestige, every confidence we who say we're leaning on Jesus functionally lodge in ourselves. I'm pointing to your self-driven understanding and my inert abilities to pull off a futile God-sized call on our humanity.

The cross is God's tool of choice. I'm remembering the *Passion of the Christ*, my own unrestrained mental and emotional rush. Big screens, right? It felt like we were part of the mixed mob of first century spectators, so many physically and emotionally present in more ways than I could ever have imagined. A woman in the theater shrieked, "Stop it, please! Stop hurting Him!" Others, myself included, released floodgates of silent tears, repressing volley after volley of agonized groans. Many sat in numb disbelief. I've never seen, never experienced anything like it before or since. *Surreal* is the word, truly transcendent.

Given such incomprehensible cruelty dispensed at the hands of calloused executioners, it's no wonder a fledgling bunch who were sold out to Jesus were believed they'd seen the last of Him. Three days seals it. Engaged then by the newly resurrected Master, Mary's white knuckled grip ensures for her, if for no one, He won't get away this time![5] Imagine the looks on collective faces that wouldn't give so much as a shred of credence to the lady's testimony as Jesus—He's just there, *poof*, like He never left—greeting them in heaven's peace.

What Else Would He Say?

Worlds had shattered with no pieces of any appreciable size to properly reconfigure. Imagine then that Jesus's greeting comes with the hope and promise of heaven's wholeness. Shalom it is as jaws drop in amazement. "Look at Me," He urges. "See My hands. Take a close look at My feet. Check out My side. Touch Me, guys. I'm not an apparition."[6] Too good to be true? It would seem so, yet the peace He brings comes as a poignant in-your-face reminder. "Peace I leave with you."[7] Words spoken when? The last supper, remember? A point in time when peace seemed most elusive and so incredibly distant.

Who'd have guessed the gift of peace came packaged with Gethsemane's unfathomable agony and Calvary's cross! I didn't, much less a group of floundering first century disciples devoid of hope and understanding come dawn's first light of day number three, yet Jesus had promised. What do you do with that? The bottom drops out, and I find myself realizing, now I do, how much I'd filtered Jesus—His words, the whole of His substance and person—through a distortion lens of misgiven thoughts and shattered emotions calling it truth.

165

"Not as the world gives."[8] That's it. Three years and some change have been strategically invested in lives that will never be the same. If they only knew. Saying yes to the King Fisher has proven more than radical; it overhauled and redefined the stuff of life as they, and everyone else, connect the dots. A fallen world has me, myself, and I to lean on where the good, the bad, and the ugly square off and bleed to no avail. They're cut from the same cloth. Peace the world offers is thin water no one can sail or navigate properly, gnarled chaff and unwanted grit that need sifting to get to the genuine article. Jesus, He's the wheat!

"My peace I give to you,"[9] says more than those at the table bargained for. We're not talking peace in the generic sense. This is "My peace," a commodity the world knows nothing of whose foundation and substance is in Jesus and nowhere else. He's the wellspring and fountainhead. So where do we see it, His peace? Try starting with a newborn baby, all snugged up and cozy, wrapped in swaddling cloths and not a care in the world, Herod and his devious intentions notwithstanding.[10] "Peace on earth," heavenly angels promise, and here's the launchpad, surrender in eternity that births new hope through a new humanity in Christ.[11]

We find our Lord resting peacefully in the stern of a crude fishing vessel as rain and swells driven by gale force winds threaten to capsize the simple craft while the crew flounders.[12] Early on when a mob in mad hysterics would chuck Him over a cliff, the Master walks through their ranks without breathing hard or breaking a sweat.[13] Color that peace, then fast-forward to Gethsemane where Rabbi Jesus breaks more than a sweat. He nearly dies going toe-to-toe with horrific imaginings of hellish anguish He chooses to embrace and does it as a man, a real man—as every man and every woman—working surrender's accord.[14] That's peace!

"No!" you insist. "That's torment, the worst kind." Have it your way, but allow me an addendum. What would you call Jesus's heart anchor that connected Him to a far greater reality? Scripture insists it was joy. Unspeakable joy on the other side of Calvary made it possible for our Savior to endure the savage horrors of the cross.[15] Let's get a grip. There's such a thing as assurance, a sense of well-being that digs in and holds when mentally and emotionally we're coming apart at the seams.

Have you ever been there? It feels like yesterday when my oldest took a severe blow to the head from an eight-foot construction ladder—in church of all places—and doctors began talking permanent brain damage and the like. Two days from her seventeenth birthday, and I couldn't tell up from down. Her baby sister was nineteen when a seizure translated into emergency brain surgery. How clearly I remember the brain scan image on the ER doc's computer terminal as my wife, Bonnie, and I cried uncontrollably in each other's arms.

> Yet there was peace, not happiness,
> an anchor called assurance.

The same anchor that secured our hearts when a couple of days prior to a much-anticipated wedding anniversary my wife hears the C word with her name on it. Dinner out had a different flavor, an unanticipated celebration of God's goodness with a bitter undertaste. Forty years together, how many more would there be? Clasping hands while gazing into each other's tear-brimmed eyes my precious bride and I gave thanks surrendering to a loving Father whose grace secured us, not a disease. He had us, not cancer.

That's peace, friends, peace through tears and pounding hearts our Savior identifies with by choice. Jesus is moved beyond anything you or I could possibly imagine by human frailty and weakness, soul and body.[16] We read the certainty of His bearing our sorrows, making our pain His own. The price for peace is steep, a tag Jesus paid in full. He can, as our incarcerated brothers are fond of saying, "I feel you!" It's in the cup.

The peace He speaks of is, in fact, Himself taking us back again to the cross where the cruel chastisement securing our peace falls on Him.[17] He is our peace,[18] not some passing feel-good dream; Christ Himself is the anchor that holds and shields us. In Him, we have peace with God, who then is the peace of God when the bottom drops out while opening the possibility of peace with one another to us.[19] He keeps it real. Always.

Unbelief and the Danger of Hardened Hearts

The thought of seeing a ghost might stop a few hearts.

Maybe it's necessary. Jesus materializes, as it were, to a group who might need smelling salts, something to engage a little reality. God's in the business of exposing thoughts and intentions, isn't He?[1] Look no further. He does so in spades, unmasking unbelief, that is. It's a big one. This one bugaboo rendered an entire generation impotent. Good intentions aside, those leaving Egypt didn't so much as taste the land God promised.[2] The bull's eye is entering His rest.[3] The danger of missing it lies in hearts hardened by unbelief.[4]

Jesus called His boys to task because of "unbelief and hardness of heart,"[5] and for what? They didn't buy into the ladies' insistent "He is risen!" madness. Why the struggle? Stop and think with me a minute. When hearts are so completely trashed, as the disciples were at their supposed loss of Jesus, the first order of business is guard and protect. Does anyone know the feeling? It's understandable, except when we shut God out by filtering people and circumstances through a highly emotional grid linked with our own twisted take on things. "Knee jerk" is the word, a conditioned reflex like touching a hot stove. You don't forget, do you?

Not a chance, which is why Jesus nips this in the bud.

Hearts hardened through unbelief become self-imposed barriers to pretty much any and all sensitivity to God, and that, my friends, is scary. The bottom line being all who harden themselves toward God, whether they realize it or not, will not because they cannot enter His rest thereby proving they really don't know Him.[6] Why would someone place the full weight of their trust in a God they don't know? You see where I'm going with this? The heart of the new covenant in Jesus's blood isn't having the right "technical" information about God, as good and valuable as it may be; it's knowing Him intimately and personally.[7]

Participating in the eternal life He is.

Color that rest, a key component of the peace Christ is to us. "Come to Me," Jesus beckons that we might, by intentionally drawing close, discover Christ alone to be all we need for life and godliness.[8] Folks who kept Egypt in the rearview mirror pulled back to their detriment.[9] Good news was theirs; you'd never know it though. If you refuse to believe God, what good is He to you?[10] What good are His promises? Great question, one the I Am of eternity answers explicitly. The first covenant's lethal fly in the ointment—the covenant ratified at Sinai better known as the Old Covenant—wasn't God. It was the people, their unbelief.[11]

Enter the new, decidedly "not like the covenant I made with their fathers."[12]

It's not Sinai warmed over, a "renewed covenant," as some have erroneously proposed.[13] This, according to the original grammar, is profoundly "new in nature,"[14] an altogether new in kind, the way smart phones are a radical departure from the black rotary behemoth I grew up with. (Yes, I'm dating myself.) Apart from one meager similarity, the differences are legion. You can make and receive calls on both, but it ends there. The new covenant takes us to previously unknown turf. Quite literally it's life out of death, not Lazarus though, not this time. Lazarus is a shadow. Jesus is substance; everything the old pointed to is now real in Him.[15]

Old Covenant thinking keeps folks locked down, bound by a perpetual sin consciousness—the "I have sinned, I'm not worthy" syndrome—that's more constrictive than anything the department of corrections has ever built. The reason? Sacrifices under the Law, not to mention the Law itself, are but shadows of the cross.

The blood of animals could never perfect, or complete, anyone who comes with shamed faces rubbed in the dirt of their egregious performance failures, a glaring reminder, "Dude, you have a sin problem!"[16] Priests offering animals looked forward to a Lamb without spot or blemish, so when a resurrected Jesus appears to His own, it screams, "Friday worked!" The writer of Hebrews lays it out: "For by one offering He has perfected for all time those who are sanctified."[17]

Hearts Can Beat Again

"Why are you troubled, consumed with so much doubt?"[1] Unbelieving believers.[2] Remember how we witnessed twelve minus one placing fragile but determined necks on the line for One they deemed Master and Lord?[3] They meant it provided Jesus was with them. Apart from Him, forget it. Us too. He's not merely the object of our faith. Jesus is the Source and gut-level means, the author and finisher.[4] Joy and amazement hold a confounded lot captive in the moment. Frozen. "Got anything to eat?" He asks.[5] Knowing who the Lord is, and ever will be, takes on form and substance in His resurrection, or they and we might as well hang it up.

"If you confess with your mouth Jesus as Lord," Paul asserts.[6] It holds water only where hearts are secure in His bodily resurrection—that He, as a historical matter-of-fact, died, was buried, and walked out of His grave at the first light of dawn on day number three. Frazzled disciples knew He died. Two of their number, respected members of the Sanhedrin and committed believers, gained permission from the Roman procurator to take the corpse of One they so cherished and prep Him for burial—in spite of what the Qur'an says.[7] He died, yes, and was raised, a reality that necessarily confronts fearful yet loving doubters and skeptics alike.

Thomas wasn't alone.

Not by a long shot. The cross apart from a bodily resurrection only gathers dust, cold, lifeless memories devoid of hope. We talked about it. In creedal language, Paul lays out what he received; no inventions here.[8] This is critical, as in foundational, to hearts and minds transplanted in renewal. Christ died for our sins, a reality meticulously documented in Scripture and set in concrete for time and eternity.[9] Get this then: Christ's resurrection, His personal tour de force and heaven's final word, means nothing if there's no propitious death to give the resurrection its impact.[10] We don't need some kind of wow factor to wake people up. We need solid bedrock to build on.

And Jesus's burial?

We touched on this as well, but I'd like to drive it home if I may. Skeptics have long cast aspersions on Jesus's substitutionary death to avoid head-on collisions with the miraculous. Hey, why not? If He didn't die, there can be no resurrection. Islam, although paying token homage to a Jesus that lines up with Muslim sensibilities, insists He didn't die in the first place. The crucifixion, as the Qur'an has it,[11] was a cleverly staged illusion to throw the scent off of a Jesus Allah miraculously translated to Himself. Guess what that means? If Jesus didn't die, He can't be anyone's Savior, can He? His burial puts a serious damper on such demonic lunacy.

Three days in the tomb, isn't it? However variations on Hebraic tradition may be understood,[12] three—as days go—puts a lock on Jesus's death certificate *and ours* in Christ. Our identification with Jesus is by no means positional, if by that we mean God considers us in a strictly judicial sense with regard to Christ's crucifixion and no more. With all due respect, that's bogus.[13] Don't get me wrong. God is fully satisfied—judicially speaking—with Jesus's offering, and what that means concerning our standing with Him, but there's so much more. Our position, as it pertains to who we are "in Christ," goes deeper and wider. Something fundamental has radically changed.

The grave solidifies finality of all Calvary renders null and void.

Grace reckons on the cross where a very real record, think of it as a line item list of offenses that points an accusing finger our way, is nullified, never again to be called upon as condemning evidence.[14] It can't. Jesus paid. When He died, our debt died with Him and was forever buried, as were we.[15] Baptism lays hold of the eternal hope of our union with Christ by faith.[16] We died with Him, a supernatural reality that crucified our "old self," or "old man," our unregenerate spirits. Ask Paul.[17] And just as three days in a grave marks His death with certainty, it seals ours, knowing you and me, we were buried with Him.[18]

The boys don't get it, ladies either. Not yet. Participation in Jesus's death and burial is light-years removed from hope, much less a reality laid hold of by faith. Apart from resurrection, what is there? All Peter is left with is one stark, profoundly naked realization, "I want Jesus. I want Him, and I need Him. I can't do life without my Lord!" James too, John and Andrew wading through moments that can never be altered.[19] I can see this. I definitely feel it.

What do you do when anguish, sorrow, and bitter mourning lay claim to your heart and out of nowhere, there's Jesus...alive! Shock, fear, and amazement give way to wonder. Am I dreaming, or is this really happening? The sun burns off morning fog clouding an unsure landscape as a growing certainty of Jesus's presence calms turbulent waters. We're able to breathe, sort of. Hearts tentatively beat, then pound as a faith choice beckons.

Slide in alongside this disheveled bunch and wonder what it all means. "What do I do with this?" What gives when your heart and the life you thought you knew lay crushed and dismembered in irretrievable bits and pieces, then Jesus shows Himself? How does one make space for hope that could never have been, not with your name on it? There are no words, just Jesus. And because it's Him, He's your focal point, your choice, the only thing you need to see.

There's a method to Jesus's madness. Always. This was over the top. Impossible. Then again, that's Jesus. "Can I have something to eat?" brings them down to earth, prepping for an eye-opening Bible study and some much-needed understanding. Revisiting familiar turf through new eyes, a risen Jesus opens Moses and the prophets with a view toward Himself that newfound hearts might see the cross where it never existed.[20] Not for them. Calvary now connects the dots from start to finish. Now they can move forward.

With Peace Comes a Call

Or should I say commission?

This I can't imagine. Barely catching short, uncertain breaths, men pinch themselves as Jesus aggressively leads off, "As the Father sent Me, I'm sending You."[1] Say what? That'll drop you for the count. Peace the first go-around came as a call to follow. He now spells it "go," as in "make disciples" and the field is global.[2] "For God so loved the world," correct? The overflow of peace then is let it flow however, wherever; Judea, Samaria, the furthest reaches imaginable. Have you ever been stretched? This is it.

How well I know. First century dynamics play well beyond Peter, James, and John. The call to follow stretches blue and white-collar alike, fisherman or tax collector, janitor, CEO—whoever, whatever— beyond their wildest imaginations as Jesus draws folks from their world into His. Two millennia hence nothing's changed where follow becomes go. There's a paradigm here, one I didn't see coming. My fervent prayer that God make me part of the answer meant shaping through sifting, then sending. Welcome to discipleship, God-styled.

In *Problems, God's Presence and Prayer*, Mike Wells portrays the believer God strategically shapes as a lump of clay in His hands, the Jeremiah motif.[3] The potter's workshop is equipped to the hilt, and He only uses effectual means to achieve His desired goals. People, circumstances, and demonic forces are often tools of choice as the Spirit Himself directs and selectively permits. It may even be physical illness, knowing for certain "only those God calls out are allowed to step forward to make an impression on the clay"—clay that never leaves the Father's hands.[4] The end result? The Father's heart is uniquely expressed for His eternal purpose.

A purpose He "infects" His church and a fallen world with.

My call, as I understand, is discipleship in the trenches.

Think relationship. You know, roll your sleeves up, and get dirty if the occasion calls for it. It's one thing to stand at a safe distance dispensing information, grading papers, and assessing class participation. Walking life out with someone is another story altogether. Sound a little like parenting? Paul gets it. "You've got so many teachers," he counsels a confused Corinthian body. "What you don't have are fathers."[5] Dad's role gets messy more often than not; changing diapers, warming bottles, and such.[6] Scary too. In that sense it's pastoral, meaning up close and very personal, a domain where hearts truly are holy ground.

"Go ye therefore, and teach all nations," speaks volumes when you realize the word *go* speaks to decisive action yet by no means "busyness." Paul talks boxing.[7] You either swing and miss or connect. The boxer who misses, then misses again is easily fatigued. Put him in with a solid counterpuncher who studies his opponent, and it's all over. The guy will systematically dismantle him. That's Paul. His thing is to load up and connect, make every punch count. The call then isn't "get busy," but "get real." "Go" has nothing to do with making yourself a burnt offering by doing life and ministry *for* Jesus but rather doing it *from* Him.

Drawing from His initiative, His energy.

Not missing cues is fundamental: What Jesus orders begins with Him, works exclusively through Him, and comes back His way.[8] Ministry then cannot be my idea, or yours. We touched on this one too, but if you're anything like me, a little repetition won't hurt. Genesis 1 is clear. He's both the source and means, while 1 Corinthians 8:6 assures it's all for Him. Color that lunacy in a world with me and myself at the center where success is routinely measured by performance outcomes. Who's surprised when they, or we, miss God? The supposed good we generate in our own determined efforts, meaning ministry that begins and ends with us may, in fact, be a ministry of death.

Ouch! I won't make too many friends here, but I learned this one the hard way. Crash hard and burn. Where we engage, not to mention when and how, has got to start with Him, and I'm not headed for, "What would Jesus do?" You and I don't need to exercise creative imaginations, wondering, "If Jesus were here, how would He handle this?"

Why? *Jesus is here.* He is, and He's engaged. The question is, are we tuned in and open to Him? Listening ears pick up on such things. Enter Laodicea. "Behold I stand at the door and knock" isn't a call to the lost, per se.[9] It's to a church that thinks they've got everything figured out, but in reality, they're riding the fence while Jesus is on the outside knocking and waiting. Hello, is anyone listening?

Who'd have thought a schooled theologian, a Pharisee at that, would spearhead Jesus to the worst of the worst, unclean, uncircumcised pagans having no hope being without God—His presence, His truth—in a lost and dying world?[10] We know it's Paul. I'll go you one better, that an unschooled blue-collar tradesman should stand toe-to-toe with the religious elite concerning the hope of their own Jewishness. Enter one more than unlikely fisherman, our good brother Peter. The real shocker was me. Never in a million years would I have envisioned doing gut-level discipleship behind prison walls.

What is it they say, truth is stranger than fiction?

I'll bite. I did, in fact, and like a fish hooked solid, I ran and ran hard.

God snuck up on me. He knows prison ministry ranked at the very top of my "I want no parts of this" list, and not because my credo is "never say never."[11] I've heard stories. I've read books and seen movies. I watch the news. Nothing against convicted felons, I never thought I could relate. When God said, "Go!" I looked behind me the way Gideon must have. God had to be talking to someone else. I could feel where Moses was coming from when I Am showed him his travel plans. "You've got the wrong man. Who am I that I should go to Pharaoh?"[12] That's just it, Mo. It doesn't begin with you; it can't. You're bankrupt. "Eyes this way! I've got you, son." And did he jump up and say, "Let's do this thing?" Not hardly. Moses fought like a hooked fish!

That's okay, though. We're talking about knee-jerk responses, the reason believers so desperately need sifting. Our inclination, our flesh, if you will, looks in the mirror and makes a muscle. "Am I up to this?" Who, after all, wants to get in the ring with Goliath? Blessed are the inadequate; God can definitely use them.[13] I had it all figured out, what would or could unravel at my expense. You know, heckling, taking cheap shots. All right, so it never happened. Faulty imaginations. There's a lot of that in the works, always has been.

The Breath of Eternal Life

Genesis, according to John,[1] comes full circle where the unbeginning God invades time and space as He gives shape to a new beginning for a new creation.[2] You didn't see it, evening and morning the first day, etc.? Me neither. Go back to day six in Eden's garden paradise where one breath, God's breath, animates "Our image, Our likeness" while pointing to an even greater hope. I'm talking about you, me, in the stench of our sin and corruption becoming the righteousness of God, and not in our determined efforts, but rather what Jesus finished.[3]

God makes a living soul,[4] breathing life into nonlife—dirt of all things. Resurrection day, Jesus infuses men with Himself, giving those He'd personally called and chosen His life, eternal life. It's theirs now, and Pentecost is around the corner! See Genesis 1 and 2 with a view toward this new day, Jesus's new creation.

Go back and read John's text.[5] Greeting His distraught bunch in peace, Jesus bids them go. We've covered this ground some, but keep tracking. John blinks; then, Jesus pulls something that looks a lot like mouth-to-mouth resuscitation. He breathes into a handful of awestruck disciples.[6] Literally. All right, so proximity or form isn't the issue. The breath of life is. And with imagery not seen since God scooped Eden's rich soil in His hands, we witness heaven's restoration. This isn't symbolic. By direct impartation, we as born-again believers witness the onset of an altogether new race, a new humanity bearing God's personal imprint. New heavens and a new earth begin here!

How well I remember standing in front of the casket of a man I worked with. The shell of his remains testified to an emptiness igniting full-blown rage. "What a waste!" I fumed, inwardly confronting a myriad of conflicting thoughts and emotionally charged images. "This isn't life. It's all wrong!" How true. And for all the fists shaken in God's unseen face, no one looks in the mirror. God didn't choose death, man did. "How can you believe in a God who permits such evil, such pain and suffering?" fuels an all too common epithet among untold numbers of avowed skeptics. "Really? Then how can you believe in man who causes it?"[7] Hmm.

"By a man came death," like it or lump it.[8] And as noted earlier, the "What if?" road is a dead end.[9] A Lamb was slain from before creation's foundation, so let "What if Adam hadn't?" lie dead and buried. God's image and likeness will only ever be realized in the second man Paul coins the "last Adam."[10] The first is as earthy as they get; the second has heavenly roots.[11] It might help to remember that, contrary to popular opinion, Jesus didn't come to start a new religion. He started a new race that's alive with His eternal life. Amen!

Speaking of the breath of life, I'm impressed to share a piece we received from "behind the wall," a living letter testifying to grace and newness of life—Christ's eternal life.

I came into the Department of Corrections when I was nineteen years old. I have life with the chance of parole and have served thirty-seven years (forty-three now) in prison without parole. To date I have met with the parole board twenty-five times without the benefit of being paroled. Nevertheless, I am free! It is this freedom I want to testify to the glory of God.

When I entered D.O.C. I was very mentally deranged. I proceeded to tear at the flesh of my arms with razor blades. The staff feared for my safety and transferred me to the state hospital.

179

I escaped and committed eighteen crimes in the thirty-six hours I was at large. After being sentenced for escape and assaulting a sheriff's deputy, I was taken to the "Old Max" in Cañon City. I had been there three weeks when I stabbed a fellow inmate. I spent a year in solitary confinement for being too violent for the prison population. For the next twenty-three years I lived a violent life filled with homosexuality.

Three times I tried to commit suicide. The doctors considered me a helpless case. My parents died within three months of each other. I tried to join them in death, cutting my throat and nearly dying.

While chained to a hospital bed in grave condition I cried out to God saying, "God if you are real, prove it to me." A small voice deep inside me—a voice I had never heard before—said to me, "I will be with you always." A peace flooded my heart and soul.

When I was finally out of a strip cell, I requested a Bible from the chaplain. While reading Scripture, the Holy Spirit led me to II Timothy 1:7: "God has not given us a spirit of fear but of power, and of love and a sound mind." I said, "Jesus, I want a sound mind!" Having been mentally ill for most of my life, I wanted a sound mind more than any gift Jesus could give me. Since 2006 the doctors have been astonished at my recovery.

My love of Jesus and trust in Him has brought me such freedom, I will serve Him the rest of my days here on earth. Because of the violence and mental illness, my chance of being paroled can only be achieved through the power of Jesus. Having a life sentence with the possibility of parole I could someday be released. However, the freedom I enjoy worshipping God in prison, and the joy of loving my fellow prisoners keep me free inside the fences, bars and walls for as long as Jesus keeps me serving Him in this place, even if it is the remainder of my life. As Saint Paul said, "I have learned to be content in all circumstances." Praise God! I am content to be in prison. To be stable and no longer violent is a gift from God that keeps me ever walking with Him.

Mr. Dan, I share my testimony because I was a hopeless case that everyone had given up on, but not Jesus! When I share my testimony with fellow prisoners, it gives hope to those men suffering from depression and other mental illnesses. Jesus can indeed give "a sound mind." I am living proof. The joy I feel while writing this has me crying. Many times when a man tells me how depressed he feels, I cry. When they see me crying the dam breaks and they weep too.

Being an "old timer," many doors are opened to bring the good news that Jesus can heal all mental illness. At one period in my life I was on seven powerful anti-psychotic medications to keep me from being violent and self-destructive. Currently I am on one anti-depressant. All heavy medications have been eliminated. Praise God to His glory!

With love in Christ,
Michael Montgomery

Returning Home

One rookie big spender shares a few distant similarities with Peter.

The kid has a knack for recklessly dropping daddy's hard-earned cash proving he doesn't know his father; hence junior's identity crisis. Home isn't a fit for a youngster who's a stranger in his own skin. No surprise. Not identifying with dad creates issues when you look in the mirror, just as not really knowing the Master sends one fisherman in a much-needed tailspin that begins to square when a condemned Jesus makes eye contact. Peter crashes hard. An empty tomb points him homeward. And junior? Not so much, not yet.

A wandering son takes his heart and inheritance to a distant, or far country,[1] literally away from one's people. Now there's the real kick. Our young friend might have put a good number of miles between himself and his home address, yes? Not necessarily. Distancing oneself from "kith and kin"[2] has less to do with geography and more with mindset and relationship. And that means? It means he went to the Gentiles, pagans, if you will, people having nothing to do with the God of Abraham, Isaac, and Jacob. That's as distant as it gets. It's an identity thing—far from circumcision, Moses, the Torah, far from his people and Jerusalem's temple.

Be it one block removed or the other side of the world.

Far is a function of heart and mind, a choice. It's Peter's, "I don't know the man!" that leaves him floundering to stay afloat where assurance and stability slip between grossly inept fingers. He might as well have been on the other side of the world. A phantom rooster exposes Peter's nakedness, not unlike a precarious young upstart who isn't feeling all that competent or especially manly. Is it the pigs? God knows when he bathed last. Who would stand down wind? Hogs don't care. They eat, he doesn't.

Turning back begins to make sense to the kid, and Peter? He's not sure that option's open to him—not here, not now, not amid a flood of bitter tears and convulsive sobs, unlike Esau.[3] Mr. "My god is my belly" mourned in bottomless self-pity over his losses,[4] whereas Peter and junior were truly broken. Looking back, it makes sense. Everything, and I do mean everything, in one swarthy man's life was building toward this time, this cataclysmic convergence, but he didn't know what he couldn't see. Who does? You and I don't envision being moved to a place of crippled abandonment. It's not part of the dream, but guess what?

Some dreams need to be trashed.

It's anyone's guess what our prodigal misfit's intentions were. Fantasies can be misleading. Cutting loose among those having less than kosher appetites might prove novel. Eat, drink, and be merry! "Riotous living," your King James calls it.[5] I think of Solomon "testing" himself with pleasure.[6] Folks in the contemporary western world are long given to reckless, self-indulgent lifestyles, but it didn't start here, did it? A flood points to mankind's depravity, driven by malevolent thoughts and intentions continuously,[7] so who's surprised when identity and fulfillment are packaged in a few laughs or a slap on the back, a shallow sense of belonging?

Performance wears a few unexpected faces where the quest for acceptance travels the path of least resistance, and it gets scary. Do you give in or pull back? Thank God for grace with an unseen lifeline where people unexpectedly bail, and circumstances go belly up. I'm listening to Blood, Sweat and Tears's soulful rendering of Billie Holiday's "God Bless the Child" now, the gist of it being cash in the hand breeds friends, but not for long. "When the money's gone, and all your spending ends they won't be 'round anymore."[8] Famine nails a kid with empty pockets, crushing hopeful expectations. Best thing that ever happened.

Wake-up calls. Our friend might have hit snooze a time or two, three maybe. What can I say? An empty stomach is a relentless, if not brutal and demanding taskmaster. "Do something!" he insists. Vision clouds when distortions come packaged with lots of feel-good and accepting smiles. Hunger clears stubborn fog as a young man makes the connection with what had ever been yet was little more than lifeless wallpaper.

A Boy Remembers His Daddy

Sifting blasts through unwanted obstructions.

They weren't always unwanted. The kid left home, why? Appetite. Whatever it was, he couldn't find it there. Greener grass. Strange, isn't it? Big brother sticks it out, biting the bullet because he has to. Little bro isn't buying. What's crazy is Dad isn't selling, yet for some reason, both boys lock into twisted images. They were convinced. Nothing too terribly unusual here. Such lunacy travels hand in glove where dad is seen through a distortion lens. Number one son locks down in bitter legalism, pretentious breeding ground of the proud self-righteous and self-avowed victims. The younger simply cuts all moorings.

Imagine that he should crash and burn. The bottom drops, and there's nothing to sustain our former upstart, nothing and no one who even remotely cares. A nonexistent world framed on make-believe foundations strips naked a deception as old as dirt. Eden's lie works like a charm on all who would script their own story convinced, "You won't die!" The serpent's well-worn retread. Naked and ashamed sends one man scrambling, but when a pigpen is the best fig leaf life offers, a forlorn son's illusions are trashed.

The stench of hogs and a sour, knotted stomach is the glaring reality check a "know it all" punk playing calculated angles never stopped to consider. "Day labor does better than I do. My father feeds them in addition to the wage he pays, and I'm starving like a dog here!"[9] Hello? Stuff you and I take for granted, day in, day out realities that never touch bottom, or so we think, now take center stage. Sonship is an honor when it's a resting place. Seriously. Realities a dreamer routinely discards as trash with nary a thought or thank you becomes the world to one who previously considered his father a cosmic killjoy. Any takers?

We're talking treasure.

"For joy," Jesus says.[10] Remember that one? Apart from eyes that see, we'll drive right past the exit. We've all been there, done that, but when the treasure's your destination and ultimate purpose, focus changes. Think sifting where "I have sinned" is an eye opener, a complete about-face.[11] Leaving, at one time, was the kid's entitlement. Repentance sends him home. Try this one on, and see if it fits. Junior blows his wad and drowns in self-pity. Permanently? No, it didn't happen here; thank God. It does for many. Some set up camp and never leave. They don't see because they can't. Blessed are eyes that do.[12]

"I'm not worthy," a broken and sorrowful son rehearses. He's seen something. Boneheaded "gimmies"[13] decorating his past no longer fit, not to his father's contrite boy. Conviction of sin does such things. Ask Job or Isaiah.[14] Too bad we live in a day when talk of sin is passé, if not politically intolerant, places where folks suppress the inconvenient and undesirable to their detriment.[15] Look in on Gomorrah. Try a preflood earth or one Pharaoh and his insistence on having the last word.[16] The price tag on defiance is steep, but the repentant?

They're homeward bound.

The boy felt trapped at home, and when a "stuck feeler"[17] signs on as the measure of truth, reality gets twisted. Don't I know it! Choices, obsessions really, come by way of hopeful expectation, longing dreams of personal gratification. The problem is when our felt desires write God out of the picture, a spirit of entitlement develops, and why? Fleshly mindsets are persuasive and extremely convincing where it comes to any number of things we don't have yet believe we absolutely should.[18] Imagine that! And did I say idolatry? It goes with obsession and neighboring compulsions. Always. Sifting clears the cobwebs, making truth accessible in a father's loving embrace.

The Difference

Right about now someone's thinking I'm contradicting a few things I said earlier. Not so. What I'm saying is sifting (from God's end) is an intentional nudge homeward where "I have sinned" is a necessary, and typically rude wake-up call, but it's not home itself. It's not "this is who I am, this is where I belong. This is where you will always find me." No, the sin you and I have committed only proves our need for home, while "I'm not worthy" reflects what I wasn't created for. It's not an identity tag—not if you're "in Christ" as true, born-again believers. But Dad's got to drive that one home before we'll see it.

There's a difference between "I have sinned" as an impetus, or trigger, and being locked in an identity prison—a swift kick in the seat—versus the proverbial albatross hanging around tired, ragged necks.[1] One moves us off dead center; the other binds unwitting souls to performance-based outcomes. Talk about a dead, lifeless end where I'm continually having my face rubbed in the stench of my failures! It's the flip side of "I'm only human," the all-purpose rug you and I have learned to sweep our dirt under. Paul nails it. "In my flesh there's nothing good."[2] Ever. The best I can hope for in my own self-effort is sin. Period.

But you really don't hear me, do you?

You don't get what I'm saying, and I understand. I've been there, so try this: Success isn't measured by performance outcomes. It can't be. And folks who see "Thou shalt not" as God's measured ladder to success can only ever crash and burn or apply for membership as card-carrying neo-Pharisees. Been there too, so what if we take a question? Why did Jesus refer to the leaders of His time as "whited sepulchers"?[3] Give up? I'll give you a hint. They focused on achievement, what they did and how it looked to themselves and others. We've touched on this, the assumption if it looks and feels right, it must be right.

And that would be wrong, dead wrong.

"You appear spot-on, but you're lawless hypocrites!"[4] Pretending to be what one is not is hypocrisy's bottom line—actors and actresses bent on convincing themselves and personal audiences they've got a wrap on "getting it right." And for those whose imaginations are lined with mirrors, observing themselves as the world looks on (they hope) with approval or envy, we've gotta talk and talk now! When it's all eyes on me, life invariably becomes performance-driven; whereas, God, who engages the heart, is a lot more interested in motive and means. What's driving you and where's the energy coming from, you or God?

Try this on for size: If what we call ministry, not to mention the overall stuff of life, doesn't begin with God, come alive through His energy then go back to Him, "that men may see your good works and glorify your Father which is in heaven,"[5] all bets are off. Seriously. You and I don't need, much less want, wood, hay, and stubble for building material, do we?[6] I hope not. "Futility!" Paul calls it. An unbelieving world stumbles in the dark, but who can blame them? They have no God connection; His life isn't in them.[7] That used to be us.

No way, not any longer.

In Christ, we look beyond me and mine knowing humanity was created to bear God's image and likeness. Left to ourselves, we've got a gaping hole to fill, a bottomless chasm, but it is what it is when all you know, all you have, is invested in finding a place to hang your hat based on self-effort. It's a dead end for sure if everything exuding life and substance has God alone as its source, and everything apart from Him spells death. If that's so, then life and death can't possibly be reduced to philosophic pursuits where truth is up for grabs, a "choose your flavor," and it's all good. No way that's going to fly! Ever.

But God makes it easy for us. "Trust and believe Me," He says, the bottom line being dependence as opposed to our intentionally shouldering a burden that's killing us![8] There the burden lies squarely on the shoulders of independent you and self-reliant me where we find ourselves eating from the wrong tree again![9] It speaks to relationship and vital connection. Apart from Jesus, nothing works.[10] "In Him we live and move and have our being."[11]

It all comes back to one fundamental choice: Who do you believe and how does that shake out?

The Word Became Flesh and Dwelt Among Us

Jesus lays the foundation. Baptism in the Jordan prefigures His identification with fallen humanity through the cross while confirming His divine Sonship.[12] Gabriel, if you recall, informed Mary concerning her unborn baby, that He would be the Son of God.[13] Identity is everything. Jesus isn't another holy man making His self-styled mark. This one presents as the living God to every man, every woman,[14] while standing both for and as us before the Father as a man.[15] A man trashed humanity; a man—a flesh and blood man—must choose life.[16]

Turning things around is no small feat. Most are willing to acknowledge the catastrophic mess humanity and planet earth are in. Coming to terms with how we got there and what to do can be a nothing short of disaster as the pieces fall. Who's to blame and where do we go? The humanist hopes with no guarantees while the mystic seeks self-improvement through karma and enlightenment, but "it takes so long,"[17] since no one, not even the Buddha, gets it the first go-around.[18] If you're Muslim, it's a one-shot deal, a risky gamble at that.[19]

But again, it's the wrong tree, folks!

Anything truly redemptive doesn't begin with us. Try inserting me as the source, and watch as I write God out at the expense of what is authentically good and truly necessary.[20] A tree makes all the difference.

Skeptics reducing Eden to mythological ramblings don't get it. Natural minds, I understand.[21] "Eye has not seen," but for those with ears to hear, God explains Himself.[22] I Am previews His intentions to a pathetic bunch knowing only abysmal slavery.[23] And that means what to us? Doing prison time gets closer, sort of. The penitentiary allows amenities: TV and visits, possibilities beyond high walls and fences trimmed in razor wire. Israeli slaves had brick pits, scarred backs, and broken, calloused hands. Unending bitterness for many.

And Moses? Apart from his call and revelation of God, we'd be in the dark concerning a few essential realities; personal and historically. There's a much larger picture. Huge. Slaves in Egypt didn't see the movie, not so much as a trailer or behind-the-scenes footage.[24] They didn't need to. Banks on the far side of a sea called Red were the ideal place to discover, "I am the LORD your God, who brought you out of the land of Egypt."[25]

Who is He, the God who put Egypt
in the rearview mirror?

Moses shines a light by way of Abraham, Isaac, Jacob, and even predates them. "In the beginning," he says.[26] Makes sense. Creation opens wide the consummate wonder of the one Source, the LORD, their deliverer. It's called context. Who they are individually and as a people is tied directly to Him, who He is as seen through a seemingly infinite cosmos and the people factor. Enter Adam. Now stick with me on this. The first man chose independence and death, correct? The second man, Jesus,[27] opted for dependence and life—in eternity,[28] yes, and Gethsemane, but there's another significant mile marker.

Affirmation as the Father's Son on Jordan's muddy banks takes our carpenter to dry places and introspective discovery, a little undivided attention and some wide-open space with Dad. We speak of quiet time in a noisy world where audio-video wallpaper peels layer by layer. (What would we do without smartphones and surround sound home theaters?) I remember driving up Mt. Evans, the highest peak you can scale on four wheels in the United States. "Listen!" I nudged my oldest. "What do you hear?" She paused while scanning, her eyes reaching for mine.

"I've never heard so much quiet, Daddy!" Indeed, and Jesus found it in spades.

Forty days and ne'er a crust of bread prove one well-nourished soul. The Word made flesh brings Eden to the desert where a Man chooses dependence instead of preference over truth where autonomy promises freedom and delivers bondage.[29] Now there's a mouthful! You, me, not one of us was built to withstand self-determination's brutal rigors. The Son opts in as man, here and Calvary. "If you're the Son of God" is the tempter's notorious prod for Jesus to prove Himself, in and of Himself.[30]

"If You are who You say You are, fly solo!"

Pick a stone, any stone. Make Your choice. Turning stone into a loaf ain't no big thing if the Father says so. I know folks who'd rather have Jesus do that than water to wine. He nails it, though. Bread alone points to appetite. Autonomy. "I need satisfaction," and why not? There's a legitimate need. But it's not about Me, is it? Knowing who You are means there's nothing to prove. "My nourishment, my real sustenance and deepest satisfaction come by doing the will of Him who sent Me."[31] Adam hadn't learned that. Jesus knew. "I do what Dad says." Leading by feel, by fleshly desires and personal appetites negates truth.

In choosing the Father, to love, trust, and obey, Jesus chooses life as the last Adam.[32]

A Prodigal Father

Think "generous" or "liberal," as in "giving on a lavish scale."[1]

The other side of prodigal. Number two son won't get it apart from a deliberate, I'm talking very intentional homecoming. How could he? Dad made choices concerning his boy the young man will never come to terms with any more than fisher Peter could wrap his brain around the grace that owns him outside of connecting with Jesus in His resurrection. They both need a taste with their names on it as this gets radical!

Take a step or two back if you would. "I have sinned," when it's a real eye opener—a stark and what often seems a cruel undressing of motives and means—can be a lifesaver. Literally. A man or woman hearing "Guilty!" in a courtroom or "life without parole" gets more than a slap in the face. Life is over. All right, so it's a matter of degree. Ask the man slopping hogs. His world is in the toilet—himself, everything he's ever known as life, his identity—and for what? Sin. For him, it's personal as it should be. Choices point to motive.

How wrong can you get? The preference over truth crowd holds a corner on anything goes. When ideals and personal satisfaction become the measure of reality, what feels right and makes sense as I search out my unique fit adrift on a sea of conflicting messages, I can pretty much justify anything and everything no matter who gets trashed in the fallout, or how. Ask Oscar Wilde.[2] The light going on, shocking as it may be, directs a telling laser where it belongs. Again, ask Oscar Wilde.[3] Conviction points us to God.

Sin is first and foremost an assault against heaven.

Always. The self-indulgent don't get it. What is heaven to those who frame reality on the basis of existential or naturalistic precepts, godless ideals shaped by a philosophical bias? Be it through a telescope or a telling smirk through a cloud of cigar smoke, the self-sustained don't give God serious thought, even those who say they believe. No more than Cain.[4] Enter the nominal churchgoer or moral behaviorist as though a man is capable of impressing God or even doing the right thing. "I'm not so bad. I'm as good as the next guy."[5] Good? That's a God word. Jesus said so, and we fall pathetically short, all of us.[6]

Isaiah has a vision, the prodigal an empty stomach. Jesus turns Peter's way, and the fisherman's denial locks him in. Guilty as charged. Reality blooms, and David gets it. "Against You, You only have I sinned."[7] *Treason* is the word, enmity with God. Hostility. Hatred.[8] Whenever you, I, whenever anyone opts for self-rule, be it open, belligerent dissent, the path of least resistance or simply doing life my way, on my terms—ministry included—malignant toxins are unleashed. And that means what? It means renegade thoughts and actions are directed heavenward.

Extreme? If you consider the status quo a 180-degree shift in reality, then, yes, it's extreme. A desensitized world, or a church cut from Laodicean cloth, won't see what it can't.[9] Looks and smells a lot like an increasingly popular breed of emergent feel-good Christianity floating in the breeze these days, alleged believers who would redefine the Book based on subjective cultural impressions.[10] The problem with the current bent toward dismissing a truly biblical construct of the abject horrors of sin means folks won't appreciate the need for an all but unheard of radical repentance toward God, switching up my focus from me to Him to find my fit.[11]

So where, pray tell, is magnetic north?

Is it a fixed, unchangeable constant?

God knows this isn't popular talk in an increasingly global context where identity is fluid, coming back to me, what I think and how I feel wherever, whenever it suits me. How I choose to identify personally, sexually. Apart from a stark confrontation with the hellish consequences of such arrogant, suicidal thinking, you and I will consistently miss out on the awesome wonders of grace, the magnitude of grace extended to repentant souls whose eyes have been opened to reality. If he won't change up and double back, a wasteful, wayward son remains clueless to the lavish extravagance of his father's love—what it truly means to be his father's son.

Dad knows. He's been watching.[12] It's all about compassion. Sound anything like Jesus,[13] His empathetic display of the Father's attentive heart?[14] A wounded and confused son turning homeward is repentance where the rubber meets the road. Literally. No victims here, just gut-level honesty. What the kid knew of his father, but never tasted, becomes one hungry man's intentional pursuit. He humbles himself as does his dad. You heard me. Embracing the unembraceable makes a loving father one with his son's fetid stench. That's Jesus, who in making Himself one with a fallen, sinful humanity coupled with, "This is my beloved Son," makes for a dual humility there are no words for, only worship.

Note the posture of a father who's beside himself; he sees, he runs, he literally falls on his wayward son's neck.[15] And that says what? It screams agape, love that could only have God as its source. I remember a story. It was Jim Cymbala, I think, pastor of Brooklyn Tabernacle. A gutter-drunk stumbles off the street into an Easter service, unbathed in God knows how long and reeking of dried vomit, stale feces, having just wet himself. Jim sensed God's nudge to draw close, to press in and embrace a man whose ambience could gag a maggot! A pastor, might I add, with a one-time prodigal daughter. Talk about a God thing!

And talk about one prodigal father's heart! Moved to reach beyond telling symptoms to greater realities, a penitent son who wouldn't so much as think of touching the father he shamed and defaced is held close, kissed repeatedly in joyful acceptance. And honored? What self-respecting individual would have imagined dad calling for the best robe, his robe and signet? Sandals too. Slaves go barefoot, not sons. "Quickly!" he insists. "Kill the fatted calf." I hear the man. What else can be said? Is this life out of death, or what?[16]

Ask Peter

An empty tomb, now face-to-face with his risen Lord who is both Savior and Life.

"I've been here before," he's thinking, but not déjà vu. It's the same but different—a long night on the water and come morning Jesus hails bone-tired anglers. "Catch anything, children?"[1]

"Nope, not one." What's there to say? It was a complete bust. Nothing new here. It happens to the best.

"Throw your nets on the right side, and you'll get something." He knows. They're still learning. It's called resurrection, bona fide evidence above and beyond anything this frazzled bunch could conceivably ask or think. Bulging nets bear witness.

Larger than anything this ragtag mob has ever known, and He's no caricature. Jesus poured Himself into "unlearned and ignorant men,"[2] not exactly orthodox, yet look at these guys. What appeared to be another wasted night on the water is their launchpad to relearn with new hope, new understanding.

"Apart from Me you can do nothing."[3] They're beginning to realize the profound efficacy of these words. Men who three years, or so, earlier abandoned every pretense to follow a Nazarene carpenter had the rug pulled out from under them. "What kind of man is this?"[4] underscores amazement that refuses to be held in check, much less explained. The natural order of things bow to His every whim, their hearts included, slow as they may be at times. "Fishers of men," He calls them. Would there be such catches they couldn't contain?

All eyes on Jesus, guys, His initiative and faithfulness dispensed in God-sized fullness.[5]

Their best and most determined efforts could only replicate another fruitless night even if they scored. "I'm going fishing," is Peter taking into experienced hands what seems and feels right while others follow. How many pastors and missionaries have come up empty in frustrated pursuit of another's purpose-driven lead? Hatching someone else's egg doesn't work. Blessed, instead, are the meek—teachable inductees who crave knowing and hearing the Shepherd's voice, responding to His every nudge, embracing brokenness and correction—that is, sifting.

"Cast your nets to the right" followed by a hot breakfast on the beach, knowing, "It is the Lord," secures hungry hearts—the fattened calf and then some—while love draws Peter out.[6] Who is he really? Does the man himself know? Do any of them? In His time with this lot of apostolic appointees, Jesus laid a sure and solid foundation, realities that would only take root in His death, burial, and resurrection, realities found only in Him. Did they see it yet?

Do You Love Me, Peter?

The question burns. Where's He going with this? Hit rewind then pause. "He who loves father or mother more than Me is not worthy of Me."[7] Strong words, yes, but they get stronger still. "If anyone comes to Me and does not hate his own father and mother, even his own life, he cannot be My disciple."[8] What gives here? "We left everything to follow You,"[9] seems hollow in light of Peter's denial, yet the fisherman affirms what he realizes Jesus already knows.[10] His love stands as Jesus confirms Peter's call. "Take care of My little ones, My lambs."[11]

Peter's love becomes a point of loyalty again, not that Jesus is clueless, but Peter needs to connect a few dots. "Are you with Me, Peter, or is fishing your life?"[12] The Master's query is fair given one angler's grotesque fumble and others who followed suit by abandoning Him as well. Does he stick with Jesus, failures and all, or does the man play it safe with what many might see as a sure thing—his life on the water? It happens a lot, yet Peter doesn't hesitate or hedge. Our friend is all in, and his heart knows it. He's convinced.

How can that happen? The cross is truly effectual in those who respond by faith. There's much bewildered apprentices don't get until "Tarry ye in Jerusalem"[13] turns everything on its ear, but they can't shake the sense they're anchored. Peter just knows, trepidation and all. He loves out of love that first claimed his heart.[14] Jesus draws that out. For all his boneheaded choices, Peter's heart is learning its resting place. "By this the love of God was manifested in us, that God has sent His only begotten, His unique Son into the world so that we might live through Him"—right here, right now with Christ Himself as our Life, our Source.[15]

"Are you in this for the long haul, Peter?"

Many have undertaken scholarly breakdowns of the Greek text and the words for *love* used in this passage, for which we're grateful, differences of opinion and all! My interest here lies in gut-level impact, where this touches Peter and what it calls out in him. Jesus paints a new and ultraradical portrait in what has been rightly coined His passion, an altogether foreign concept. "What kind of love is this?"[16] We're talking love that reaches down and out to the unlovely and unlovable and makes them sons and beloved daughters. Amen.

Loving Jesus means loving them, the Samaritans and tax collectors, sex offenders and garden-variety felons. Remember Brooklyn Tabernacle's vile, smelly gutter drunk? "One of the least of these," Jesus says. "Loving Me is borne out in loving them. They're family too."[17] "If we love one another, God abides in us, and His love is perfected in us."[18] Not a formula, but evidence. Love poured out in willing hearts by His Spirit brings hope that compels and constrains.[19] "I'm asking again, do you love Me, Peter?"[20]

He's been called to shepherd, no holds barred.[21]

Round number three pushes Peter and pushes hard. Good. "Good?" you ask. "What's so good about it?" I'm not trying to be cute, but that's a really good question. With all our man's been through, Jesus has to go deep. Is He asking, "Do you really love Me?" or is that what it feels like. The Master, it would seem, believes His disciple but what about Peter? Does he think Jesus doubts him? His life, after all, is the cost of loving Jesus. With where he's been, you know our man will get blindsided, again. He knows it too, which is why Jesus calls him out a third time. I'm convinced.

No one has tasted the bitterness of self-preservation quite like Peter, the crushing remorse, so that's not happening. Not again. Jesus understands, Peter too, and it's not for renewed determination. That ruined him once. That's not happening here. The rabbi's resurrection puts fresh wind in his sails, affirming love on a previously nonexistent level. Peter needs to make contact with his own heart, so Jesus pushes. "Lord, I can't pull anything over on You. You know everything." Amen, so again Peter confesses; three denials, three very real confessions, three confirmations. Jesus seats our boy with Him, in heavenly places.[22]

From this position, Peter is free indeed to learn what it means to tend the Shepherd's sheep.

"If Anyone Wants to Follow Me"

Let's double back for a moment, or two.

Have you ever noticed how our vision sometimes clears in the rearview mirror? Mine does. It was important, not only for twelve, but all who could legitimately be counted Jesus's disciples. Remember when He sent seventy out for short-term missions,[1] to preach and heal the sick, and don't forget the multitudes who were touched.[2] Disciples were birthed among their ranks too. How much did any of them see on the front end? Many blew past like so much sand on a windy beach. Resurrection reflections yield a fuller, more accurate, if not stable imagery.

Bear with me then, even though you and I see through a glass darkly,[3] the fog is lifting. Consider those who were first to hear straightforward talk of discipleship while under His wing. Spectators and would-be groupies, more often than not, got upended and tossed amid Jesus's rising swells, waves breaking as nonsensical ferocity. They don't have an invite to participate in kingdom mysteries.[4] God knows it was hard enough for those who were and presently are. Who can see or hear, much less lay hold unless He first lays hold of us?

Consider, will you?

Dots connect as the gospel of the kingdom converges with talk of Calvary. The unveiling of Jesus as Messiah to a select group of apprentices is coupled with suffering and death, a proposition that breathes shock and dismay in downcast faces[5]. (We've hit this in a couple of places.) How do you reconcile keys of the kingdom with doom and gloom? But it doesn't end there. It's one thing for forerunners in the making to be blindsided with Jesus's certain demise only to learn it's not for spectators. "Following Me," Jesus insists, "means self-denial and crosses with your names on them."[6] Want grounds for sifting? Take a hard look at the threshing floor.

Self-Denial Is Gethsemane's Calling Card

Think "a place of brokenness and consummate surrender." And you thought Peter's sifting unpacked itself in the high priest's court-yard? Oh, that's part of it, but wasn't our friendly fishmonger asleep at the wheel, so to speak, abandoning his call to "watch and pray," and not just Peter?[7] Others dropped the ball. Great observations. We can't lose sight, though, of sifting in action when confused apostolic newbies first stepped into this garden altar. "My soul is grieved," mourns Jesus, "to the point of death."[8]

Had He ever come apart with such raw, unbridled passion con-cerning Himself? Not hardly. The Master crashed hard at Lazarus's passing,[9] breaking down in convulsive sobs over Jerusalem's rejection of her Messiah,[10] but this? This they'd never seen. The boys were clueless as to the burden He carried, angels too.[11] They had no idea. The weight of the world doesn't come close. He bears the brunt of the ages, of time and eternity. Eden's animal skin coverings point to it,[12] as do Old Covenant images,[13] but none could possibly convey the look in Jesus's sad, anguished eyes, the tormented soul Peter con-fronted in the company of a rattled James and John.[14]

They were crushed as well as confused.

The Call to Discipleship Is Radical If Not Impossible[15]

A call no one hears or resonates with if they're not one of His.[16] God knows it's true. Saying yes to Jesus spells death to everything this crazed bunch has ever known as life. Us too. Everyone who's heard heaven's ultimate reckoning. Jesus is by no means icing on the cake, or God forbid, an embellishment to anyone's resumé.[17]

Calling Zebedee's sons, not to mention Peter or Levi, from respective workstations takes on meaning and substance in their collective responses to Him. What can I say? Leaving everyone and everything says something about His claim on their hearts whether they realize it or not. Not yet anyhow. Identification with Jesus in His death definitively separates His beloved disciples to Himself. The cross is now the lens they begin to view God, themselves, and the perverse world around them through.[18] Where information comes on a need-to-know basis, the only thing they need to know is Jesus. He's it, the sum total.

But there's a context.

Our Lord speaks of His imminent rejection and death, but only—now get this—only in the context of resurrection.[19] He's got to. Apart from resurrection, the Galilean's death is, it's one of many unfortunate departures fraught with pain and suffering. Did I say misunderstanding? Many see it that way. He doesn't. Death here has nothing to do with martyrdom, a man giving Himself for noble, if not worthy, convictions. That's not Jesus. Never. He's a Savior dying for us, as us, and discipleship for the likes of those who believe can only mean participation in Jesus's death before we can ever hope to share in His life. In that order.

"In Christ" addresses our covenant union, Jesus's love commitment for better or worse, binding us to Himself with His death as our point of entry. This, friends, is where we're joined to Him spirit to Spirit.[20] And as grizzly as all of this cross talk may sound, it's heaven's emancipation proclamation signed in blood. Every last one whose heart is assured in the knowledge that we, in fact, are the purchase of blood, have now been liberated, set free from sin and death's stranglehold. "He who has died," says Paul, "is freed from sin"—free from its relentless guilt, shame, and condemnation, free of its insistent tyranny.[21] Free indeed.[22] Jesus isn't morbid; He's honest.

And He's not a heavy-handed, despotic cult leader—no Jim Jones, no David Koresh.[23] His emphatic assertion, "If anyone comes to Me, and does not hate his own father and mother and wife and children and brothers and sisters, yes even his own life, he cannot be My disciple"[24] reeks of cultic extremism unless you know Jesus. Again, think context. This time, it's the boundaries of life and death. Our first parents were persuaded, "You won't die."[25] They were suckered in by what appeared to be good and honorable intentions.[26] Us too. Every generation since Eden builds on the same worn-out retread. "Life can be found in yourselves."[27]

Sorry, it's still the wrong tree.

The one who "cannot be My disciple" disqualifies themselves with their stubborn insistence for doing life on "my terms, not His." The price tag hasn't changed since Eden, folks. Death is death no matter how you slice it, the wages of sin as Paul has it.[28] The question is: Who, or what, will you align yourself with? A man who can't navigate beyond the blind deafness that frames the only world he knows, me and mine sound untouchable depths for him. So, when Jesus comes with a sense of unbridled urgency dripping with blood,[29] we smile and shake doubtful heads. Who's going to take you seriously, Jesus? Who would want to be your disciple?

Who indeed? Believing and learning what it means to trust Jesus does more than put a fresh spin on things; He redefines reality. "I am the way," stands as the compass's fixed reference point, a new magnetic north!

"I am the truth. I am the life."[30] How's that for arrogance? It's not if you truly are. Bring on the naysayers, the cocky challengers! Where's the harm when nothing can be done against the truth, only for it?[31] Staggering, right? When Jesus speaks of discipleship in terms of ultimate allegiance, it's about ultimate truth and life at its source, how the whole ball of wax[32] comes together; not as concepts or principles, but as a Person.[33]

What Sifting Comes Down To

How many times had what we might construe as a morbid, satanic threat run us off the road? Have you ever wondered what would happen if God allowed the devil to have his way with you or me? Satan's incessant demand to get in on Peter and the others, sifting them like so much wheat, doesn't exactly conjure up warm and fuzzy images, does it? You might as well ask God to tell Satan where you live, as in, "Have you considered my servant?" having your name inserted for Job's. I'll pass, thank you. Why so fearful? It's that tree again, isn't it? Touché, it certainly is.

The fear of death gives birth to every fear imaginable, which is why Jesus went for the jugular, "that through death He might render useless him who once held the power of death in his barbarous clutches, while liberating those who through fear of death were held captive with every breath."[1] It's scary at times, I won't deny it, but in order to secure our freedom and ultimate wholeness, Jesus had to take you, take me to Himself on Golgotha's tree, into the grave and back as day three's dawn breaks with new life, new resilience.

> If that's true, then:
> His death is our death.
> His burial is our burial.
> His resurrection is our resurrection.
> And now
> His life is our life.

Sifting is the outworking of Calvary's grace through faith, most often by way of brokenness, repentance, and surrender. Believers readily acknowledge as I did for years, "Jesus loved me and died for my sins." And? "Well, He forgave me so I can go to heaven when I die." But is that all there is, forgiveness and heaven? "I'm not sure I get you," someone says. "What else is there?" Forgiveness and eternity in heaven is the sum and substance of our salvation in Christ for many, if not most, evangelical believers. What about you?

I'm not trying to ride anyone; trust me, I'm not. I am concerned, though, where we dock our boats with regard to the hope and assurance that's ours in Christ. Targeting forgiveness and heaven as the end all to Jesus's passion as it touches us on this side of the grave is, it's unfortunate. This is one of those places you and I can't afford to stop short of the whole counsel of Scripture. "At the right time," Paul assures, "Christ died for the ungodly."[2] No arguments here. We who believe are saved, as in delivered, from God's fiery wrath.[3]

So far so good, but does Jesus's death save us? What do you mean?" someone fires in return. "Of course, Jesus's death saves us!" Does it really? Go back to the text where Romans 5:6 rapidly segues to the seemingly unthinkable. Enemies, treasonous traitors like you and me, were reconciled to God, but how? What was the means of grace used to accomplish such a feat? *We were reconciled to the Father through the death of the Son*, or so Paul says.[4] Reconciliation, that's salvation, isn't it? In part, yes, but there's more to being saved than you or I may have thought.

We Think Threshing and Winnowing, How About Cutting and Ripping?

Cut through the fog of so much confusion, our twisted distortions. Without exception, sifting has got to do some serious cutting. I'm thinking of a man right now. Molested as a boy and not once. Repetition has a way of setting things in concrete, as well as on edge. "It's who I am," makes for a lonely, desolate prison, a life sentence for untold numbers with no parole, no discharge. If not for grace, you take your last breath here. "But God," cuts into dark hopelessness, and Jesus steps in. For some, it's only so far. A man can be saved and still not walk in his deliverance, never find green pastures, still waters that are uniquely his.[5]

Forgiven with the hope of heaven only goes so far. We build layers, don't we? Barriers to pain, fortresses secluding wounded hearts from fresh reminders of skirmishes, some ancient. Rejection mostly. I brought a message one Sunday to a group of inmates that came back to bite me in a letter:

> *Wow!* I barely made it back to the shower and turned on the spigot full blast before the tears that ripped open an old wound started to flow. I was finally able to stumble to my cell, as it was next to the shower, and collapse. Thank you and damn you for pulling that old wound open and helping me know that I am not alone. I was stopped by three other men. The four of us admitted we all had been victims of the same kind of sexual predator in different places and different times. "We need to hear this type of gut-wrenching message more often," one of these men said, as we all had tears flowing as we walked back to our cell houses.

> Can I please share my story? I mean, honestly, you started this, and I would like to use your honesty and bluntness to finally cleanse and stitch this old and ragged wound up for the final time.

Something about having scabs pulled off old wounds screams for more than the hope of heaven. The cross cuts hard and deep releasing us from the bondage and consequences of sin pointing us to freedom and wholeness. Forgiveness as we've known it may prove shallow over against the true riches grace exposes as lonely hearts languish, hungry for something more. God strips us down.

We need deliverance, genuine freedom from the bondage of guilt and a relentless taskmaster, the power of sin.[6] Deliverance is one edge of salvation's double-edged sword, and it cuts with surgical precision. The other is wholeness. No hack job here. God knows His business and does a thorough job. We're the clueless ones having no idea how deep sin's cancer goes. We need deliverance. We need wholeness. That's salvation in Jesus, a complete package. Reconciliation through His death opens the door to a mind-boggling "much more" reality. "Having been reconciled, we shall be saved," not by Jesus's death, but *"by His life."*[7] Amen, it's true!

Forgiveness and the assurance of our justification by grace through faith lays a rock-solid foundation, yet Major Ian Thomas, world missionary and founder of Torchbearers International asks: "Does the knowledge that your sins are forgiven—for His dear sake in itself—equip you for a life of God-life?"[8]

What does "equip you for a life of God-life" mean? Glad you asked. Do you agree that doing life on Jesus's terms is a God-sized proposition? The Master is clear. "Apart from Me you can do nothing."[9] And that means? The short answer is bearing fruit, walking as believers in the obedience of faith.[10] Paul's letter to confused Galatians contrasts our own self-sufficiency with Christ as our life in the Holy Spirit.[11] They're polar opposites! The fruit Jesus speaks of has Him alone as its source.[12] The alternative? The plastic fruit we spoke of. It looks convincing, but try eating such man-made fare.[13] There's no life in it, no sustenance, no real satisfaction.

If you agree Adam made the wrong choice, that men and women weren't created to be independent or self-contained free agents, then you and I are on the straightaway. Apart from Jesus, we're incomplete and far less than human. All right then, what do the likes of us who trust Jesus need from Him to pull off a life only God Himself can live? Again, the Major asks for us to honestly consider:

> "Does the knowledge that your sins are forgiven because you have claimed Christ as your redeemer...
> You have pleaded His precious blood.

You've named His name.

You've called upon Him.

And you have been accepted by the Father in the Beloved.

Your name has been inscribed in the Lamb's book of life.

Would this rich assurance of your eternal destiny and security in itself impart to you any capacity to live a different kind of life from the life you lived before you were redeemed?

Take a Few Steps Back and Consider for a Moment

Christ's substitutionary death and propitiation cannot be short-changed.[1] Big words, right? But I'm not trying to come across as a theologian writing from his learned ivory tower. If anything, I'm hoping my vulnerability throughout has been loud and clear. I'm not talking down or attempting to one up anyone. In pulling a few concluding thoughts together, I pray words and key concepts from Scripture can be used of God.

Jesus died both for us and as us. We've said that repeatedly, and I make no apologies for reiterating it. He's our substitute, taking what you and I could never bear, and us with it, making full compensation for what we couldn't possibly repay. "As a result of the anguish of His soul—meaning Jesus—He, the Father, will see it and be satisfied."[2] That's propitiation. Christ's substitutionary death and propitiation are foundational, realities you and I, as believers, lay hold of by faith through the lavish grace that claims us.[3] We desperately need this, but does the knowledge of the forgiveness it secures, that "Jesus paid it all!" change the essence of who we are? Does such staggering insight make us different people, men and women, young and old, having the ability to live new and radically changed lives?

As it stands, we have in Jesus the best fire insurance going, not to mention reservations for the other side, but what about here and now? In a world that promises an overabundance of trouble, where does "life and that more abundantly" factor in?[4] Where's the easy yoke, the light burden Jesus promised? That's for this side, isn't it? How does it work? I can't do it, so I agree with Jesus.

Oswald Chambers rightly observes the hinderance to our spiritual growth that occurs when a believer insists on claiming his or her individuality as rightful turf.[5] That's our flesh, guys, the nefarious self-life that forever looks for ways to enthrone me and mine depending on how life looks and feels at any given moment. It's the same drive and determined self-effort that would have the last word, win, lose, or draw. The cross is where it's sifted out, the long and short of it being an intimate and very personal knowing that makes it real, seeing with eyes wide open the truly finished work of Calvary, then choosing to embrace by faith our place in the wonder of who Jesus is.

Think identification and participation.

"I have been crucified with Christ," is Paul's very real and very personal touch point connecting him in vital union with Jesus.[6] He sees and owns it. The gift of life in Christ Jesus comes to us by way of the gift of death. *We died with Him.* Paul's confession to a confused Galatian church bound in Jewish legalism isn't one of a super-saint or spiritual gold medalist; it's foundational to all who are in Christ— our co-crucifixion.

The light goes on, and a man sees. He knows that he knows.[7] A woman encounters her Gethsemane and the choice, a very real faith choice, to participate in Christ's brokenness, His surrender for us, as us, that becomes His surrender in her. We come in weakness. "Jesus, I need You. Work Your surrender in me. Be my surrender." Amen and amen. Life's unique scenarios provide a taste of His substitutionary suffering and death, and a genuine discovery of His substitutionary life, Christ in us the hope of glory.[8] "The life I now live is not my life, but the life which Christ (Himself) lives in me."[9] No positional mumbo jumbo,[10] this is real.

Salvation that begins and ends with forgiveness linked to life on the other side fits believers for heaven while leaving us "hopelessly inadequate for earth."[11] Back to Major Thomas to tie up a few loose ends:

>"The life Jesus lived qualified Him for the death He died."
>
>But it doesn't end there.
>
>"The death He died qualifies you to receive the Life He lived."
>
>"That's the genius of the Gospel."

50

A Critical Sidebar

I'm thinking about a woman right now.

Folks labeled her "sinner,"[1] respectable types as they saw themselves. Sinner, as was generally understood, was an all-purpose term for measuring lowlifes. Everyone knew their loathsome ilk—uncircumcised Gentiles and dirtbag Jews such as lepers, common criminals, street walkers, tax collectors, and so on. This one came looking for Jesus. However she might have gotten wind of the Master and the grace He so freely dispensed, this lady was on a mission; forget the consequences and nix public opinion.

Why else would such a woman risk entering a Pharisee's home? Awakened to her own desperate situation, this first century Esther is determined. "If I perish, I perish!"[2] Only one thing mattered, Jesus. Brokenness for this lady spells hope in a way she never dreamed possible. How many attempt to justify choices and lifestyles to their detriment because it's all they know, all they're aware of? We wholeheartedly agree, but what happens when previously nonexistent possibilities dawn, brimming with altogether new light and it's got your name on it?

Jesus reclines at the dinner table, and she bursts in sobbing.

See this as one of those places where you and I have got to allow ourselves to be touched in deep places by the impact of the moment. It's not a Bible study—not for her, not for Jesus, certainly not for Simon the Pharisee. He's incensed. And Jesus calls Himself a prophet? Really? How can a "holy man," if that's what He is, allow common street scum to contaminate Him like this? Doesn't Jesus get it? This sad excuse for a lady who flagrantly touches Him, "was the kind they buy and sell."[3] Talk about treading shallow water!

Legalism is performance driven to the hilt, while brokenness energized by grace plays out as hearts that can't run any longer, refusing to hide or make excuses for sinful choices. No one had to convince the lady she'd blown it. The law God had given Moses sounded depths only Jesus could negotiate. Vibes she picked up from the Savior previously left her bent and determined to get a real taste.

"As the deer pants for the water brooks, so
my soul pants for You, O God."[4]

What can I say? The man who's legitimately hungry, the woman who's parched and knows it needs no arm twisting, no persuasion when the oasis finds them. Jesus availed Himself to such, the worst of the worst. Don't get me wrong; there are many who suffer and suffer badly, folks who wallow in self-pity basking in the their own warped determination. "It's my way or the highway." Too bad. They either haven't seen the oasis or suffered enough. Sounds a lot like the gentleman Jesus was having dinner with. I've been amazed at those for whom coming to prison was their wake-up call, a profound realization, "My God, I'm so thirsty!" You bet it's true.

"My soul thirsts for God, for the living God."[5]

Think, "where your treasure is, that's where your heart will be."[6] There was a time when the lady's treasure was elsewhere. No-brainer, right? Be it cash or power, she was invested, "following the hookin' game."[7] Whatever her reason for doing an about-face, not unlike the prodigal we spoke of earlier, you and I could speculate endlessly. I'll suggest it was Jesus. The Law exposed her; He offered love.

Remember, will you, our hearts have an insatiable desire, a craving for love and acceptance on a level only God is capable of delivering. Looking in all the wrong places does what? It's like heroin or meth. The itch destroys you. God knows we've seen it. Yes, but seeing Jesus as treasure, I'm talking real treasure, ultimate treasure, has a definitive impact on choices. There's something about thirst honed to a razor's edge where treasure is seen as...well, as treasure, priceless treasure! "For joy"[8] says it all. For joy we abandon what we were convinced was so necessary, so absolutely essential. Treasure seals the deal. There's no comparison! Such things happen when you've tasted, when you've truly seen. This one's tasted, they've truly seen.

All of this as a lead-in to the real game changer: "Your sins have been forgiven."[9]

I speak this way with regard to earlier remarks some may construe as my downplaying the significance of forgiveness that's ours in Jesus. Not so, friends. The "certificate of (sin) debt"[10] anyone of us owes is above and beyond my ability, or yours to reconcile. Knowing this, how can we not esteem the stroke wielded on our behalf that makes acceptance and new beginnings possible? Ask the lady. From where she sits, hers is a life sentence that it could never be commuted. So for her, there's nothing to lose and everything to gain.

Grace does things to people because it's Jesus, His heartbeat. To Him, floundering sheep without a shepherd's lead and nurturing touch are sad, if not pitiful.[11] So, guess what? Word gets out and folks come running. Imagine that! The impact is such that the hope and wholeness He dispenses may, in fact, find itself linked with repentance.[12] Funny, isn't it, how grace, genuine grace, alters our perception of God and ensuing choices you and I make?

Consider, will you, that hope and wholeness are inextricably linked with forgiveness. It's true. The word quite literally speaks to release from debt or obligation, release from penalty.[13] Jesus paints a classic portrait of a king settling accounts with his slaves, one in particular who racked up a debt he couldn't remit in twenty lifetimes. Moved with compassion, his majesty wipes the slate clean.[14] That, friends, is forgiveness, complete and total. Imagine then a lowlife hooker's moral debt!

She loves much who has been forgiven much.[15]

Two scenarios: one who values little,[16] one who values much.[17] Many are clueless regarding the value of personal forgiveness because they can't wrap their brains, or hearts, for that matter, around the price heaven paid to exonerate them. Is it priceless treasure that overhauls your understanding toward God and yourself. Or are you wearing the infamous older brother's "poor me" shoes?[18] It's in the eyes, whether we see treasure, or "Oh well, if I have to."

Forgiveness means sin's barrier has been removed[19] and the highway is wide open. For what though? A rock-solid God connection beginning in the here and now, that's what. Countless believers set their sights on heaven, our eternal home. True enough, but as good as heaven is it's more of a glorious PS than a main course built on life and godliness.[20] There's a union that's never been, guys—Spirit to spirit.[21] And for those of us who've been born of the Spirit, it means an altogether new life source to draw from by faith. Chew on that a while, will you?

Christianity 101, right? Foundational precepts, yet how many believers cross the bridge from forgiveness to seeing Christ as their functional life source? I didn't for ages, more than ten years after Bible school. Knowing Him as Savior, yes. Lord, possibly, but not early on. Life, not so much. For some, not ever. Think of a lamp plugged into a wall outlet with a switch that has never been turned on! I say this knowing the agonizing frustration of being forgiven and called while functioning as a broken cistern. Real talk. Treading water in hopes of "power when the Holy Spirit comes upon you"[22] means little in rip currents of exhausted, clichéd answers.

"Lay it all on the altar," we were told in Bible school. And that means? Surrender, yes, total surrender for those having ears to hear. I heard try harder. It gets old, though, doesn't it? Trying harder in the name of Jesus. "Give up yet?" sifting confronted me. I hadn't seen that Jesus is a living doorway, a narrow gate by all appearances, opening to a broad, spacious horizon that never ends. You and I have only to say amen and enter in by faith.

The Resurrection Factor

The life Jesus lived can only condemn us if we're doing A-B assessments, Him versus you or me giving it our best shot. It isn't pretty, I promise you; not to God. Our attempts to do life out of our own self-effort are nothing short of one colossal disaster. Again, think trashed, filthy rags.[1] Sifting nails it. Literally. To the cross it goes, our best, our worst, our everything, and us with it. Jesus did that, but remember the context. Resurrection completes the package. If Jesus didn't get up and walk out of His grave, forget it. The whole thing's a wash, a frustrated exercise in so much futility that's far beyond us.

We were joined to Jesus in His death and burial, crucified in the totality of our self-made nightmare, then laid to rest. Three days, if you remember, says it all—the finality of His death, the finality of ours. Finished is the word, paid in full, victory secured—a fixed certainty we need to lay hold of as a grace through faith awakening. "He is risen!" sums things up knowing Friday worked. Amen, it's true.

So where do we as believers fit in?

No zombies here. No one's breathing new life into corpses. In Christ, you and I are new creations alive with His resurrection life, an altogether new species according to author and professor of theology, David Needham.[2] We're not retreads, the same old clunkers issued new titles and registrations. Let me see if I can explain by going back to my story. What grace did with me was scandalously supernatural. My body looked the same, but inside, deep in the core of my being where I am most truly me, I was different. Something radical happened. I felt clean and loved with no qualifiers, no if, ands or buts, and did I say new? It's hard to explain what it's like to be wanted or valued, to be safe.

I touched on this earlier and need to double back, see if I can bring further clarity. How do you, how does anyone, come to terms with a sense of newness that militates against all we've ever known? Can it be real? There's no rationale, no logic I was aware of, no argument to support what had become of me, the loser who would never amount to anything. How was I to know God had, by His Spirit, taken me into death, burial, and resurrection, a reality I would need to repeatedly reckon on where the cross is both foolish and offensive?[3]

I'm in good company, alive for the first time and clueless.[4] Jesus's life was mine, but what good did it do me? "Forgiven, that's what you are. You've been cleansed." Good stuff, for sure, but not the complete package. The gap in my understanding as a neophyte in Christ is one you could drive a truck through with room to spare. Again, I'm in good company. Assaulted by a dark and hostile world tripped me up big time. What I couldn't reconcile was my own confusion over identity. Who was I really, and what does it have to do with Jesus's resurrection here and now?

I benefitted, yes, down the road in the sweet by-and-by, but now? I couldn't see it. The nuts and bolts of my soteriology—the salvation that's ours in Christ—was cut and dried. I'd been forgiven and clothed in a righteousness not my own. True enough, but who am I? The search for self-worth was forever taking me back to the bleak mirror of my performance failures. What was I doing with what Jesus entrusted me with? Had I buried the lone talent I'd been given?[5] Would I ultimately be exposed as worthless?

If we can't see beyond forgiveness and our Lord's imputed righteousness to what's been imparted, you and I will never move beyond grossly distorted images of what we think we've received. I'm speaking, I trust, to a few who've scratched confused and frustrated heads over multiplied identity crises in the face of rejection and repeated performance failures whose hearts and minds desperately crave more than what they've tasted.

Am I talking to you?

Resurrection connects the dots where it speaks to our immediate participation in Jesus's death and burial. It's no longer positional. Vine life isn't imputed; *it's imparted.* His risen life is ours. We draw on that!

The Profound Mystery of "I"

Recent weeks have found me taking a hard look at "I."

Pronouns get tricky at times. To who, or whom, are they referring? What is it about them? Slow down, and be prepared to ask a few questions. You might be surprised. I know I have. I've been chewing on a verse in Paul's second letter to a young man he's invested himself in, a father to an adopted spiritual son, if you hear what I'm saying. In 2 Timothy 4:7, Paul's life is winding down with a very real sense he's drawing close to the finish line. A prisoner in Rome and forsaken by many, he remembers in anticipation and rock-solid assurance:

> I have fought the good fight, I have finished
> the course, I have kept the faith.[1]

Makes for quite an epitaph, I think. The man's not dead, but his reflections warrant serious consideration, seeing as our friend puts fresh wind in the sails of one who's just hitting his stride. "Preach the word," he counsels. "Be ready in season and out of season."[2] Powerful stuff in light of valued insight Paul doubles back on from his rearview mirror. For a man who has navigated one minefield, then another, that's saying a lot, and he's not bragging. My question is who's the "I" Paul sees in the mirror?

I ask this knowing a time I myself would have seen the "I" writing to Timothy as Paul the self-made man. The Damascus road cut him down, and he got back up. Renewed in zeal and a second wind, this one-time Pharisee was determined. "I'll show you, Jesus. We'll win the world, You and me!" Why not? His passion to take everyone out who named the name of Jesus was second to none. Momentum like that makes him purpose-driven, a man on a mission. Now Jesus is his spearhead. Such a one could press and press hard, train like an Olympic athlete, and run for the finish line with eyes fixed like hot steel on his personal prize.

Imagine his five-star, award-winning acceptance speech: "I have fought the good fight, I have run the race and finished the course, I have kept the faith." I did that. Jesus should be glad to have a man like me. Really? All right, so I'm overstating things but not by much. Saul of Tarsus was a proud man; make no mistake. He'd have held his head high, chest out waiting for a well-earned gold medal, his crown. It's no wonder God had to let the air out of his tires and pull him out of the loop for three years to decompress and reprogram the man.

Is This the Man Writing to Timothy?

Not hardly, but I didn't see it. I couldn't. The Paul I knew stood tall, God's man of faith and power who never balked or trembled in the face of opposition. Sorry, not even close. "I was with you in weakness," is the man's open confession to Corinthian misfits, "in fear and much trembling."[3] That's not a Damascus-bound Pharisee talking. This man's been broken. The "I" writing here has been sifted, hasn't he? I read his words but still didn't see. Again, I couldn't. The boy who'd never amount to anything needed a hero, a superhero he could look up to who, unbeknownst to me, would leave me crushed and condemned!

I'd never be able to lace, much less fit in his shoes. Words to a young evangelist, to "fulfill your ministry," found me gasping for air. Okay, so God's hand was on me, and I knew it. It didn't matter, not if He expected a finish like Paul's! I'd be embarrassed to even show for the qualifying trials, much less step in the ring to fight or run. And keeping the faith? Not like him, not ever.

Want some good news? I don't have to. Ever. That was never God's intention.

Not for me, not for you.

His plan A was always sifting, as in Calvary. In God's economy, there's no place for the self-made "I," the "I" who's got to buck up and try harder. None whatsoever. The self-made, self-sufficient "I" has no meaningful substance, and certainly no future. And self-aggrandizement?[4] The toilet, that's where it goes.[5] Ask Paul. "Circumcised the eighth day, an Israelite of the tribe of Benjamin, a real Hebrew and committed Pharisee," and so on and so forth.[6] It stinks; it stinks to high heaven.

Is it any surprise the call to discipleship is neither self-indulgent nor self-reliant? Not when following the Master is seen through Jesus's eyes. "Take up *your* cross," sort of personalizes things, doesn't it? And He's not speaking in metaphors. The cross is gut-level reality, the threshing floor where stalks are trampled and thoroughly crushed, broken for sifting. Precious wheat is winnowed, separated from so much useless chaff it had come to identify with—the self-life. Yes, it's that vile, narcissistic identity thief, the "I" who would reign in open defiance to God. *Treason* is the word and rightly so, the treason of "I."

Who Then Is the "I" Writing This Letter?

Apart from the cross, you and I will never know.

Paul knows. The apostolic mentor pouring into young Timothy isn't climbing the corporate ladder any longer. He's not trying to impress anyone. That man died, and no one is more aware of it than he. The "I" bent on making a name by showcasing his achievements was buried in Damascus where new birth means new life.[7]

Think context, only this time we're not going back to other parts of Timothy's letter, as rich as it is. There's another letter, one Paul wrote to disoriented Galatian believers as he confronts them and their damnable distortions head-on.[8] Nothing new. Paul was forever going nose-to-nose with Judaizers who openly defied the simplicity and truth of salvation by grace through faith—Jesus plus nothing. The Law has more than done its work exposing our noxious corruption in sin while finding us "Guilty as charged!" And the sentence?

Death, what else?

You want to talk passion? The head of steam-stoking Paul makes sense. Who but a former self-made, self-reliant "I" could see and diagnose their error with such exacting precision? Hindsight may sometimes exceed twenty-twenty when you've got new eyes, a new Source complete with a new and altogether different operating system, which enables one apostle to cut through so much fog.[9] He sees, he knows. Jesus Himself is his discernment. The Law Paul so vehemently weighed in on cuts the man down and summarily executes him.[10]

This is critical. Writing to a church suffering from a severe case of identity confusion, he makes it clear. "In Christ" is the death knell to one-time identities, and he makes it personal. "I have been crucified," he avows. "I no longer live."[11] Quite a testimony, wouldn't you say? But this is real, folks. No graphic imaging. This is real, as real as it gets.

Think of the apostle's death as a matter of historic fact. Okay, when? The Romans separated Paul's head from his shoulders somewhere around AD 67, but what gives? His letter to the Galatian church was written ten to twenty years earlier where he speaks of another death in AD 33 as his own. When Jesus was crucified, Paul was crucified with Him. Put a lock on it. His beheading was little more than a formality—Paul's homecoming.

A lost world and Christians suffering from identity confusion will forever be looking in the wrong direction where it comes to sorting fact from fiction. My point? Fix your sights on AD 33. This year of our Lord marks a timeline Paul, and all who are in Christ, need to reckon on through an effectually new set of eyes. "I have been crucified" marks the death of the self-made "I," the unregenerate self, who had nothing beyond me and myself to draw from. The death of "I" is real and definitive for one reason, "I have been crucified with Christ."[12]

The self-made "I" is dead and buried. He's not the one writing; that "I" no longer lives. He won't because he can't. Jesus died once. Paul says so.[13] Peter says so.[14] The writer of Hebrews says so.[15] And that means? It means death in totality, in finality to all who, like Paul, participate in Christ's crucifixion. We were crucified, dead, and buried, but death doesn't have the last word. Friday worked. There's a new "I," Christ in me.

Go Back to Galatians 2:20

The "I" who emphatically points to his own co-crucifixion with Christ is the "I" who no longer lives, our one-time Pharisee. Two "I's" in this passage, the first is crucified, dead and buried—a done deal. Paul's testimony is not, and cannot be, a work in progress. He's not saying, "I am currently in the process of being crucified with Christ," any more than Jesus's crucifixion is still a work in progress. Sorry. When Jesus said it's finished, it's finished. Kaput. Finito. Translations rendering this, "I have been crucified with Christ," are correct. It's not progressive. The spear in Jesus's side is proof. To be crucified with Him is definitive; Jesus dies, Paul dies. We die.

And he's not saying, "God sees me as crucified with Christ, while my old self—my unregenerate spirit—is still alive and kicking." Not even close. I understand why folks, even studied theologians, balk at taking Paul literally. I have as well. It happens when personal experience fails to line up with Scripture. Been there? Frustrating, isn't it? Try reckoning yourself dead to sin while attempting to put a hammerlock on temptation.[1] Forget it. The power of sin gets the upper hand every time, doesn't he? If you don't cave, you still lose. There's no sense of freedom, only tension. Am I right? God knows how many times I've been there.

You have, I know, but check this out. What is true of your forgiveness is true of your deliverance.[2] It's done, finished as Jesus said. Paul's co-crucifixion and ours can never be rendered effectual by determination and renewed self-effort. It can't! Our eyes must be opened, to see and acknowledge as a matter of fact the cross is a finished work with our names on it. The apostle's old man was crucified, dead, and buried when Jesus was crucified. There's a second "I" in Galatians 2:20, an altogether new "I." "The life I now live isn't mine," Paul insists. "It doesn't have me as its source." Why? "Christ is my life. He's my Source. Jesus lives His life in me."

Faith discovers and chooses to reckon.

How Many Have Wrestled With Their Personal Assurance of Salvation?

What, I'm the only one? I don't think so. The devil loves wreaking havoc with us here, but before we take this any further, I need to be clear concerning who's a legitimate heir to such assurance. This isn't complicated. "Repent and believe the gospel," Jesus said.[3] When? "Today if you hear His voice."[4] It's time to get radical—a radical change of mind concerning God—a radical about-face.[5] Repentance toward God and faith in our Lord Jesus Christ,[6] a heart cry that sticks and changes everything after a real conviction of sin and personal need.[7]

I'm about to get in trouble with somebody, but oh well. The truth is, seeker sensitive environments are big at drawing people in, young folks mostly. Not exclusively. Make Jesus attractive, but how? Present Him in terms of blessing, that is, His benefits. Nothing out of the ordinary here. From the beginning, our Lord had groupies, endless numbers who were drawn to Him for self-serving reasons, and Jesus called them on it. "You don't want Me for Me. You're only interested in the perks."[8] Numbers are always attracted to a feel-good Jesus.

Don't get me wrong. Jesus is attractive; to the hungry He is, those who genuinely thirst. The real Jesus. The truth? He isn't seen; He doesn't show in some of these warm, fuzzy settings. I'm talking the real Jesus. Laodicea unknowingly shuts Him out.[9] Too bad. "Say this prayer," is no guarantee of authentic repentance, that or deep conviction of sin. I say this for the benefit of those who struggle, as in knockdown, drag-out wrestling matches with their own assurance of salvation, as well as walking in freedom. Got questions? Ask God. "Come to Me," beckons Jesus.[10] He'll put you on the straightaway.[11]

Reformers stand firm on an assurance of justification by faith. "But I don't feel forgiven" doesn't hold water for those who've genuinely placed the weight of their trust in Christ and Christ alone. "For by grace are ye saved through faith," yes or no?[12] So be it then. What about Paul's co-crucifixion? What about yours? Doubt and suspicion concerning the historic fact of your co-crucifixion, or mine, solely on the basis of feelings and repeat performance failures is no more valid than "I don't feel forgiven today."

> Stuck feelers and performance failures are not,
> and cannot be, the measure of truth. Ever!

"I" number two in Galatians 2:20—the "I" who lives expressly by faith in the Son of God—is the "I" writing to our dear brother Timothy. Don't get it twisted. The "I" who unashamedly confesses to fighting the good fight is the "I" who confesses Christ as life to a Galatian church that doesn't see it for themselves. Paul sees, knows, and confesses. Calvary apart from our immediate and very intimate participation is so much wood, hay, and stubble. It's incomplete, a cross offering forgiveness but no built-in deliverance, no real "oomph" to fight the good fight, let alone finish the course or keep the faith. Calvary minus our "Amen!" by faith has no power in the here and now.

"That I May Know Him"

Of all the purpose statements a sifted man might make, this nails its mark.[1]

Kind of reminds me of David. "One thing have I desired of the LORD, that will I seek after."[2] The pursuit of God.[3] Our king seeks I Am as his permanent residence, and for what? A man after God's heart would continually behold the beauty of His presence in ongoing fellowship. What passion! In the same way, Paul presses on. He presses in craving intimacy. Talk about a 180! The "I" who once sought top billing by crushing the church humbles himself to serve the Name he so openly despised—not just talk, participating in Jesus.

Priceless. This apostolic mentor of Gentiles has entered the most holy place, Christ's blood cleansing and going before him. "So, let us know," Hosea urges. "Let us press on to know the LORD."[4] Paul gets it. People once held at a distance[5] are urged to draw near with confidence, to aggressively press in and not hold back. Say, "Amen!" knowing we can trust Him implicitly.[6] Staggering, absolutely staggering.

You and I, so many who call themselves Christians, read Paul and take in his teaching, but does anyone hear the man's heartbeat? I didn't, not for years. The broken, sifted heart is in a place to listen and be moved by another's passionate cry. The "I" writing to Philippian believers reckons on the cross as a vibrant, dynamic reality in them. These folks aren't bystanders. They're participants, actively engaged with him in the gospel, and so Paul presses, desiring they should see. He presses hard. "That I may truly and deeply know Him."[7]

Intimately, fervidly.

Reflections shared down the road with Timothy are, as he speaks, being worked out in the trenches, and it's real, so incredibly solid. Off the launchpad, Paul's words exude passion, the infectious kind. Confidence in God melds with longing for family in Philippi. Letters from prison are precious. They are to us. This one lights a fire in my heart. What can I say? Considering all the man's been through, he virtually ignites. Remember the launchpad for his connection with these folks, a public beating and a night in the city lockup?[8] Not exactly what you'd call a country club missions trip, and there's more.

Whipped like a dog, repeatedly beat down and shipwrecked.[9] That's serving Jesus? How could anyone in his, or her, right mind even think about pressing into that? No great shakes for those looking on from a distance, but for Paul, this isn't a Bible study! Listen to him: "Trash it all! Just give me Jesus!"[10] Locked down and restricted, yet what joy, what liberty he senses, soaring unhindered. Mounting up on wings like an eagle, is he?[11] I never saw it, not like this—the relentless zeal. He's either mad or in touch with a far greater reality.

And there's no fine print.

Jesus is straightforward. He's wide open with the cost of discipleship. Deny yourself, take up your cross, and so forth. Yet who but those who've been sifted at Calvary's tree can pull-focus in a world having little to no depth of field?[12] New eyes open heaven's door to searching the unsearchable. What kind of love seeks us out, compelling Paul to press, then press harder?[13] Naturally speaking, it makes no sense, this otherworldly desire. "Joy deeper still than heartfelt pain."[14]

I go back to an interview actor Jim Caviezel gave concerning the physical, emotional, and mental stress he endured making *The Passion of the Christ*. The long and short of it? Jim nearly died. Fumbling under the prodigious weight of a real wooden cross, he, like Jesus, collapsed on the Via Dolorosa[15] separating his shoulder.

The worst of it? Prolonged hypothermia, six months I believe, and pneumonia, requiring open-heart surgery postproduction. Prepping himself for death, he prayed. "I don't want people to see me. I want them to see Jesus…a visceral effect to finally (trigger them to) make a decision whether to follow Him, or not."[16]

Topping it off, our brother was struck by lightning while filming the crucifixion. Why do such a thing if not for supernatural love compelling him?[17] God so loved the world, yes, but what does it mean apart from the immediacy of One who gave Himself in a way that, quite literally, causes hearts to leap and dance? It stirred Mr. Caviezel to risk both his career and health, while claiming more than one Pharisee among other Jewish leaders.[18] Why would such love lay hold of anyone the way it does, love that gets folks pressing?[19]

Paul presses knowing the treasure. He speaks of the surpassing value,[20] or worth,[21] the supreme excellence[22] of knowing Jesus over against former pursuits.[23] There's no comparison. A man who's had the glitter and glitz this world offers sees it for what it is, or what it isn't.[24] Have you been there yourself, searching blindly, if not desperately, for significance in people and fleshly pursuits? Recognition maybe? Choose your poison. The real deal, real treasure exposes the facade of earthly gain. Eyes that dump outhouse refuse where it belongs![25]

The Much-Needed Intimacy
of Agape, Our First Love

Knowing God is a believer's birthright.[1]

We've said that, but who avails themselves?[2] Knowing comes by abiding, drawing near, and making ourselves at home.[3] "Don't be a stranger," we say, and to whom? Folks we'd like to see more often. Why the distance? Maybe they're caught up in other things. Themselves perhaps? Is this the body Jesus spoke to in Revelation 2, the church in Ephesus? They had so much together, it seems—deeds, doctrine, perseverance, an impressive resumé, for sure. "But I have this against you," and it's a big *but*, "abandoning your first love."[4] Ouch!

It's possible then to be occupied in the name of Jesus, yet abandon Him? Evidently. He says they've fallen.[5] Hard to imagine, isn't it? So much that's right, or so it seems, yet Jesus points to a higher call birthed out of a new heart connection—first love stuff. *Priority* is the word. A newborn church reflects something genuine through their desire for apostolic teaching coupled with fellowship, the breaking of bread and prayer, freely giving themselves to one another.[6] What happens, though, when such spontaneous heart cries become little more than decorative ornaments, as in going through motions out of a sense of duty, you know, Christian obligation?

Or worse. What happens when doctrine, programs, and social outreach become ends in themselves? I'm talking purpose-driven as opposed to Spirit led. Given a push the wrong direction, it could conceivably morph into lukewarm with Jesus on the outside looking in.[7] I'm serious. Consider the fallout within many mainline denominations, and God knows the independent, nondenominational types who've gone awry. Jesus calls for repentance, a radical turnabout in thought, word, and deed among those who claim His name.[8]

Speaking to those who've lost touch with
the truth and power of grace.

Sifting is needed where the love God uniquely is has been lost and grace misconstrued.

Ask Paul. Grace unpacked for a Roman church comes by way of Calvary.[9] That's how Corinth got it.[10] How about one confused lady who encounters grace as a Person? "If you knew the gift of God," Jesus probes, "and who it is that's speaking with you."[11] Who'd have guessed? Folks with Law on the brain think Moses, but truthfully, most don't get it.[12] Why? They don't see Law as a love confrontation with the wonder of God over against our shared sin problem, then pointing us to grace.[13] The real hoot is Paul, or should I say Saul? The time was our friend considered God's Law as heights he successfully scaled.[14] Then comes our Lord.[15]

Funny how Jesus's hillside chat puts an entirely different spin on Moses, the way He exposes us by raising the bar.[16] Sort of shoots down, "I'm as good as the next guy," by pointing us beyond our bankrupt limitations, doesn't it? But seriously, what does His, "You have heard it was said, but I say to you" approach do to you?

Does Jesus run you off the road or leave your heart pounding? Do you feel like throwing in the towel or reaching out to Him? Has "I'm only human" worn thin because you find yourself sensing, "I was made for something more?" Amen, I hear you! Humanity was made to bear His image and likeness.

No cop-outs. Yet apart from Jesus, apart from His cross, we're hamstrung, finished. Rededicating tired, worn-out rededications won't get it. We crave His broken body and shed blood—the Savior's love poured in vacant hearts. Renewed pledges on our end means nothing apart from His love commitment. Singer and songwriter Don Francisco vows, "I could never promise you on just my strength alone," knowing the very real frailty of human flesh.[17] His especially. "Words that last a lifetime would be more than I could say."[18]

Folks bail on first-love commitments where intentions wear thin, be it marriage; it could be Jesus. Infatuation burns hot and burns out quickly. Think with me. Whether it's a smile that makes us feel special or a message calling us to "lay it all on the altar," there's no life in it, no substance apart from His love commitment.

And it comes together how?

On the Night of His Betrayal

Jesus blesses bread, and He breaks it.[1]

"I'm giving it to you," Paul says, "the way God gave it to me."[2] I hear the man, yet I never understood the rationale for his marking this night with Jesus's betrayal. I get that Passover's fullest intention comes together in the covenant meal we call the Lord's Supper, but why home in on Judas? How does his noxious treason fit God's predetermined plan and foreknowledge?[3] Is it possible Jesus's giving Himself needs to play out against a backdrop not unlike Eden's unbelief and flagrant disobedience? It wasn't so much the temple's elite and their malice of forethought,[4] as it was betrayal masquerading as loyalty.

My trusted friend lifted his heel against me.[5]

Do you see it? The thief seduces one of Jesus's own a stone's throw from Eden's garden paradise.[6] Did Judas see it coming? Not hardly. The self-absorbed rarely do. When did the devil get in on him? No one else saw or suspected. Was it talk of rejection and death that uncorked Judas's plan to ride the Jesus wave for all it's worth? That would be my guess. Palm Sunday's triumphal entry might have put fresh wind in his sails until the Master upended the status quo by cleansing the temple and pulling rank on them. Imagine their disdain!

And it's downhill from there. "But what about the people? Weren't they all in with Jesus?" Great question with "were" being the operative. Momentum builds, and the crowd is on board, but put folks at risk, and watch them fold. This is people we're talking about, and Judas is the kingpin where, "It's all about me!" is the anthem. Always. There's your motive, gang. What else is needed? If the well's running dry, get the last dip! I know this is conjecture on my part. Call it an educated guess since not much is written. See it as my thoughts as to why Judas might have betrayed Jesus. It fits, though, doesn't it? It fits like a glove.

Consider the impact.

David got a taste where his backbiting son, Absalom, persuades the king's trusted advisor to jump ship and side with him.[7] Oh, it gets ugly, heartrending really. There are others; one prophetically pointing to Judas and his vile co-conspirators. "They have spoken against me with a lying tongue,"[8] but Judas specifically. "Let another take his office."[9] Read Psalm 109 for yourself, a passage Spurgeon in his *Treasury of David* admits, "the soul trembles to read."[10] Amen, I agree. Is David's outpouring prophetic insight into the heart of Jesus?

And that means? It means the gospel text regarding Judas's betrayal can't possibly be broached through stoic lenses, as though, "It's only Judas. He's just doing what he had to do." Not so! Not ever! Jesus anguished in ways you and I would die trying to wrap questioning souls around. Think about it. One who prayed, "Father forgive them," from depths of agony we'll never connect with, rightly condemned him whose birth is his own damnable sorrow.[11] Sound cold? I understand. It's what makes a gospel of grace so abhorrent to the self-righteous and by contrast renders Judas's betrayal second only to Lucifer's uprising as heinous acts of treason.

I'm serious, but don't get me wrong. I am in no way diminishing the tragic significance of Adam's fall. A man chose death. Its ripple effect; you tell me. Watch the news; study a little history. How about your own life? Apart from God, sin is mankind's only option—our best, our worst. Everything. Yet blood was shed to cover Adam's debacle, not so for Judas. He teams with Lucifer. Both got next to divinity in ways few had known or imagined possible. I'm talking up close, extremely personal. Both flat-out rejected Him.

Where It Comes to Judas, I Think of Esau

Both sold out. One over a bowl of soup. Weigh that against thirty pieces of silver. All things considered, it's six of one, a half dozen of the other—a fairly even trade-off considering the price both men inevitably paid. "What will a man give in exchange for his soul?"[12] Scripture speaks of Jacob's twin as immoral and godless.[13]

Sounds like Judas. Both display "poor me" trade-offs. What can I say? Tears don't mean much where self-pity writes the script. Esau sought repentance but couldn't lay hold of it; whereas, Judas, I believe, knew there was no reverse gear. Might he ease his conscience by returning blood money? No? Then it's suicide.

There are others, like Saul and his all-out betrayal of David. This king felt threatened. We're talking big time. Rhyme or reason go strange places, especially where obsession kicks in. Saul was obsessed. Judas too. The issue, though, is wrapped up in Jesus. He freely chose to lay down His life, but how? The means of our Lord's death is one of context. It's the cross, yes, by way of betrayal with a kiss. Take a good hard look. People vowing, "All the LORD has said, we're all in; we'll do it."[14] Honorable intentions all the way, yet when Moses goes missing, a golden calf becomes I Am's stand-in.[15] Then come a horde of Canaanite deities, Baal et al.

Who's shocked then that Jesus should come to His own to the tune of envied rejection?[16] Consider it the ultimate consummation of adulterous betrayal, as in, "Someone's sleeping in My bed." You don't get it? Rewind to Jesus's triumphal entry, the day we affectionately coin Palm Sunday, as the Master rages with fixed precision in the temple. Overturning tables while expelling thieving merchants is light work for One whose heart pounds in jealous abandonment over a faithless bride in His Father's house.[17] He's thinking first love.

And Judas?

Consider the price he accepted. Talk about a cheap shot! Let me explain, if I can. The going rate for treason, as Judas would have it, was identical to compensation rendered for a common slave gored by another man's ox.[18] Are you kidding me? This is the value of Israel's Shepherd, thirty measly pieces of silver?[19] What does it say about the sheep? Our Lord considers them harassed and helpless, a flock with no one to look after them.[20] He has compassion as opposed to Judas who only has space for calculating his own self-interest. You know the type.

Funny, isn't it? The appraisal unbelief gives a Lamb without spot or blemish, over against Jesus's passion for the helpless. How narrow is the focus versus "Greater love has no man than this."[21] Love poured out, love poured in.[22] Love with God alone as its source and energy makes the gospel so profoundly, if not scandalously other than a confused, unbelieving world—one Judas stands in bold proxy for, in flagrant pursuit of me and mine.

Wrong tree again, and it doesn't
get any worse than this!

We're talking self-serving independence to the nth degree. How can someone, how can anyone be in such close proximity to deity, to "you are the Christ, the Son of the living God," then openly oppose Him? "It'd have been better for Judas if he'd never been born."[23] No kidding! Yet with the devil's mad pursuit of autonomy—his "I will ascend," maneuvers—and Judas playing into old snake eyes' hands,[24] none of it hindered God's eternal purposes. They establish them! The predetermined plan and foreknowledge of God, remember?[25]

Betrayal, an Unlikely Canvas

King Jimmy has it. "With desire I have desired to eat this Passover with you before I suffer,"[1] the idea being, "You guys have no idea how much I (Jesus) have longed for this moment!" How could they? Anticipation marks each commanding pulse of a heart given to heaven's love commitment confirmed in a covenant meal. Think of it as an eternal bond in the heart of God. What is it to us? You, me, untold numbers run through familiar motions "taking communion" oblivious to realities coming together on earth and in the heavenlies.

Talk about a study in contrasts!

Commitment to the Father and His purposes versus "What's in it for me?" My guess is Judas slept through "Blessed are the poor in spirit" and the vine-branches lecture where Jesus touches the obvious. "Apart from Me you can do nothing."[2] No threat, no heavy handed edict, just gut-level reality. It's where "abide in Me, abide in My love" connects the dots.[3] Color that rest. Adam chose death. Judas, in self-imposed ignorance, turned on Him who would take that death to Himself.

On the night Jesus was betrayed, He faced the arrogance of independent insolence head-on. "Not My will but Yours" never bodes well for the reprobate or faint of heart. Judas embodied both. Indeed, none but Jesus, knowing what He knew, dare breathe such a broken and surrendered prayer. "My body given for you" quakes as "My soul is crushed with grief."[4] Ruptured capillaries are the giveaway. Look at Him. Anticipating the worst, the Savior releases sweaty streams blood. "Remember," He tells us. Look and remember. Remember often.[5]

Remember the garden. Judas knew the place. He knew it well. Accompanied by soldiers, six hundred or so, the betrayer shows his true colors. For three years, Judas blended, a chameleon of sorts. Who'd have known? I'm not sure he did. Hanging out with Jesus, handpicked at that, it was a ride unlike anything the man had ever known. He was one of the guys, a trusted trainee. Imagine the shock when he shows as an outsider, and Jesus calls him on it. "You betray Me with a kiss, Judas?" An expression of intimate endearment turns bitter.

Wormwood they call it.

Funny that C. S. Lewis should peg a demonic trainee that way.[6]

It fits though. Peter wept when confronted with denial of his beloved Lord and Master. Judas abandons in self-pity. The difference is huge. Read the Book. Scripture, no doubt, gives us a greater volume on Peter, but where God is concerned, we get what we need. The long and short of it? Where it comes to Jesus, Peter's is a heart connection, and the roots go deep. We see it repeatedly. This swarthy fisherman may yield to some in theological understanding of his Nazarene rabbi, but not love. Not appreciation. Not so with Judas. He's the consummate opportunist, a chameleon who could blend with his hand buried deep in the moneybag.[7]

And he ate with Jesus. "So what?" you ask. In Middle Eastern cultures, breaking bread together is reserved almost exclusively for immediate family ties, this one especially. We call it communion, and rightly so, a place of intimate participation in His body and blood, a covenant meal. Judas did so knowing his intent to betray One whose broken body and shed blood were given for a fallen world's redemptive ransom. Mr. Iscariot, by choice, made the table of our Lord his own morbid, demonic travesty where Satan enters him to Judas's demise.[8]

I can't begin to underscore the solemn significance of all that plays out here. Cultures where covenant—blood covenant specifically—means little, if anything, don't get it. A bond sealed in blood is traditionally the way select individuals, like David and Jonathan,[9] or groups (tribes, nations, etc.)[10] commit themselves for their mutual benefit on pain of death to any and all who dare violate vows binding them in "covenant love." Understand it as the intentional outworking of all they've agreed to. Blood is shed marking the permanence of agreements binding them as one, while a meal including bread and wine is shared to commemorate their union.

The covenant in Jesus's blood binds heaven and earth, as we've previously noted, in an altogether new covenant—new in kind, not latest and greatest.[11] Whereas Adam stood as every man and every woman in his choice for death,[12] Jesus stands as covenant representative for an altogether new humanity.[13] It's what the words "in Christ" points to. Pulling it off is fearful beyond words, but this is covenant love in His blood.

Do you see it?

Judas's betrayal becomes the canvas committed love's portrait is painted on.

He shares in the body and blood as a cover to morbid intentions, eating and drinking his own condemnation. I say the words but can't begin to imagine. Judas can't either. "It can't be me, Rabbi?" stands as little more than a ruse to deflect attention while trying Jesus. He knew, sort of. It's only after Jesus's condemnation is sealed that the veil is lifted as "I have sinned!" finds the real Judas out. Bottomless guilt and endless shame plague one soul who can never find relief in this life or the next. Ever. Ask Jesus.

"But how could he do it," someone asks, "knowing who Jesus is?"

"Ah, Watson, therein lies the crux," notes Holmes.[14] Did Judas know the Lord Jesus, who He really is? Time to hit pause then rewind. Mark speaks of Jesus traveling with His boys through the villages of Caesarea Philippi, probing, "How do folks talk about Me? Who do they say I am?"[15] Remember? It's a hoot really, the endgame being, "Who do you say I am?" That'll stop you cold, the answer especially.

"You are the Christ," is a decidedly Jewish wake-up. "Son of the living God."[16]

So where was Judas? Did he call in sick that day? Nope. All present and accounted for. Mr. Money Bags was part of the mix. So he heard? He heard words, all right, but did he get it? Okay, okay, let's not get ahead of ourselves. Time for reality check. Peter confessed Jesus, right? Right. Jesus affirmed him, right? Right. All the boys heard him, right? Not right. Say what? Take two steps back. If Jesus's top twelve were present, wouldn't they all be tuned in? Not so much. There are ears, and those that actually hear. Huh?

It really isn't complicated.

A veritable universe spans the difference between ears, and ears that hear, eyes, and eyes that see. Jesus directs us to Isaiah 6 where people with 20/20 vision still don't make the critical connection, by engaging listening ears.[17] And that means? It means Judas could be present with the rest who saw and heard could himself be blind and deaf. Absolutely. Apart from a heavenly lights on, any and everyone on the planet will find themselves condemned to forever wander in darkness. The reason? Spiritual realities require Spiritual light.[18] Peter was all in, as were James and John, Bart too and Andrew, but so what? Innate desire and self-determination won't cut through the fog.

Judas could be the lone blind man at a sculptor's unveiling, hearing impaired at the symphony. If the Father hadn't made the connection for him, he's one in twelve who sets up camp in his own private world, and he doesn't know it! He really doesn't. When the others come unglued at the thought of losing Jesus, they're working from an altogether different context. They live in a different world. Literally. And Simon Iscariot's boy is left flirting with the only players who share remotely similar interests—priests, elders, and the like.

So, it's every man for himself, is it? Ask Judas who makes his move to, "get while the getting's good." Caiaphas and his sorry bunch cheer in vindictive agreement as the blind lead the blind to a bottomless pit.[19] And Jesus? He willingly empties Himself on betrayal's gaunt, lonely canvas.

Out of the Gate Paul Presses Hard

A self-made Pharisee can only rage at a name his heart is dead to. Surprised? I hope not. The Damascus road gets Saul's attention where a new and unfamiliar door opens, his heart. Love lays hold of him, love this man had never imagined, much less gotten a whiff of. What kind of love would allow itself to be betrayed and shamefully brutalized, then call others to enter in, to actively participate in the fellowship of His humiliation and suffering? It's the father taking the prodigal back only to be slandered along with him.[1]

Jesus does such things, the God of Abraham, Isaac, and Jacob touching untouchables, making Himself one with them and their fetid—dare I say gag a maggot—stench. Making them one with Him. I don't think we appreciate, or even begin to see, how truly offensive God's love is to the likes of an upcoming Pharisee from Tarsus when it comes packaged as Jesus. Red-faced, explosive rage erupts at the thought of His name. Stephen is stoned, and Saul ravages the church until love sabotages his madness.[2] He didn't see it coming.

"Who are you, Lord?" is the terrified response of a man who doesn't know up from down. Not for long. Three days in the dark, water baptism, then filled with the Holy Spirit pave the way to a world that, outside of Christ, never existed. How is it Jesus said, "Unless you're born again you can't see, or even enter the kingdom?"[3] He sees now, and the man, whose mission it was, to dismember the church does a 180-degree about-face and heads to the front lines, preaching Jesus in the synagogues and on the street. Color that radical.

Okay, hit pause, will you? Moving beyond this penetrating phenomenon doesn't make sense just yet. How can anyone dive face first into the power of His resurrection much less get close to fellowship of His suffering apart from the intimacy of knowing Him? I can't. This was my turning point. The God who confronted me thirty-some years earlier in profound brokenness made Himself clear. I didn't know Him. My God distortions were the primal root of so much hell, so much pain and confusion. If I didn't know Him, how could I possibly know myself?

Knowing the Father through the Son is the effectual essence of eternal life.[4]

Imagine Paul should be so compelled, and not for information. Jesus Himself was the curriculum for twelve blue-collar nobodies. Has anything changed? Sinai came with the Torah, but people intentionally held I Am at a distance. They were flies in the ointment creating the need for a new and better covenant, "not like the covenant I made with your fathers."[5] All right then, what about this covenant makes it new and better? For starters, the Levitical priests will be passé, and why? "All will know Me."[6] Simple. "From the least to the greatest."[7] No one's exempt.

Such a promise! No wonder Paul presses and presses hard to lay hold of "that for which also I was laid hold of by Christ Jesus."[8] Knowing Him is the ticket, the whole ball of wax. Knowing about Him only? Shallow water at best. Again, this isn't for a select few. Paul stands shoulder-to-shoulder with the rank-and-file "until we all attain to the unity of the faith, and of the knowledge of the Son of God."[9]

It's called growing up.

Paul Isn't the Only Sifted One Who's Pressing

I'm thinking of a man who at fifteen went to prison for shooting and killing his mother. Jesus, I know, took him to the cross along with another teen, a dark, Gothic cultist. His crime? Strangling a classmate, a young lady whose only point of agitation was caring enough to openly share the love of God with him. She, like Stephen, was a precious falling grain of wheat only to prove Jesus's living axiom. Dying, a grain of wheat bears fruit, and lots of it.[1] What about men charged with arson? Three come to mind, one whose children died in the fire. News items, for sure, in heaven as well as earth. Heaven sees with far greater clarity.

Brutality unspeakable. We've heard more than I can count—in prison, in the courtroom, one-on-one. The so-called success stories? They're as bad, possibly worse. Ask Paul who looking back on his overt success qualified himself as "chief of sinners."[2] What can I say? Positively programmed flesh tends toward a sense of having arrived, if not well on your way. Such folks typically don't see themselves in need of a Savior, or if they're a committed part of church leadership, sifting. Those whose sin has found them out tend to be more open to brokenness leading to surrender. It hurts, but the outcome spells relief.

A man locked up for decades shares his most recent path of brokenness and sifting:

> Father has bestowed grace on me!
> Dan, since I entered this program, I experienced more pain, anguish and heartbreak than I

have ever known. Yet with each self-revelation…
my trust in Him grows sweeter and stronger.
So many blocked memories have opened. Each
enlightenment brings more contentment…
Through all of this my heart draws closer to God
than ever before. I'm grateful and bow in humble
adoration and offer the fruit of my lips—the sacrifice of praise.

What peace comes from allowing Jesus to
correct my perceptions and give me right thinking. The insight that comes with submission and
surrender brings such freedom! Truly my soul
soars to heights previously unknown…

Dan, Bonnie, the beauty found in knowing
that what I don't understand today, *I will* understand "bye-and-bye." Tears of gratitude flow from
my eyes as I pen this. I've longed my whole life
for this part of my journey. Does it sound out
of my mind to say, "Lord, allow Satan to bring
affliction?"

Since coming to this program there have
been so many personal revelations about myself
that have brought deep anguish and pain. Yet
through the storms there was an inner strength
that anchored my soul. As my after-care, you
need to share my journey. You'll see the anguish
and sorrow looking back at the harm I caused.
Without His strength and understanding He has
brought me, I wouldn't have been able to cope.

Knowing my Abba/poppi has made me
new, adopting me as His cherished child. "By
their fruits you shall know them." Being an open
book…has allowed others to come to the same
saving love I experienced… There are those who
in the quiet of their cells have found the courage
to bring their "stuff"—shame, pain, bondages,

wounds—to Jesus because I shared my freedom from my past. Freedom to face every day...surrendering each day.

Sifting Seeks Ultimate Reality

Think doctrine where the rubber meets the road.

Knowing by participation, but how? What dynamic brings it all together, the power of His resurrection?[3] Sounds mystical, doesn't it? Ethereal even. On this side of Calvary, we learn union begins in death, but death apart from resurrection is worse than pathetic. Hope is hopeless. Life is lifeless, an illusion, but life out of death? Imagine the power when it's Jesus's own resurrection life. "It's not my life,"[4] Paul asserts, and how right he is. "Christ lives in me."[5] He said it, but that's Paul. What about us? Can you or I dare make such a claim?

Do we actually believe it?

"Take it by faith," we're told.

I get what they say, but what does it mean, really? Grace by faith, right?[6] God said it. I believe it. That settles it. We've all mouthed such noble platitudes, yet no one I've ever spoken with has been able to avoid running off the road, spinning frustrated wheels in the middle of Romans 7. "I don't do what I most deeply want to do; I do what I hate!"[7] Been there? God knows I have. There's no greater frustration for one whose life is Christ and doesn't realize they're trying to pull God-life off by human effort. Don't I know it?

But like Peter, Paul, and so many others, He lets me fall flat on a face that already has egg on it. Sifting. I hadn't learned that "nothing good comes out of my own self-effort."[8] A world weaned at the breast of self-sufficiency programmed the lot of us to try, then try harder. It's the self-made "I." Apart from Jesus, it's all we've got. Not anymore. It took time for Paul to catch on. Romans 7, remember? The will to do versus the wherewithal to pull it off. A world celebrating self-made types isn't big on weakness. Christianity is.

"Come to Me," Jesus beckons, and to whom? He calls the weak, the crushed, and the destitute. He calls the helpless. Strange, isn't it? One who claims unfeigned allegiance, even death as the cost of discipleship, reaches out to the feeble. It only *seems* strange. The poor in spirit, those who are totally bankrupt and bereft of hope seem least likely to present as potential discipleship candidates, and they are His target audience.

Why would Jesus reach out to the likes of these?

In a word, we're talking weakness, and not as a liability. We've been around this tree a number of times, and I make no apologies. A world that heralds strength and awards creative ingenuity has little to no room for those it perceives as less than. Not Jesus. The good stuff is hidden from "the wise and prudent"[9] and given to the fragile, the impotent who can only depend on Him. Hey, that's it! The cross is God's threshing floor to sift and winnow, exposing the helpless child who chooses to embrace weakness as his own.[10]

The apostle wears it like a banner, doesn't he? "I'd rather showcase my weakness if the resurrection power of Christ can be my sustenance."[11] Earthen vessels are nothing really. Life is in the treasure. And that means? It means we, like Paul, learn to exercise the gift of faith we've been given, as in "the faith of the Son of God," by placing the full weight of our trust in Jesus who loved and gave Himself for us—that is, "faith in the Son of God."[12]

Working Out What Jesus Is Working In

We're in Philippians 2 now, trembling in fear. Verse 12. Trusting Jesus gets scary at times—going where He directs, doing as He says. "Are You kidding, Lord? I can't do that!" Life in the minefield, that's Jesus. Working out the deliverance from sin He secured and taking us on to wholeness are faith choices. Do we believe Him?

Jesus truly is at work, but we'll never know apart from the choice to put one foot in front of the other trusting Him to direct and secure our steps. We have new "want tos," altogether new thoughts and desires God Himself has written on the tables of our hearts. His resurrection life is the power to pull it off. The paradigm shift from self-sufficiency to the "I" who trusts only Christ is beyond radical. It's the infant resting secure in loving arms.

Isn't that what Jesus promised? Praying, "Show me the rest, Lord!" is more than, "Can You give me a hand with this?" It, in fact, is complete and total abandonment to His will and purposes. "Thy will be done," etc.[1] Takes your breath away. What do you expect from, "Take now Thy son" but an emotional free fall?[2] You don't believe me? For Abraham, his view of Mt. Moriah is but a stone's throw from Gethsemane.[3] And you thought his was an outsized Bible study, didn't you? He's there for our benefit, but there's more, much more. Abraham looked to Jesus as his only hope and expectation; now He's ours and not from a distance.

Yes, but do we believe it?

I'm not pushing. No, maybe I am.

The ripple effect in a pool marked by easy believism is a feel-good Jesus on my terms. I've seen it too many times, so I've got to be honest with you. There is no shortage of twisted thinking where it comes to the gospel. What do you do when "My yoke is easy"[4] stands in stark opposition to "strait is the gate and narrow is the way?"[5] The long and short of it is Jesus. If He's an add-on, or a term insurance policy, and not the total investment of your heart; don't expect much. "For where your treasure is, there your heart will be also."[6] If *He's* your treasure, the straight gate and narrow way opens wide to rest with joy unspeakable and full of glory.[7]

I know where I've been. Others too. Peter speaks of "precious and magnificent promises,"[8] and for what? So we can stand at a distance telling the old, old story?[9] I don't think so. The promises are the priceless link to your immediate participation, and mine, in Christ as our very Life, not just Lord and Savior. "The life I live"[10] is vine life with Jesus as its source pouring Himself—literally not figuratively—through Paul. He writes with a sincere hope and expectation that a faith response will look expectantly to Jesus. "Lord, You know I can't do this, but I'm moving forward in obedience, trusting Christ Himself to be my energy and strength."

The Power of His Resurrection and Fellowship of His Suffering

I'm confused. Didn't Jesus's resurrection follow His suffering?

I thought so. Why then would Paul link his passionate desire to know Christ in the power of His resurrection with the fellowship of His suffering in that order? There's no question you and I, as believers, find our connection to Jesus in His death first. Paul too. "I am crucified with Christ" precedes "the life I now live."[11] A no-brainer for sure. And I'm not looking to make a trick question out of this. The answer lies in yet another question: How can Paul, or anyone, participate in Jesus's suffering apart from the power of His resurrection?

True enough, but how does Paul or anyone share in Christ's suffering? Didn't He say, "It is finished," that is, "paid in full?"[12] He did, and it is. Accounts have been settled. There's nothing more to pay, no debt whatsoever. There is, however, another component. When Jesus died, the plug on suffering in a fallen world wasn't pulled, not by a long shot. Another no-brainer? Absolutely. Consider suffering as the overflow of Adam's race as a whole over against redemptive suffering in the name of Jesus. The difference is astronomical.

Adam's literal historic fall plays out in a multiplicity of ways where life hurts and hurts badly. Think conflict—conflict with God, conflict within, conflict without. Writing eternity's I Am out of the equation lights a fuse where life explodes, often without notice. Pundits who'd use this to dismiss any and all God talk have missed the boat. He's not the source of pain and suffering; we are. A sovereign God has made a sovereign choice, one that ultimately shapes what it means to be truly human. Choose God and live; choose self-sufficiency and die. Adam, as we know, opted to fly solo. He chose independence, and so has every generation since. Imagine then that God should be so emphatic: "Cursed are those who put their trust in mere humans."[13]

A Man then must make the choice to turn this incontrovertible mess around. He does. The last Adam, Jesus,[14] takes to Himself both the fetid stench of humanity's corruption, in conjunction with our abysmal pain and suffering—making it His pain, His suffering. How? By offering Himself as the consummate lightning rod for the Father's wide open, unrestrained wrath. Get it? I wish I could say I did. Oh, I can fill in the blanks on the pop quiz, but wrap my brain around the cup Jesus drained; I can only worship.

But embrace the fellowship of His suffering?

That's a tall order. Only the sifted need apply. Only the truly sifted will. We're talking participation—not spectators, not academia.[15] And it's His suffering—active, gut-level participation in Christ's own agonizing torment. Lay hold of that, will you! All who are legitimately in Christ, those born of the Spirit, have, in fact, participated in His death, burial, and resurrection. No way around it. Now, if you hear the man, to beg participation in Jesus's redemptive suffering, to be poured out for a fallen world simply takes my breath away.[16]

Lots of People Really Don't Like Jesus

His name, meaning who Jesus legitimately is, has endured fierce hatred and abuse like none other. You don't agree? You're thinking about the adoring crowds, aren't you? Many who later demanded His execution. And we don't want to forget untold numbers who historically recast Jesus in a more humane likeness that's socially, if not politically acceptable.

Do you remember our earlier discussion concerning Satan's bull's eye? He specifically targets those created to bear God's image and likeness. Why? The real target is God. Anything to hurt Him is fair game. And Jesus? He's the seed of the woman who crushes the serpent's head.[1] Get Jesus, and it's a lock on the enemy's game. He wins! And although snake eyes has set enough in motion for humanity to self-destruct, he zeros in on the promised seed.[2] (Hint: Israel is the womb giving birth to that seed.)[3]

Note then the onslaught of grief this Hebrew nation has sustained historically. It's all about Jesus who will ultimately bring complete restoration to His people.[4] He is their identity whether they see it or not. They will. The church, in the meantime, catches flak from every angle imaginable and Paul gets his share from Jew and Gentile alike. The straight gate and narrow way claim exclusivity an unbelieving world wants no parts of.

Yes, but don't people adore Jesus?

On their terms only. They've adopted a persona that doesn't exist calling it Jesus, reshaping Him to fit their own sensibilities. The real Jesus is offensive,[5] an archetype a tolerant crowd wants no parts of. He warned us. Oh well, nothing's changed in over two millennia, and didn't Jesus say we'd be martyrs? Witnesses, that's it.[6] Same thing. The idea here is bearing witness with one's life, laying it down if necessary. Whatever the occasion calls for. The redemptive work of Calvary claims us as participants, to witness with all we are, all we have, to suffer maligning and abuse, death possibly. It's not just a Bible study. Read *Foxe's Book of Martyrs*.

Knowing Him, knowing the power of Christ's resurrection, to actively participate in His suffering is beyond where most would even think of going. Apart from such, we're spectators, nothing more. This is reality, folks. Threshing, sifting, and winnowing are God's work to establish reality. "Don't be surprised, or think it's strange," counsels Peter.[7] Think what's strange? Fiery trials. "Threshing is not a soft and kind thing," observes British author and Bible teacher T. Austin-Sparks. "It may be very hard, it may seem very cruel, but you all agree it is very necessary."[8] Imagine eating bread whose wheat hasn't been threshed and sifted…well, trying to.

Paul understood. "I die daily," he affirms as his credo without a moment's hesitation.[9] The path our apostolic companion walked was a minefield, as we said. His life was always on the line. Paul's morning coffee brewed with the sense it could be his last. Repeatedly whipped, beaten, stoned, and imprisoned, in danger at every turn from man and beast not to mention the elements coupled with hunger and thirst, sleepless night after sleepless night, and all in the interest of nurturing care for the churches of Jesus Christ.[10] Not exactly what some might see as your best life now, if you hear what I'm saying. Knowing his co-crucifixion sustained Paul.

So Why Would Jesus Lay Hold of Me Personally?

I avoided sifting.

I thought I was. Silly me. Sifting was an answer to prayer, yet how could I know? My anxious heart pounded in quiet desperation while taking aimless potshots at molding life on my terms. It was killing me. Literally. The Christian counselor I sought out blasted me point blank, "Do you want to die?" Wow! I surely didn't see that coming. Blind searches for empathy proved more of a quest for pity, and the truth leveled me. It's a good thing my wife was there to scrape my remains off the floor. So many props I'd carefully constructed had to be knocked out from under me. I needed it badly. Thank God for His love commitment that took the wind out of my sails.

Allow me, will you, to take a few steps back and fill a few blanks in. Bonnie and I were engaged when at nineteen I went off to Bible school. It was God's doing, and we both knew it. What *I* didn't know was God's strategy: Questions come before answers. Questions and more questions. Answers? I couldn't see the horizon. Time to sort through ever-growing confusion didn't exist, not with the academic load—not for me.

It got worse after school. Learning a trade, my tent-making endeavor, scrambled seemingly nonexistent brains more than they already were. "Where do I fit, Lord?" I mused. I had no idea, not so much as a clue.

Self-imposed distractions designed to provide relief from, "You'll never amount to anything" aroused increasing tension. I didn't see it. Years later after a near nervous breakdown and an ulcer, God began connecting a few dots. Oh, the relief of sifting! You heard me. I still didn't know where I fit, and I'm not sure I cared. Vocation as identity wore thin. This too spelled relief as I discovered the satisfying joy of knowing God, over knowing about Him. I began to discover a certain oneness with Paul.

"Lord Jesus, I want to know why You laid hold of me!"

Articulating the desire to genuinely know Him who loved and gave Himself for me is…there aren't words. All I can say is the passion to know the Father through the Son began to override my own self-centered, self-interest in pursuit of discovering a new "I" who had been crucified with Christ. How do I say it? Galatians 2:20 had my name on it. I felt like our Chinese brother Watchman Nee when he began to see his own co-crucifixion, how he wanted to run through the streets of Shanghai, shouting, "I died! Isn't it wonderful?"[11]

It's the essential "knowing this" of Romans 6:6. I died, and an altogether new "I" lives. This, if you will, is the most real, the most authentic me there is, or could possibly be. There's no dying to self,[12] as many have espoused, but rather reckoning by faith on our blessed co-crucifixion. On the basis of knowing, you and I can then consider ourselves dead to the power of sin and alive to God.[13] Amen and amen.

He Laid Hold of Me to Know Him

Instead of leaving me out in the cold, the words of Jesus bore me up with renewed hope:

> Come to Me, all who are weary and heavy-laden, and I will give you rest. Take My yoke upon you and learn from Me, for I am gentle and humble in heart, and *you will find rest for your souls*. For my yoke is easy and my burden light. (Matthew 11:28–30, NASB; emphasis mine)

Sifted and extremely grateful.

Appendix: Some Foundational Realities

In clarifying a few thoughts as we wrap up our study, it seems a fuller understanding as to why sifting like wheat might be important to God, first and foremost, then us. Please don't allow yourselves to get derailed by what initially comes to us as Satan's tack on upending God's precious elect. The thief comes to steal, kill, and destroy, no doubt about it, but why miss the greater reality? "I came that they might have life; real life, abundant life."[1] Whatever space the slippery one is given to maneuver in, it's solely that I Am might see His heart and sovereign purposes established for time and eternity.

A fundamental error when coming to the New Testament Scriptures is forgetting, therefore omitting, much of the Old Testament foundation the New is built on. God's heart is global; make no mistake about it, so His claim on Abraham comes in the context of his "seed,"[2] Him who is the hope of all nations and the people who bore Him. And that means what? It means from Genesis through Malachi, we need to look for Jesus, that's what! "Moses wrote about Me," as did the prophets.[3] In Him, the New fills out the Old, and vice versa.

Imagine yourself in Isaiah's shoes for a moment, Ezekiel maybe. Talk about head scratching! The Spirit of Christ burned hot within, yet they were clueless as to who, what, or when God was pointing them to in the midst of unspeakable pain and conflicting turmoil.[4] You know it's true. God's people earned it in spades with unbelief at the helm. Nothing new.[5] Few cared to listen. What happens, we ask, when even the slightest desire for God flatlines, where me, myself, and I are consumed with me, myself, and I? Forbidden fruit has an enticing glow in the light of personal gain and the promise of limitless satisfaction.

Enter the seduction of idolatry.

"You shall have no other gods before Me,"[6] isn't the insistent demand of a heavy-handed despot, not when love, as God calls it, has no fine print, no back door. In a day when newlyweds are given to originality, scripting vows that feel warm and fuzzy, "'til death do us part" doesn't always find a niche. An open-ended approach is in vogue these days. "As long as we both shall love," as opposed to *live*, fills the bill, spoken or unspoken. Color that fear, not love. "Cleave to Thee only," is God's way. Faith agrees as "I will" speaks to the promised discovery of commitment "for better or worse." So much for vows gone sour at Sinai's fiery alter.[7]

Covenant is what God is about, committed love.

Couples standing before "God and these witnesses" bind themselves to each other in hopes of solidifying a lifelong union. That's how it used to play out on a fairly regular basis, a road paved with honorable intentions. Now shift gears to "we agree" as it affirms a cowering and uncertain lot. "We agree to everything the LORD says, and we'll do it!"[8] The weakest link is what? The people, right?[9] We're talking about a newly formed Hebrew nation coming to God with the best of intentions, folks whose lives were molded in Egypt. Now what? Thick smoke and fire, thunder and lightning. The mountain quakes violently as do Moses and the people.[10]

Think "convergence" as eternity meets time and space history in remembrance of love. I'm thinking Abraham and sons[11] as God points Moses back to His standing commitment. "I established My covenant with them," a pledge He remembers with the intent of securing Israel as a people.[12] When God reaches out as He's done through Moses, there's continuity. Four hundred years of silence is enough to put you, me; it's enough to put anyone in a state of forgetfulness. Not God. For Him, remembering means continual watchfulness, hovering over and nurturing a people who couldn't see much less hear Adonai, yet love kept endless watch.

That's God, the love He is—in Hebrew *hesed*, meaning "covenant love." When humans commit themselves, it's in hopes of creating a bond that holds through thick and thin. Again, not God. His commitment brings the sum and substance of who He is to bear. Covenant love isn't something He shoots with high hopes for. It's who He is, His very essence. And the people? They're another story. If anything, this sad bunch proves what multiplied newlyweds have confirmed. As it depends on them, the commitment is a wash, yet God persists.

The covenant consummated at Sinai, otherwise known as the Old Covenant, went belly up because people were the hinderance. A letter to a group of Messianic Hebrews nails it cold. "For finding fault with them."[13] What about the boys Jesus called? They're sincere, aren't they? Absolutely. It's what Peter, James, and John don't see that becomes their undoing. I'm talking about their flesh; all they are on their own. "The spirit is willing," Jesus affirms, but the flesh? Forget it.[14] It's weak and that by design. Left to ourselves, the best we can do is sin.

Sorry, it's true.

The quaking bunch we left at Sinai pulled back. They were scared. You'd be too; we all would. The God of their deliverance is fearful beyond words, a consuming fire as the people will readily attest.[15] Good call, bad response. Moses was quaking in his boots too. Having more than a little experience of the One who claimed them as His own, Moses begged his brethren to hold with him, hold together, but no. Not knowing the heart of the LORD their God, they refused. Sounds like the people's downfall. That's a flesh thing from start to finish.

The Greater Intent

In liberating a tired and sorry lot from an oppressive Egyptian yoke, freedom points back to God. *He* is their freedom. We tend toward fantasy, images of a world free of restrictions filled with end-less choices—freedom to do whatever I want, however, whenever it suits me. I remember. I also remember the cost. It's the grand illusion: I won't die, I'm in control—Eden's original lie.[16] What a joke! So, when the LORD of all conscripts Moses, His message to the people speaks of a God-sized deliverance by way of judgments on Egypt with one fixed assurance. "I'm going to take you as My people, and I will be your God."[17] Amen. Amen.

"My people," that's identity, a profound if not heart-pounding reality, one that separates Israel all people, all nations. "Your God" opens His heart to them. The unbeginning "in the beginning" God who framed the cosmos and sustains it by the word of His power chose to establish His eternal purposes in the context of relationships as the personal God of Abraham, Isaac, and Jacob—now as the beneficent God of Israel.[18]

This, friends, is love talking, covenant love that commits to making Himself known to "My people." "You've seen what I did to Egypt, how I carried you on eagles' wings to bring you to Myself."[19] Drawing close is where freedom is potentially realized, and rest. Release from Egypt makes it possible.

> Distanced by time and geography, western
> minds typically don't get it.

The consommé of world religions may prove itself a quicksand to all who get sucked in by the "eeny, meeny, miny, moe" crowd who see nothing but a mystical coexistent mishmash. Six of one, a half dozen of the other, so choose your flavor! All things being equal, that would be fine, but supposing they're not? Supposing one stands alone, a one of a kind God among a pantheon of pretenders? What if He then, for reasons known only to Himself, chooses a people as His one of a kind possession, His people? Mythology and active imaginations don't factor in. He's got to show them, personally teach these folks there's no god like their God.

He alone is God.[20]

Their God is different, so His people are different—not in themselves but because of Him. He makes them one of a kind, a holy nation, people who stand out for one reason, who they are because of Who they belong to. *Unique* is a good word, the right word for a God who stands as the sole qualifier in a seemingly endless cosmos and infinite heavens worthy of such majesty. In that sense, there are no words, no close contenders.

Appendix: Our Hebrew Friends Didn't Get It

The book of Judges is a roller coaster of ups and downs showcasing boneheaded choice after boneheaded choice. Confusion takes center stage as God's people try finding their fit in a dark, unbelieving world in their own backyard. These people didn't know God, so they couldn't possibly know themselves! Sinai's Law became one gargantuan, "Wet paint. Thou shalt not touch!" sign. And that, my friends, is God's genius![1] The best intentions of a confused and floundering people to do the right thing get derailed by what? Themselves, their own corruption, but who knew it?[2] They didn't. God had to show them, and it involved a trip to prison.

God sent Jeremiah, His covenant attorney, to warn His beloved that their adulterous bent was a costly proclivity. Fleshly appetites come with steep price tags, don't they? Sure, but it'll never happen to me. Guess again, folks. Feel-good preachers bring a different report until the cops show up, handcuffs and all, hauling busload after busload to the DOC Babylon.[3] "Get used to it," he chokes through hot, bitter tears. "You're doing seventy years—day for day—no good time, no early release."[4] That's life for most, life without parole.

All part of God's plan

His plans. A future with genuine hope is defined and shaped by God. That's good. He alone makes our individual and collective futures real in the best and truest sense. I'm talking substance, a rock-solid foundation. The itching ears fraternity would have us see life almost exclusively on our terms, the way you and I prefer things to shake out, yet it may not work.[5] It might blow up! "Don't trust your own smarts," we're counseled and rightly so.[6] Apart from God exclusively as our magnetic north and integrating point, we eat from the wrong tree every time, doing what's right in our own eyes,[7] and that, my friends, spells disaster.

Okay, I'll admit. I can't imagine hearing "life without parole" then in the next breath, "But it's all good!" I might want to hurt somebody. Lay hands on them. It happened to Jeremiah. He ended up in jail because jealous leaders and two-bit prophets in the people's camp blamed him for their miserable lot, yet this was love talking, love on an order the creative imaginations of men couldn't invent. God's committed love.

The way to understanding is prayer.

"Seek Me," says God.[8] Seek and keep on seeking. Push like a woman in the throes of labor. Don't presume. This isn't time in the department of corrections; it's God. Freedom has a context, remember? Relationship. "Seek Me." You got seventy years, but there's no statutory release date, no mandatory dress-out of Babylon. You heard me. Connecting with God's plans—His future, His hope for us—is a call to press in through prayer, turning a deaf ear to all pretended prophets who tickle and titillate in the name of God with promises that don't hold water. Forget them, will you? We need to touch and be touched by God, His heart for us.

Apart from that, we may never leave Babylon!

No threat. The choice is ours. Shifting hearts into neutral won't get it. There's no coasting, no cruise control. "You will seek and find Me when you search with all your heart," God assures them.[9] Press in by faith. *Restoration* is the word, and God truly wants to restore His people. Through the cross, He's made every provision necessary, and it's a gift! Two thumbs up to Larry Crabb for pointing out how grace, under the new covenant, renders our screw-ups null and void. They're no longer a barrier to God's blessing any more than our attempted goodness is needed to receive blessing.[10] If there's an obstacle, it's us, our stubborn unbelief. God longs to satisfy and make good to us the deepest desires of our hearts, desires we've been oblivious to.

No "gimme, gimme; I want, I want." God's plan, His ultimate intention, is to restore the root of our captivity not just outward manifestations. He goes for the jugular, addressing the driving force behind the cruel and bitter yoke we've so readily given ourselves to.[11] There's no place, no good reason for willfully staying locked in a connection that's held us captive in the past. (You remember Romans 6:2, don't you?) If the chain binding us to the power of sin has been severed, who in their right mind would want to continue as though it hadn't? That, friends, is lunacy! Freedom isn't biting the bullet in hopes of getting a better handle on life.

Freedom Is Jesus[12]

No cliché. Reality. Whatever angle anyone hits this from, the cross is where it comes together, or forget it. You end up lost or feeling like it. It is what it is. Many get paroled, many discharge prison sentences, and many come back. Many leave Babylon only to exchange it for Persia or Rome. Freedom isn't getting out of prison or adopting socially acceptable behaviors. Freedom comes by death.[13] For as many as have sought to keep hurtful addictions in check, higher powers and all, they don't get it. Not just the bad stuff, the good too. Flesh, whether negatively or positively programmed, is still flesh. It's got to die, not be managed—all of it.

Now there's a can of worms. You and I weren't fitted and framed for self-sufficiency, but guess what? It's all Adam left us—the self-contained life—the good, the bad, and the ugly. Left to ourselves, it's all we've got. Parade the highest and best, showcase the most beautiful, and either hide or lockdown the bad and the contorted ugly. It all needs to go, but no. In pride and mammoth ignorance, we celebrate one and condemn the other. Who's surprised whenever shallow flesh management programs go awry because they don't get to the root?

Not me. Programs which focus, almost exclusively, on thought patterns and habits are doomed out of the gate.

It's why Jesus isn't in the recovery business. He doesn't recover alcoholics, dope fiends, or sex addicts. He executes them and out of death raises up altogether new men and women who are alive with His life. If all you've got is flesh management, i.e. concerted attempts through self-effort to change thoughts and behaviors, the best you can hope for is muzzling the mutt that needs to be put down and replaced—a rabid Doberman with a golden retriever! Harness the addict to avoid certain people, places, and things, and a fear-based identity will emerge as their prison until a box with their cold bodies is lowered into the ground, where they are finally liberated.

It's how they see it, or so I'm told.

Too bad. God's plan dials in a future and the best hope possible by giving us the death we so desperately need. (See Romans 6:2 and 11.) at Calvary. Ours. Jesus takes us to Himself. What's His is ours. The gift of life, eternal life Jesus promises—His life—begins with the gift of death. Anyone who's united with Christ in His death is freed from that cold, ruthless taskmaster the power of sin—free from guilt and condemnation's shame and damnation by grace through faith.[14] Knowing is all the difference between walking it out and wishful imaginings.

Appendix: Same Story, a Different Angle

Jeremiah cried his eyes out as a people who were chosen to grow into a saving knowledge of their God hardened themselves toward Him. They didn't know God, so again, how could they have so much as a clue as to who they were? Nix on both counts, but who's surprised? Something about being self-absorbed puts up barriers like two confused brothers we spoke of. The younger has plans. Hopes for his future involve dad, not personally but for his liquid assets, an inheritance he couldn't wait for. The boy's plans are costly. Big brother's cost him as well. Neither knew his father. Neither knew himself or each other.[1] Sad. It happens frequently.

Among the initial wave of exiles, priest Ezekiel ben-Buzi gets a taste of Babylon firsthand. Like Jeremiah before him, his was a prophetic mantle shooting straight from the hip as God directs. No feel-good message, no popularity contests. Many to whom he ministered lapsed into full-blown denial while others completely closed up and shut down. No laughter, no songs of Zion. The pain was excruciating, so why even try? Hang up your harps, gang![2] Consistent with a heart that refuses to throw in the towel on a people He loved and committed Himself to, God relentlessly persists, but He won't candy coat.

I poured out My wrath for the blood
they shed and judged them.[3]

People were scattered far from home.

Those not having Hebrew roots may not make the connection. To a Jew it was everything. The sifting God does among them severs this people from the one thing that above all else anchored them as a people, the land of God's covenant promise.[4] Whatever else identified our Hebrew friends in their confusion, the land of Abraham's sojourning marked them as Jews one to another. This too is God's genius. Were it not for Jerusalem and it's temple, the people, no doubt, would have amalgamated in murky seas of Gentile nothingness.

Oh, they trashed the gift of God's precious land along with the temple, yet this singularly unique piece of real estate on the Mediterranean etched indelible boundaries that kept them afloat as a people, if nothing else. The heartbreak lies in this unusually privileged bunch not seeing the God who made them stand out. They're His people, first and foremost, His personal possession. The land points back to Him, not them. Time for a wake-up call. It's one thing for God's own to think and live like foreigners and quite another to be dragged kicking and screaming for a seasonal transplant in the stench of foreign soil.

> Son of man, when the house of Israel was living
> in their own land, they defiled it.[5]

The image God paints of their idolatry is sick, putrid really—a woman's menstrual discharge—so in pulling everything together, Adonai lays it out in no nonsense terms.[6] How desensitized have those shaped for God's image and likeness become, wallowing in sludge and hailing it as the good life? Pathetic. Yet His purpose truly is for restoration, and His calling stands,[7] but first things first. God's people profaned His holy name while the world around was checking them out. Unbelievers, nations where the Jews were exiled watched and listened as Abraham's sons and daughters presented a severely distorted image of the God of Abraham.

"I'm going to do something," the LORD God decrees, "but I'm not doing it for you. I'm doing it for Me, for My holy name."[8] To quote Hamlet, "Aye, there's the rub."[9] Seeing as the earth is the LORD's in all its fullness,[10] He loves men and women, folks from every tribe, tongue, people, and nation.[11] It makes sense that His greater purpose in creation is propagating the awe and profound uniqueness of His Person. Think about it. All that God is, as He is seen and worshipped in the heavens, will ultimately be celebrated globally.[12] Filling planet earth and all that is.

My Holy Name

This one's tricky.

Not really, but it seems that way at times. I remember, from a very young age, seeing the marriage of "God" and "holy" as synonymous with "pure" to the nth degree, undefiled and incorruptible. It fits, in part. God *is* purity on a level not one of us could possibly wrap our brains around if we tried. So, forget His being dirtied or soiled even a little. Ever. It's the name part that gets us, "My holy name." Don't take His name in vain, one of the big ten, got me early on. What does it mean? Don't say or use His name in any coarse or jesting manner?

"What's in a name?" Juliet wonders in Will Shakespeare's romantic drama.[13] It's the person, not their proper name that counts, isn't it? Ah, but what if they're one and the same—the name and the person? Some religiously hold if I don't speak or even attempt to write God's name, I can't possibly violate His holiness. Others are convinced not using "God" or "Jesus" in openly cursing makes them good to go. As a teenager, I remember a college ministry coming to our church, inserting a clever observation in their program: "Contrary to popular opinion, God's last name is not damn." Cute. I get the picture, but they're missing something.

The name *is* the person, and where God is concerned, that's everything. Try it this way: It's possible to get the words right, follow every accepted religious cue, and still fall flat. Jesus marked the leadership of His day by their flagrant hypocrisy. Read Matthew 23:15–36. Scribes and Pharisees, et al., performed for men and God, yet Jesus says they bombed. One Pharisee, in smug self-assessment, gives thanks that he stands taller than his peers and common sinners in personal piety. Talk about nerve! Our Lord speaks of a day when ministries will be trashed for their "Look at Me!" approach and what I call plastic fruit. "I never knew you!" He insists.[14]

65

Appendix: God's Name
Zeros in on the Heart

Think "desire" and "motive."

Ask, "Who is God, really?" and you'll learn what folks believe both by their words and actions.

"I'll follow you, Lord," pretenders insist, "but I've got things I need to address first."[1] And you're trying to convince whom? Performances (allegedly) designed to please God scream, "Legalism!" and reek like an outhouse, so God isn't impressed.[2] He gags while choking on the foul stench of a thieving marketplace His house in Jerusalem had become.[3] And the prodigals? They got waylaid at happy hour. Unbelieving Babylonians don't know what to make of the parade of fish,[4] better known as the incoming newly exiled Israelis. "Aren't these the LORD's people?[5] Why are they here and not in His land?"[6] Why indeed, and what had they been chasing? Treasure.

The great commandment—the Jewish Sh'ma Yisrael recited morning and evening—is the people's designated response to their loving God who uniquely stands alone. And they are to what? Love Him back, and not casually. "You shall love the LORD your God with all your heart and with all your soul and with all your might."[7] That's the design, a tall order however you hit this, but what can I say? God is all there's room for if all of me and all that I possess are what He wants. "Trust in the LORD with all your heart."[8]

Is God being selfish? Not when you realize He's it, the complete package—no flaws, no missing pieces. Apart from Him who so graciously gave us form and substance, you and will never take our next breath, much less our next step. And that goes for the planet; the entire cosmos from vanishing point to vanishing point.

All of it.

I may get myself in trouble, but here's what I mean. There's no hierarchy, no pie for us to divide. It's not as though God is first; therefore, He gets the biggest and best slice, family comes second, job third, hobbies and leisure fourth, etc., etc. That's nuts! You and I aren't artificially segmented. By design, we're a unified whole, and He is all in all. God then is tied into everything that touches me, every person and part of my world. It's all His, and rightly so. My choice and yours can lay securely founded in knowing, "In Him we live and move and have our being."[9] He holds us together.[10] Embracing this hopefully translates into a radical discovery: My life and unique self are in Him, or guess what? They're nowhere.

And that means what?

Loving and trusting God with all my heart and soul is a proposition that's bigger than me. It truly is. Think I'm crazy? All right, so how does the thought of complete and total surrender strike you? Surrender what? Surrender everything, all that concerns me and my loved ones for God to do as He will. Does it take your breath away? I hope so.

The truth is I need Him whether my life is on the line or I'm getting groceries out of the car for my wife. God isn't a spectator assessing my performance. He's in the mix! Tucking my grandbabies in at night, teaching them to pray or ride a bike is my sleeves rolled up, in the trenches love to God, and I need Him to pull it off.

All of creation, each microscopic protozoan to the far reaches of distant galaxies, is centered in Jesus. He made it and keeps everything ticking. The only reasonable and most appropriate response then for those called and chosen by Him is faith that finds its resting place in His love—faith that responds in love.[11] That's our choice. Think worship. With all of my heart, with all of my soul, with all of my mind and strength, which can only be His strength. I bow down because love constrains me, His love.[12] I bow to Him as I love my wife and kids. I bow in serving Him in my ministerial calling. I bow in my unique enjoyment of life. I bow in my pain.

Too bad our Hebrew friends didn't see that. Their treasure was somewhere else—hungry hearts in hot pursuit. I've been there, and I understand Jesus: "Wherever your treasure is, that's where you'll find your heart."[13] Are you surprised the Babylonians couldn't connect the dots concerning their Hebrew captives? I'm not. "These are supposed to be the LORD's people, and they're doing what?"[14] Hey, I smoked pot and snorted coke with a crew who couldn't believe I went to Bible school then buried myself in porn. When folks making professions of faith blend like chameleons with an unbelieving world, it breaks my heart. I've been there; I know the fallout.

They Don't Have a Clue

Who He really is.

And like me in my former delusion, along with a few precious Israelis, none of us got it.

Sure, God is different, completely and totally other. That's holy for starters. Take a walk through history and observe cultural imagery given to deity. The Greco-Roman world made gods and goddesses "in our image according to our likeness"[15] as outsized men with female counterparts, aberrations and all. Ancient Egypt had a thing for human-animal hybrids; whereas, the Far East has traditionally been given to a mixed bag of self-denial, mysticism, and bizarre humanistic forms, lots of them. The pantheist sees God in creation, every tree, every rock, and every flower. The atheist sees none of it. There is no God, big G or little. Agnostics aren't sure.

Ancestor worship travels the globe in multiple religious expressions. Islam stands firm. There is no God but Allah with Muhammed as his messenger. Period. It's legalism to the hilt, guys. There is no personal touch as Allah is too removed, far too lofty for intimacy with humans. He cannot, and will not, condescend to take on the likeness of sinful flesh. The other extreme? God is Santa Claus, the jolly elf in the sky. He makes a list, checks it twice, and we still make out like bandits! With all due respect, friends, God is none of those. Not even close. To know Him, His holy name, means God has got to make Himself known as only He can.

Holy, as it concerns I Am, gets radical. I'm talking *far* above and beyond any concept or imagination construed by man or demon.[16] It means God sits by Himself in His own category, a uniqueness He shares with nothing and no one. God is separated to Himself, making the people He's uniquely chosen as His own His holy ones—His saints. God, by His choosing, has separated them from other people and nations to Himself. He calls them My people, and not by meritorious entitlement. His choosing makes them saints, His people.

And they're clueless.

Apart from His profound uniqueness, their calling means little.

A low view of God gives birth to countless evils, as the self we see in our soul's mirror is a mess! Knowing this, I'm not in the least shocked or amazed when our brother and good friend A. W. Tozer categorically insists our thoughts about God may, in fact, be the most important thing about us.[17] In confronting a confused and unrestrained people with their bold-faced profanity of God's holy name, the root of their confusion is exposed. If you don't know God, you can't possibly know yourselves.

Isaiah saw God, then himself.

The shock value must have been staggering, if not violent, rattling him to the core. "Holy, Holy, Holy, is the LORD of hosts."[18] Listen, please. When a fallen and depraved world is all we've known, even the meek are desensitized and don't know it. Absolutely. Sin means doing life on our own where even our best misses the mark by a mile. Foul, filthy rags, remember? Everything outside of faith, that is. Believe God, and it's an entirely different story.[19] Ask Abraham. Given Isaiah's calling and the imagery God commissioned him to paint, the prophet needed to see just how level the playing field was among "a people of unclean lips."[20]

What can I say? We're dealing with God-sized issues where He, and He alone, must provide seeing eyes and minds capable of making the connection.[21] Left to ourselves, we might find company in a group quaking at the smoke and fire of Sinai whose knee-jerk response was to pull back. Fear and ignorance distanced a stubborn people from love that sought to liberate them, while Moses probes and pushes for a more intimate close-up.[22]

Forget Max Ehrmann and his winsome imaginings of peace with God, "whatever you conceive Him to be."[23] That's a short road to a long disaster. We can't elevate our highest and best imaginings exponentially in hopes of getting somewhere in the ballpark. It won't happen. It can't, not when grossly limited, if not distorted human apprehensions clog the gears. Moses begged God to see His glory and was told he couldn't bear it.[24] Whatever Isaiah saw, it reduced him to nothingness. Only God the Son incarnate can explain Him.[25] So whether it's Peter, Israeli captives in exile, or us, sifting is needed since His holy name has been badly contorted.

Appendix: "It's not for Your Sake I'm Doing This"

Exiles get sifted in the DOC Babylon, Peter, and the boys at Calvary.

Both spell death to everything these folks have ever known as life. It's the cross, all of it. One prefigures what the other lays hold of. Either way, it's death, and in either instance, "It's not for your sake, it's for Me and My name." Okay, okay, stop right here. Does this seem cold or more than a little egotistical for the LORD to take such a blatant "Me first" approach? (I'm remembering my eleven-year-old daughter asking, "Why does God want people telling Him how wonderful He is?" as though our worship and heartfelt praise made up for something He was lacking.) Has God displaced Israel and Judah along with the people of this world to save His own face?

Is God that insecure?

Whoa, now that's twisted! For anyone to suggest such lunacy only proves the magnitude of our ignorance. We obviously don't have a clue who He is, His holy name. Let's double back and try walking this out, okay? God so loved the world, right? And to reach them, He has to vindicate the unparalleled uniqueness and consummate perfection that separates Him from all pretenders and fabricated imaginations. Do you see how it must be so? People respond to what they construe as being valid and true as it frequently corresponds with deep emotional ruts. Think "dead end." God then must break through so much fog to set the record straight if He is to enfold the lost and ignorant to Himself.

And this what really blows me away:
He's going to do it through people!

And not just any people. If there was ever a reason to bow down in jaw-dropping awe and dumbfounded amazement before Him who has no equal, this is it. *This is it!* I'll be the first to admit, when God chooses the likes of those who've so completely and thoroughly run His name through the mud as the means of vindicating His holy name to unbelieving pagans,[1] it doesn't make sense. But if anything confirms the God of Abraham and His eternal gospel as it comes to us in Jesus—that it's no invention of man—words spoken through Ezekiel to all-out rebels and blockheads stop us cold. We're talking grace, the harvest sifted.

Read with me. I'm in chapter 36 beginning in verse 23 of the New American Standard Bible. "I will vindicate the holiness of My great name which has been profaned among the nations, which you have profaned in their midst," God says, but here's the bomb. "Then the nations will know I am the LORD when I prove Myself holy *among you*." Say what? God intends to prove His holiness in and through the jokers who profaned His name?

You got it? The ESV says, "when through you I vindicate my holiness," and the pagans will see it! The God whose person and character are so far removed, above and beyond any earthly construct or imagination, has done the unconscionable! It's beyond staggering. Try to wrap your brain around Isaiah's vision of the sovereign Lord, high and lifted up, where six-winged creatures worship God without ceasing above and around His throne. "Holy, Holy, Holy," seraphs cry, underscoring with true finality the profound otherness and untainted completeness of Him who has no equal.[2] Above all, He is holy.

Theologians speak of the attributes of God in ways the cerebral among us might, without realizing it, attempt to dissect Him as a biology lab project. Big mistake! A frog or human cadaver is one thing, the Almighty? Not even close. Louis Berkhof scores a grand slam in recognizing "God and His attributes are one."[3] Ask Isaiah, then the angels whose calling and proximity have them in the immediate presence of the Shekinah glory perpetually. They cover their eyes, feet too. Moses couldn't bear the glory of His holiness. Again, God said so.[4] Isaiah, you remember, came apart. Unclean lips. The thoughts and intentions of the man's heart were exposed.[5]

Holiness does that.

The greater context of God in His holiness generates fearful awe of who He truly is as it comes together in all His majestic fullness. Omnipotence, omniscience, and infinity, even love grows shallow and downright pallid apart from "Holy, Holy, Holy." In His presence, the unpretentious, the humble and contrite alongside perverse and hopeless degenerates; all as the purchase of grace are broken before Him. Dare I say sifted?

Incredulous as it seems, God has purposed the impossible, proving His holiness in and through a motley crew, who by nature are anything but holy or sanctified in their own right. Making the likes of these altogether new creations is a God-sized hurdle. As such, you and I have got to give some serious thought as to what crushed and trampled wheat tossed in the wind of His Spirit looks and feels like. I'm talking about our desperate need for brokenness, yours and mine. You know, sifting. It's important to God and essential for us.

Endnotes

[1] Isaiah 55:8
[2] Hebrews 11:40b
[3] John 15:1-11, I John 5:20 and Colossians 1:27
[4] Philippians 1:21

Chapter 1

[1] Staves, meaning clubs
[2] Luke 22:24
[3] Go to Matthew 20, and read verses 20 through 28 where a mother steps in an attempt to secure preferential treatment for her sons, which really stirs the fire.
[4] Luke 22:24–27
[5] John 19:26
[6] Matthew 26:47
[7] Luke 22:61 (NASB)
[8] See Hebrews 4:12–13 for soul and spirit, joints and marrow along with the thoughts and intentions of his heart.

Chapter 2

[1] John 1:41
[2] That's Cephas, the Syriac surname Jesus gave Simon Bar-Jona. The Greek rendering is Petros, or Peter, as we know it. Read John 1:35–51, but zero in on verses 41 through 43.
[3] Coffee
[4] My loose paraphrase of what I truly believe captures the apostle's heart in 1 John 3:1.

5 Matthew 14:18–20 (NASB)
6 John 1:50 (KJV)
7 John 14:9
8 Referencing the Talmud, a comprehensive body of Jewish civil and ceremonial law as well as legend made up of the Mishnah (considered the authoritative exegesis of the oral tradition of Jewish law—the first part of the Talmud) and Gemara (rabbinical commentary of the Mishnah—second part of the Talmud).
9 Mark 3:14
10 John 18:33
11 Matthew 11:28
12 John 14:6
13 An expression appealing to what the user sees as ultimate authority.
14 1 Corinthians 1:30 and 2 Peter 1:3 NASB

Chapter 3

1 Zs meaning sleep
2 We're talking Peter here, Simon Bar Jonah.
3 Isaiah 11:6
4 Luke 8:26–27
5 As in Klu Klux Klan
6 To the nth degree meaning to the utmost, as far as you could possibly carry something.
7 That's cellmate, his exclusive touch point with humanity in a small enclose with bars the department of corrections calls home when they lock down.
8 We're in Genesis 2:16–17 where the boundaries of life and death are framed.

Chapter 4

1 Ephesians 3:20
2 See Isaiah 6, starting at verse 1 and settle in on verse 5. That's the idea.
3 Luke 5:8
4 Luke 5:10

5　Read the whole thing for yourself in Luke 5:1–11.
6　The account we're discussing here can be found in Matthew 14:22–43.
7　Daniel 3:24–25
8　Matthew 8:27
9　Not "in toto," meaning this isn't the whole package.
10　Matthew 8:27
11　John 15:1–17
12　Matthew 14:31 (KJV)
13　Matthew 26:33

Chapter 5

1　Matthew 16:16
2　Genesis 22:18 and Galatians 3:16
3　See Luke 24:27 and John 1:18, 5:46, 14:9.
4　Hebrew for Jesus the Christ—the Messiah
5　Unlike those who've been raised in western traditions, our Jewish friends didn't see themselves apart from their forefathers. This is a God thing. Who they are and where their hopes are anchored is inextricably linked with Abraham and his hopes, along with Isaac and Jacob, specifically the God of their fathers. That's the plan, at least, but in the face of Roman tyranny and no word from YHWH in four hundred years, what can I say? It wears thin at times.
6　The Apostles Creed, a succinct summary of first century apostolic teaching.
7　Mark Lowry, © Word Music LLC
8　Matthew 16:17
9　1 Corinthians 1:21
10　Matthew 11:27

Chapter 6

1　Matthew 3:4, a diet of locusts and wild honey
2　We're back at John 1:35 but taking it all the way through to verse 42.
3　Romans 5:12

4 Again Romans 5:12 along with verse 18.

5 Isaiah 61:1–2 (NAS)

6 Isaiah 64:6: Filthy garments as per some translations. However you slice it, it's an ugly mess.

7 Taken from Ira Levin's novel of the early seventies and later movies portraying programmed wives in a small chauvinistic Connecticut community.

8 Not circus clowns. It's a song written by Stephen Sondheim for the 1973 musical, *A Little Night Music*. One of the leads is devastated by rejection and seeks a little meaningless relief. Theatrically speaking, if the show bombs, send in the clowns.

9 Isaiah 53:4: Grace meaning the Lord Jesus Himself.

10 See Matthew 9:26: To a deeply wounded and discouraged people, the promise of covenant love resounds: "The steadfast love of the LORD never ceases; his mercies never come to an end; they are new every morning; great is your faithfulness" (Lamentations 3:22–23, ESV).

Chapter 7

1 1 Samuel 31:1–2

2 2 Samuel 9:4

3 1 Samuel 16:14

4 Psalm 105:15

5 1 Samuel 18:3: Although this passage doesn't specifically mention blood, it's what they did—a given.

6 1 Samuel 20:15 (NASB)

7 Samuel 9:1

8 2 Samuel 9:1, my paraphrase

9 2 Samuel 9:3, again, my paraphrase

Chapter 8

1 Romans 5:6

2 Galatians 4:4

3 *Kairos* is the Greek term addressing a fixed point in time as opposed to "chronos," an expanse of time.
4 Genesis 12:1
5 John 1:45
6 See Romans 8:29
7 John 1:49
8 "Making book," a gambling term meaning to place a bet.

Chapter 9

1 See John 5:26 and 1 John 1:1–2.
2 Chapter 3
3 Luke 7:36–50
4 John 8:2–11
5 I say "snooty Samaritans" because these precious folks held themselves aloof from the Jews as much as the Jews did from them. The Samaritans were convinced that theirs was the pure and true religion of ancient Israel, a debate the woman at Jacob's well attempted to engage Jesus in. John 4:12, 20.
6 Nathaniel Hawthorne's novel written in 1850 that speaks to the shame of an adulterous woman in Puritan Boston who is obliged to wear the scarlet letter "A" on her dress the way men in prison are dressed in orange to mark their shame for stepping out of line.
7 To call something "a wash" renders the situation null and void. For Jesus, there is no Jew-Gentile distinction. "Nix' is synonymous with "wash" as Jesus cancels cultural male-female issues.
8 2 Corinthians 5:21 (NASB)
9 "Cellie" meaning cellmate in case you forgot.
10 John 9:25
11 1 Peter 1:8

Chapter 10

1 Matthew 16:22
2 Matthew 16:23
3 Matthew 26:73

4 Mark 14:70 tells us Peter cussed, as they say, like a sailor.

5 Luke 22:31

6 The "rock" is literally what Peter means and *Diabolos* is Greek for the "devil."

7 Luke 22:32

8 To get lost or take a flying leap are two figures of speech that pretty much saying the same thing: Go away and never come back!

9 John 10:10

10 Hebrews 12:27

11 Job 1:1, 8

12 Job 29:17

13 Old Scratch is just another name for the devil as he shows up in literature, one of the more noted being a short story written by Stephen Vincent Benet called "The Devil and Daniel Webster."

14 Those downplaying the significance or validity of oral tradition don't understand its reliability where God is concerned, the One who on paper and off watches over His word to perform it (Jeremiah 1:12).

15 Job 1:20

16 Matthew 16:22, 26:51 and John 18:10

17 Matthew 27:18

18 John 3:6

Chapter 11

1 Frat parties, meaning college fraternity parties

2 To "play gay" meant giving myself for sex part-time to a nightclub owner who promised to advance my music career, an option I wasn't even remotely open to.

3 Luke 15:11–17

Chapter 12

1 Job 1:8

2 Job 1:10

3 Job 1:9

4 Genesis 1:29–31, Job 38:41, Psalm 104:14, Luke 12:24, 2 Cointhians. 9:10, Ephesians 3:20, Philippians 4:19

5 Romans 1:5

6 John 15:5

7 Psalm 19:1–6, Romans 1:20

8 Genesis 3:4, my paraphrase

9 Would the man and his wife become like God? Context is everything. The slippery one did not say omniscience, omnipotence, omnipresence, or any supernatural "God qualities" would be theirs. The temptation, if you read the text, is, "You will be like God," in this sense only, the personal knowledge of good and evil (Genesis 3:5). And that means? In choosing not to believe the One who gave them life, our first parents followed the serpent's seductive lead in writing their own declaration of independence. They could choose for themselves what fits and what doesn't, what is good and what is evil. In so doing, they severed their relational connection to Him who was their functional source of life.

So, did they become like God? He says yes (Genesis 3:22). The two would now choose for themselves seeing as that's all they had. When you're God, all you need is Yourself, when you're not, oh well, you and I are in deep, deep trouble. No tree of life. No way, no how.

10 I selected only two of God's divine attributes as for instances. Omnipotence speaks to His all-powerful status, while omnipresence says He's everywhere present containing all of outer space within Himself.

11 Genesis 3:5

12 Satan, formerly Lucifer, heaven's star of the morning (Isaiah 14:12)

13 Psalm 90:2

14 Various other translations render this in terms of names written in the Lamb's book of life before the foundation of the world. So what? It's six of one, half dozen of the other. A Lamb is slain, and names are written. The context is eternity.

15 And time begins when exactly? When there was evening and morning, the first day (Genesis 1:3).

16 John 10:10

[17] Colossians 1:19–20 says it pleased the Father that all the fullness of God should come together in the Son and through Him to reconcile the stuff of earth and heaven to Himself through the blood of His cross.

Chapter 13

[1] Genesis 3:4–5 has the serpent laying out his fundamental thesis: God is holding out on you!

[2] Genesis 1:1

[3] Revelation 4:11

[4] Isaiah 46:10 pretty well sums things up.

[5] 1 Corinthians 8:6 and Colossians 1:17, but not without considering Colossians 2:9

[6] Romans 11:36—Lock, stock, and barrel: a figure of speech meaning absolutely everything.

[7] Ezekiel 36:16–38 with special emphasis on verses 22 and 23. This prophetic reference speaks directly to the heart of New Covenant realities that come alive in Jesus. A "me" centered focus—our inheritance from Adam—would have us viewing Calvary's redemptive gift through self-centered eyes. It's understandable considering the impact the cross has on us as believers. New life from an altogether new life source, new hope for the here and now, not to mention eternity.

Everything changes concerning us, yet if you and I don't look beyond ourselves, we won't make contact with a far greater reality, one God unveiled by way of the prophet Ezekiel: "It's not for your sake I'm doing this, but for My holy name." Now there's a kick in the teeth. It makes sense, though. If the chief end of man (as stated in the Westminster Confession) is to glorify God, it's only right that He should "vindicate the holiness of My great name" as a first order of business. Wouldn't you say?

[8] Ephesians 2:6

[9] Matthew 11:28

[10] Isaiah 6:5, "I'm a man with unclean lips who lives among so many others who are just like me!"

[11] Genesis 3:21 and 22:1–13

12 Exodus chapter 12

13 1 Peter 1:11

14 Imagery of Abraham preparing to sacrifice "your only son, whom you love" (Genesis 22:2) is typically cast as one of dad with his prepubescent boy, a little guy, as we say. Could be, but not necessarily. Terminology used in this passage is wide open in this respect. What you and I need to realize is Isaac was old enough to understand and give himself to follow dad's lead. Imagine, though, what he thought and felt!

15 1 Corinthians 5:7

16 Mark 14:27

17 SLR meaning single lens reflex, a camera using a mirror and prism. In my case, it was 35 mm.

18 A term of endearment used by many for the small school that sat on a knoll in Lima, New York.

19 Shoo-in—a sure thing, a done deal

20 Run of the mill meaning average

21 Think Gethsemane.

Chapter 14

1 John 17:3

2 Isaiah 45:15

3 1 Kings 8:43, Psalm 46:10, 102:15, 126:2, Ezekiel 36:22–23 and 37:28.

4 Romans 1:18–20

5 Exodus 20:18–21

6 Galatians 3:24

7 Jeremiah 31:34, Hebrews 8:11

8 2 Peter 1:1 (NASB)

9 2 Peter 1:1 (ESV)

10 1 Peter 1:23

11 2 Timothy 2:15

12 Hebrews 11:4 says it all. The difference between Abel and Cain's offerings comes down to one word, *faith*. And that means? It means Abel believed God; whereas, Cain sought to perform to gain acceptance.

Chapter 15

1. Luke 22:14
2. Strong's *Exhaustive Concordance*
3. The convergence of all the right and necessary components at precisely the right moment.
4. Luke 22:15, my paraphrase
5. Exodus 12:5 and 1 Peter 1:19
6. From "O Little Town of Bethlehem," by Phillips Brookes somewhere around 1865
7. *Old Testament Bible History*, Alfred Edersheim, p. 79 Wm. B. Eerdmans Publishing Co. 255 Jefferson Ave. Grand Rapids, MI 49503
8. Exodus 12:9
9. A small Greek island in the Aegean Sea
10. Revelation 1:13–15 (NASB)
11. The tabernacle, and later the temple, included a bronze altar on which substitutionary animals, that is, bulls and goats, were offered in flames after shedding their blood to atone for the people's sins (see Exodus 27:1–8). Who's surprised then that the Lord Jesus, in His exaltation, should symbolically present Himself as One who walked through the fiery furnace of judgment to secure us to Himself?
12. Luke 22:15—Literally, as your King James has it, "With desire I have desired to eat this Passover with you before I suffer." The picture here is one of earnest and deliberate passion.
13. Passover being the celebration of deliverance from the tyranny of bondage and marriage the binding of two as one, she by coming under his name, his banner.
14. Rabbi Daniel Thomson from YouTube video "Messianic Rabbi at Christian Church" https://www.youtube.com/watch?v=o6rFs4QB-Pqo published October 25, 2012 by Emmatec Studios
15. Matthew 26:29 (NASB)
16. Philippians 2:5–11
17. 2 Corinthians 13:8
18. Although not expressly stated, Adam chose to violate covenant, God's covenant of life. Foundational components comprising covenant were present, conditions the first man (humanity's covenant

representative) chose to turn his back on taking the human race with him—all of us.

[19] Covenant representative of an altogether new humanity.

[20] The new covenant in Jesus's blood is not, and cannot in any sense be, Sinai warmed over as some have suggested, a "renewed" covenant. "Kainos," the Greek word for "new" where Jesus's covenant is concerned means "new in nature" (per Kittel and Freidrich), as in an altogether new kind—new and decidedly better. See Hebrews 8 zeroing in on verse 6.

Chapter 16

[1] Matthew 26:34
[2] Romans 7:18
[3] Tree surgeon: a licensed arborist
[4] Mike Wells, *My Weakness For His Strength*, 2011 Abiding Life Press ISBN 978-0-9819546-2-2
[5] Genesis 12:1
[6] Genesis 22:2
[7] Hebrews 11:17–19
[8] Galatians 3:17 (NKJV), referencing Deuteronomy 21:22–23
[9] Matthew 26:35
[10] My own loose paraphrase of Matthew 26:40–41
[11] Matthew 3:12 (NKJV)
[12] Matthew 4:17
[13] Many see the Baptist pointing to Messianic judgment of the wicked as portrayed by Jesus as wheat and tares in Matthew 13:24–40, or a dragnet cast into the sea in verses 47–50.
[14] Check out Job 21:17–18, Psalm 1:4, Psalm 35:1–5, and Isaiah 17:3

Chapter 17

[1] Ecclesiastes 2:22
[2] Anabel Gillham, "Death of a Doer" part 1 from their e-mail periodical *Lifetime Weekly* on Wednesday April 22, 2009, 3:11:37 PM MDT

3   Snake eyes in the game of craps is rolling two, one pip on each die. It's a loser's roll. To fold is to quit, to forfeit whatever one has invested in the game, be it craps, poker, whatever.

4   Matthew 11:28, my paraphrase

5   Matthew 23:5

6   From the Westminster Shorter Catechism: "Man's chief end is to glorify God and enjoy Him forever."

7   Isaiah 64:6

8   2 Timothy 3:7

9   Jeremiah 2:13

10 Romans 3:23

11 Deuteronomy 6:5, Matthew 22:37, and Luke 10:27

12 Again Romans 3:23

13 Romans 7:22–23

14 Romans 7:18

Chapter 18

1   "Stuck feeler" is an expression that, as far as I know, was coined by author and Bible teacher Bill Gillham speaking to those times when we allow our emotional jam-ups to become the measure of truth.

2   The thief who comes only to steal, kill, and destroy, the accuser of the brethren (John 10:10, Revelation 12:10).

3   Toss Peter aside, fire him.

4   Romans 11:29

5   Luke 6:12–16

6   John 15:5

7   Psalm 22:1, Matthew 27:46, and Mark 15:34

8   John 15:16

9   2 Peter 1:10

10 2 Peter 1:1b

11 Hebrews 7:25

12 Luke 22:32

13 Genesis 3:15b

14 Job 1:20–21

[15] Try 1 Corinthians 2:14 on for size.

[16] Spend some time in Romans 7, but zero in on verse 18.

[17] Philippians 3:1–9 is a great summary, but look at verse 8. I'm referencing the King James Version on this: "Yea, doubtless, and I count all things but loss for the excellency of the knowledge of Christ Jesus my Lord: for whom I have suffered the loss of all things, and do count them but dung, that I may win Christ."

[18] Galatians 2:20 (KJV)

[19] Isaiah 53:6a, Judges 29:25b, and Proverbs 3:5—The heartbeat of sin: every man, every woman going their own way per their own understanding. It may help to spend some time in Genesis 5:5, 8:21 as these verses present God's assessment of a natural man's heart, then swing over to Genesis 11:1–9 to see where it leads.

[20] Romans 3:23

[21] Colossians 1:27

[22] Matthew 10:39 (ESV)

[23] "Old man," or "old self," meaning Peter's unregenerate spirit that Paul points to in Romans 6:6, Ephesians 4:22, and Colossians 3:9, while "flesh" speaks of all that we are apart from Christ—which is us trying to make life work on our own from our strengths and weaknesses by way of the limitations (and did I say distortions?) of our own understanding.

[24] Psalm 127:1

[25] See Hebrews 12:27

Chapter 19

[1] Proverbs 26:11, I2Peter 2:22

[2] DOC being the department of corrections. In this context, we're talking about someone going back to prison, be it a parole violation or picking up new charges.

[3] Ephesians 2:10a

[4] Addressing fundamental needs such as food, clothing, housing, transportation, periodic urine analysis, parole office visits, attending required therapy groups and classes, staying within prescribed physical and social boundaries, etc. may keep someone in line,

keep them from going back to prison, but there's more to the story. There's the soul and spirit God connection that involves people—themselves and others. Folks can jump through all the required hoops like a trained dog and still blow it if they see God, themselves, and those around them through a lens that doesn't correspond with reality. I'm talking Jesus and vine life (John 14:6).

5 Cellmate

6 Knowing is Romans 6:6, leading to what it means to be "complete in Him" (Colossians 2:10).

7 "Cough up," an idiom meaning to "come up with."

8 1 Peter 1:23

Chapter 20

1 Matthew 19:16–26, Mark 10:17–27, and Luke 18:18–23

2 Numbers 11:5

3 Three hot meals and a place to sleep.

4 Matthew 19:16–24

5 John 4:10

6 Matthew 13:44

7 John 8:4—If she was caught in the act, where's the guy?

8 Exodus 2:14 and Leviticus 20:10

9 Romans 7:5

10 Romans 3:31

11 Isaiah 5:20

12 Malachi 3:6

13 Psalm 29:2 and 96:9—The beauty of holiness is what you and I were created for, a beauty that begins and ends with God and God alone.

14 Genesis 1:17 (KJV)

15 Numbers 32:23

16 Forest green happens to be the color Colorado has chosen to dress inmates in, that and orange for new arrivals and those who step out of line.

17 Pardon my anthropomorphism, treating sin in human terms.

18 John 10:10

[19] John 8:34, my paraphrase

[20] John 8:44

[21] Romans 5:20, 7:5, and 7:7

[22] Galatians 3:24

[23] Psalm 32:3–4

[24] Brent Curtis and John Eldredge, *The Sacred Romance*, p. 1 Thomas Nelson Publishers 1997, ISBN 0-7852-7342-5

[25] Psalm 139 shows how much David realized the necessity of heaven's scrutiny and divine restoration.

[26] Psalm 34:8

[27] 2 Samuel 12:7 is the bull's eye, but read all of the first twenty-five verses to get the full flavor.

[28] Psalms 32 and 51 ring true. Yes, David was a fallen man in need of cleansing and restoration, yet stirrings in deeper places point to realities the good king was created for. Memories of Eden bleed through. We're talking the image and likeness of God here.

[29] Psalm 42:7

[30] Matthew 14:22–33

[31] H. David Edwards 1973—one of the wisest, well read, compassionate, and most balanced people and Bible teachers I've ever known. I owe so much to this man, his personal input during my season in Bible school.

Chapter 21

[1] Hebrews 12:25–27

[2] See Genesis 3:12 and "The woman You gave me."

[3] A presenting problem being the reason someone seeks assistance, a counselor maybe?

[4] Genesis 2:25

[5] Psalm 13:2a

[6] A character from Washington Irving's short story published in 1819 about a man from the NY Catskills who slept for twenty years under the influence of a magic potion, of sorts, missing the American revolution. Oh, how his world changed!

Chapter 22

1 Read Joshua chapter 7 for full disclosure.
2 Genesis 38 tells the story.
3 1 Samuel 15, the entire chapter
4 Judges 13–16 pretty much covers it.
5 Gregory Boyle, *Tattoos on the Heart*, p.43 Free Press a Division of Simon & Schuster, Inc. 1230 Avenue of the Americas, New York, NY 10020 ISBN 978-1-4391-5315-4.
6 ibid.
7 ibid.
8 "When first we practice to deceive" (Sir Walter Scott).
9 Interesting figure of speech, as though committing a new crime with its consequential sentence can be likened to "catching" a cold, or other viral ailment.
10 See if Romans 1:32 fits here. I think it does.
11 One of the key names I personally grew up with, remember?

Chapter 23

1 Genesis 19:23–26
2 Acts 5:1–11
3 Get the full context in 2 Samuel 13:1–19.
4 See 2 Chronicles 32:21 and Proverbs 3:35, respectively.
5 1 Samuel 17 and 18
6 Hebrews 12:17
7 2 Samuel 12:1–15
8 Read verses 1–3 and 14–22 of Psalm 25 for the framework, then go back to the rest to see how it all fills in.
9 Isaiah 50:6 (NKJV)
10 *International Dictionary of the Bible*, p.130 Merrill C. Tenney 1963, 1964, 1967 and The Zondervan Corporation 1987 ISBN 0-310-33190-0 Zondervan Publishing House.
11 Isaiah 50:6c (NKJV)
12 That's the gist of the first half of Isaiah 53:4.
13 Isaiah 53:5 (ESV)

14 Isaiah 50:7 (ESV)

15 John 19:30

16 Colossians 2:13–15 are inferred with part of verse 14 quoted. It wouldn't hurt to turn over to Hebrews 2 and chew on verses 14–18.

17 2 Corinthians 5:21

Chapter 24

1 Crescendo—a musical term meaning to build, to get progressively louder and fuller.

2 Allow me space for a little creative imagination. Hours on the water, then out and about with Jesus would give more than sufficient cause for the sun to do its damage to anyone's clothes.

3 Luke 24:33–49 and John 20:19–29 for this and more.

Chapter 25

1 Understand that Satan didn't come, hat in hand, to God's throne politely requesting permission. The best sources I've investigated stand firm that this is not so, which makes all the sense in the world. Consider the accuser's posture where Job is concerned. He pushed and pushed hard. Satan demands God give him permission to have his chance for a shot at Peter as if it were his personal entitlement.

2 Acts 2:23 (NASB)

3 John 3:16

4 Galatians 2:20

5 Luke 22:31, J. B. Phillips, *New Testament in Modern English*

6 Luke 22:31 (AMP)

7 "Tête-à-tête" is French for a private conversation or interview between two people.

8 Simon Barjona is Simon son of Jonah. That's Peter!

9 John 18:15–16

10 John 18:15

11 Mark 14:51–52

12 Matthew 11:3 and Luke 7:19

13 Luke 1:66

14 Luke 1:76

15 A "yes man" is typically the spineless flunky whose only valued function is to mindlessly agree with the boss. Not so with John. Saying yes to God put him on the firing line, ultimately costing him his life. To be left "holding the bag" is a US idiom, taking the blame for someone else's doing, being the fall guy.

Chapter 26

1 A voice spoke from the heavens, "This is My beloved Son," but who heard? The Son did. It was for Him, and the Baptist took note. The people? It might as well have thundered. See John 12:27–30 where the Father again audibly speaks, but it falls on deaf ears.

2 John 6:35, 7:37, Matthew 11:28

3 Matthew 11:4–5

4 Matthew 11:6

5 James 4:3

6 John 6 might be good to read here, the whole chapter.

7 No need to run for office when all authority in heaven and earth are Yours, is there? It's not a popularity contest, and there's no struggle for the King to maintain His status. He's King of kings, Lord of lords.

Then there's this thing called tolerance, a curious term in the current political climate where "different strokes for different folks" no longer holds water. Open dialogue allowing for differences of opinion is more than passé. If you don't approve me and my position, you might find yourself charged with a hate crime. Where the university once was a proving ground, a place to consider for different folks with ideas. No more, not if your difference is perceived as a threat. Protests to keep free speech under wraps get violent at times.

8 Matthew 1:5 nails it. Rahab of Jericho was a known harlot. Ruth hailed from Moab, whose people worshipped Chemosh the

destroyer, a cult Solomon brought to Jerusalem (1 Kings 11:7) and was later crushed and removed by Josiah (2 Kings 23).

9 "It's all good," being vernacular for, "Hey, no problems here."

10 As in Santa Claus, or Saint Nick, the jolly old elf who for many has replaced Jesus at Christmas.

11 Mark 1:4, Matthew 3:2 and 4:17—A radical change of mind playing out as radical change in choices.

12 Luke 9:23

13 Matthew 11:29

Chapter 27

1 John 18:37–38

2 Dogmatism being an emphatic insistence of concepts or principles as incontrovertible truth

3 See Acts 17:19–21

4 A term used of political liberals having an inflated opinion of their own uniqueness coupled with an unwarranted sense of entitlement who are easily offended.

5 "Coexist" bumper stickers and posters make a broad ecumenical statement embracing Islam, LGBTQ, evolution and special creation, Judaism, neopaganism, Taoist Yin and Yang representing harmonic balance between dark and light influences, last of all Christianity.

6 John 1:1–3, Colossians 1:16–17, and Hebrews 1:3

7 Ephesians 1:10

8 Romans 11:36 and John 14:6

9 Luke 2:52

10 Hadiths are words, actions, and habits attributed to Mohammed passed on by oral tradition.

11 There is no deity in Buddhism, strictly speaking.

12 Alleged founder of Taoism whom scholars believe never really lived outside of mystic imaginations.

13 Krishna, a major deity in Hinduism, is said to have been born in northern India more than three thousand years before Christ. Lord Krishna is revered as the eighth avatar of Vishnu.

14 I say embarrassment knowing no one but Jesus can pull off what He commands. Hence John 15, Christ in us doing what only He can.

15 John 10:10

16 1 John 4:7–21—God alone is the root and substance of such love, which is why He had to offer Himself as a gift (John 3:16). Apart from first receiving such love (agape), you and I can only attempt to replicate it, a cheap facsimile—typically eros, possibly phileo or storge, but not agape (Greek).

17 John 15:1–11

18 "Lord of the Dance" on Steven Curtis Chapman's "Speechless"

19 John 15:5

20 Colossians 1:27

21 In thought or intention

22 His own possession, His disciples including you and me.

Chapter 28

1 Matthew 5, 6, and 7

2 Matthew 5:3

3 His divine lead off pointing us where He would focus our attention.

4 Again, Matthew 5:3

5 Read the opening paragraph's of Watchman Nee's "The Normal Christian Life."

6 Philippians 2:6–8

7 John 10:37–38, 14:8–10

8 One of Mike Wells's observations I can only say amen to.

9 John 14:10 (NASB)

10 Luke 2:49 and John 17:5b, my paraphrase

11 John 17:20–23

12 Romans 8:15

13 John 15:4

14 John 15:5

15 I Corinthians 6:17 (ESV)

16 Galatians 5:22–23

[17] V. Raymond Edman, *They Found the Secret*, p. 169 Zondervan Publishing House Grand Rapids, Michigan 49530 ISBN: 0-310-24051-4.

Chapter 29

[1] "Iffy" being maybe, maybe not. Doubtful is the word, I think.

[2] Marijuana.

[3] A pastor I served with hit me with that question when, overcome with confusion and lots of emotional pain, I was trying to connect a few dots.

[4] My job as a graphic arts cameraman often had me working with sensitive panchromatic film emulsions that could only be handled in total darkness.

[5] Galatians 6:8

[6] See John 10:10

[7] Please understand these are my distortions talking.

[8] Job's wife, if you recall, encouraged her husband to seek relief through a common misconception. Curse God, and He'll take you out!

[9] Matthew 11:25–30—A question I sometimes put to folks is, "How does your life as a Christian feel to you?" Hard? Impossible? Not once have "easy" or "light" been mentioned. Common frustrations. Common ignorance.

[10] It's the basic gist of Psalm 13 verse 1a.

[11] Psalm 42:1

[12] John 10:27

[13] A cessationist being one who's convinced the supernatural gifts of the Holy Spirit ceased with the death of the first century apostles and the completion of the canon of Scripture. I would direct my precious Calvinist friends to D. Martyn Lloyd-Jones's *The Baptism and Gifts of the Spirit* by Baker Books.

[14] Psalm 42:2a

[15] To be "slipped a Mickey" means drugging someone without their knowing, typically in their drink.

[16] 2 Kings 4:38–41 tells the story of a man who in gathering herbs and gourds for a stew didn't realize he'd gotten poisonous wild gourds. As is with many Bible teachers and pastors, his intent was sound, but what he failed to understand was toxic and would have brought death had it not been for divine intervention.

Chapter 30

[1] British pastor and author Alan Redpath on suffering.

[2] Romans 7:24

[3] Romans 7:18

[4] V. Raymond Edman, *They Found the Secret*, p.54 Zondervan Publishing House, Grand Rapids, Michigan 49530 ISBN 0-310-24051-4.

[5] American missionary John Hyde, better known as "Praying Hyde," sought God for effectiveness in prayer to break through demonic Hindi strongholds, while Scotsman Andrew Murray discovered surrender and abiding.

[6] Then the LORD God said, "Behold, the man has become like one of Us, knowing good and evil" (Genesis 3:22). Carefully reread all of Genesis 3, then go back and see what we said in chapter 12, and please don't forget endnote 9. Multnomah Bible College teacher, David Needham, puts it this way:

God's life flows from no higher source than himself; he draws on no moral law outside of himself. So now Adam and Eve were on their own, severed from any higher source—any moral law other than their own—even as God is on his own. It was in that tragic sense that they became "like God." At least part of what Satan told them was true. They were now independent creatures, cut off by choice from God's will, from his perfections, from his purity. (David C. Needham, *Alive for the First Time*, p. 30 Multnomah Publishers, Inc., ISBN: 0-88070-738-0)

[7] John 17:3

[8] Romans 8:15, Galatians 4:6

[9] I remember first hearing this twisted Beatitude from one of my high school teachers.

[10] No doubt someone will recognize my reference to Johnny Lee's 1980 country song, "Looking for Love," from the movie *Urban Cowboy.*

[11] 1 Thessalonians 5:24

[12] Mark 1:11, Luke 3:22 then 1 Peter 1:12

[13] Hebrews 1:5

[14] In Luke's genealogy of Jesus, the "supposed son of Joseph," the good doctor traces everything back to Adam who he calls "the son of God" (Luke 3:38). In blatant rebellion fueled by unbelief, this first man and his lady intentionally chose death, thereby severing the love connection binding son and daughter—descendants included—to their Father's heart. The Son, in restoring what was lost, brings many sons and a multitude of daughters to glory (Hebrews 2:10).

[15] It's true Jesus pleased the Father always (John 8:29), yet His Sonship was never conditional. The Father's public acknowledgment of His Son was just that. "He's My boy, and that pleases Me" (Luke 3:22). Whatever Jesus did was birthed out of the inseparable Father-Son love connection that made them One.

[16] 1 Corinthians 15:45—He's Adam, and not the first. Jesus is the last.

[17] John 20:17

[18] Romans 8:15, Galatians 4:5, Ephesians 1:5

Chapter 31

[1] From Rogers and Hammerstein's movie and musical *The King and I.*

[2] "My Way" was written by Paul Anka and made popular in 1969.

[3] Isaiah 53:6

[4] Ecclesiastes 1:9

[5] Acquaintances or friends who possibly grew up together

[6] Think context.

Chapter 32

1 Isaiah 65:17 and 66:22, 2 Peter 3:13, Revelation 21:1
2 Read Romans 8:19–23 with new eyes and heart.
3 Genesis 3:17–19
4 The 1925 *State of Tennessee versus John Thomas Scopes* trial established precedent for teaching the theory of evolution in public schools. The rest, as they say, is history, especially for those Bible teachers who tucked tail in embarrassment and turned giving birth to a new breed of critics.
5 Check out Matthew 19:4 where in quoting Genesis 1:27 he corroborates the account Moses gave us.
6 2 Corinthians 13:8, my paraphrase
7 Revelation 21:5
8 Ezekiel 36:25–27
9 John 1:13, 3:3, James 1:18, and 1 Peter 3:3, 23
10 Hebrews 8:6, 13—The word "new" in verse 13 is taken from the Greek "kainos" meaning new in nature, an altogether new breed, as opposed to "renewed." This isn't Sinai warmed over. It's a new kind of covenant, as distinct in its own right as, "Beam me up, Scotty" is to Henry's Model A.
11 See 1 Corinthians, the first couple of chapters as a launchpad, then feel free to study the remainder of Paul's insightful letter.
12 "Sizing up"—to evaluate, thinking we have someone figured out
13 King James rendering
14 Complete Jewish Bible and NIV
15 Amplified
16 1 Corinthians 1:10–17 and 11:18 set the stage for Paul's concern over developing schisms in the church.
17 1 Corinthians 3:1–4 and Hebrews 5:12–14
18 1 Corinthians 11:19
19 1 Corinthians 12:16 and 21 pretty well sums things up.
20 Philippians 3:12
21 *The Calvary Road*, by Roy Hession, p. 21 Christian Literature Crusade Fort Washington, PA 19034 SBN: 87508-336-X.

22 *Shattered Dreams* by Larry Crabb, p. 52 WaterBrook Press, 2375 Telstar Drive, Suite 160 Colorado Springs, CO 80920, a division of Random House, Inc. ISBN 1-57856-506-5.

23 ibid., p. 52

24 Colossians 2:10

25 *The Ultimate Intention* by DeVern Fromke, p. 47 Sure Foundation Publishers Box 74—Route 2, Clocerdale, Indiana 46120 ISBN: 0-936595-02-7.

Chapter 33

1 We're back at Luke 22 moving on to verse 32b.

2 Luke 22:53

3 Acts 2:23

4 To "hit the wall" connotes a sudden loss of strength and energy like a marathon runner whose stamina unexpectedly gives out.

5 2 Corinthians 5:16b

6 Galatians 5:17

7 The gist of John 1:18

8 John 5:39, Luke 24:25–27, 44, Acts 13:27

9 Genesis 16:7, 13, Exodus 3:2, 6

10 Genesis 12:7, 17:1

11 Daniel 3:25

12 Luke 2:10

13 Luke 22:42

14 Philippians 2:8

15 Matthew 16:13–14

16 1 John 1:1

17 Luke 10:23–24

18 Isaiah 6:9, Matthew 13:14–15

19 Watchtower being Jehovah's Witnesses who stand firm on Jesus being Michael, the archangel. LDS, or Latter Day Saints, that is, Mormons see Jesus and Lucifer as spirit brothers, making them equal opposites.

20 Arabic name for Jesus

21 John 6:44, 65

22 Matthew 11:25, mostly paraphrase

23 Matthew 13:10–17

24 John 16:7

25 "All in" is when a poker player has put all his chips in the pot. At that point, they can't do anything more. All their chips are invested.

26 Mark 10:28

27 Matthew 13:44

28 Matthew 9:9–10, John 4:1–42

29 Matthew 16:24–25

30 My paraphrase of Bonhoeffer's thoughts taken from *The Cost of Discipleship* by Dietrich Bonhoeffer, p. 63 The Macmillan Company, 866 Third Avenue, New York NY 10022 Fourteenth Printing 1973.

31 Mark 14:27 taken from Zechariah 13:7

32 Mark 14:50

Chapter 34

1 Luke 24:5

2 Sabbath

3 Luke 24:6

4 Luke 24:11

5 Although not one of the twelve, Cleopas, or Clopas, was obviously a committed disciple, tradition holds him as the brother of Jesus's earthly father, Joseph.

6 2 Corinthians 5:16

Chapter 35

1 John 5:39

2 Genesis 1:1 to Malachi 4:6

3 Matthew 7:12, Luke 6:31

4 John 15:5

5 Mark 3:14

6 John 7:37

7 Matthew 11:28
8 Colossians 1:17
9 John 14:6
10 John 3:3, 5
11 1 Corinthians 2:14
12 1 Corinthians 2:9
13 Isaiah 64:4 and 1 Corinthians 2:9

Chapter 36

1 Luke 24:25
2 Read John 11:1–46
3 John 10:18
4 ibid.
5 Luke 24:25
6 2 Peter 1:19
7 Luke 11:29–30
8 Luke 24:26
9 1 Corinthians 2:9c
10 Isaiah 53:1 (NKJV)
11 Luke 24:26 (NASB)
12 Psalm 2:9
13 Isaiah 50:6
14 Romans 11:36 (NASB)
15 Luke 24:23
16 Luke 24:26
17 From Isaiah 53:10
18 ibid.
19 Matthew 16:24
20 Romans 6:6
21 John 8:36
22 Romans 6:7
23 Romans 3:25, 1 John 1:7, and Isaiah 1:18

Chapter 37

1 John 6:68
2 Psalm 34:8
3 John 1:35–40
4 John 6:35 and 7:37
5 See 1 Corinthians 2:3
6 *Brubaker*, starring Robert Redford, is a graphic 1980 prison drama based on a newly arrived warden sent to reform a corrupt system. *The Shawshank Redemption* focuses on a man unjustly convicted of murder, and his subsequent prison break.
7 Psalm 42:1 (NKJV)
8 ibid.
9 John 6:68, my paraphrase

Chapter 38

1 Luke 24:36 and John 20:19
2 Luke 24:34
3 Matthew 14:26
4 Hebrews 12:27
5 John 20:17
6 Luke 24:39, John 20:19–20
7 John 14:27
8 John 14:27
9 ibid.
10 Matthew 2:1–18
11 Luke 2:14b, Philippians 2:6–8, and 1 Corinthians 15:45
12 Mark 4:37–38
13 Luke 4:28–30
14 Luke 22:42
15 Hebrews 12:2
16 Hebrews 4:15
17 Isaiah 53:5c
18 Ephesians 2:14
19 Romans 5:1, Philippians 4:7, and Ephesians 4:3

Chapter 39

1 Hebrews 4:12
2 Hebrews 3:19
3 Hebrews 4:1 (although it wouldn't be a bad idea to read chapters 3 and 4 in their entirety)
4 Psalm 95:8 and Hebrews 3:8, 19
5 Mark 16:14
6 Psalm 95:10—Knowing God's ways lie at the core of knowing Him. They'd seen I Am in action yet didn't have a clue concerning His heart for the people He longed to embrace as His own. They never hugged Him back.
7 John 17:3
8 2 Peter 1:3
9 Exodus 20:18–19
10 Hebrews 4:2
11 Hebrews 8:7–8a
12 Hebrews 8:9
13 I've heard this from a splinter faction of the Hebrew roots movement behind prison walls.
14 "Kainós," from *Theological Dictionary of the New Testament*, abridged in one volume by Geoffrey W. Bromley, Gerhard Kittle and Gerhard Friedrich editors, p. 388 Copyright 1985 William B. Eerdmans Publishing Company, 255 Jefferson Avenue. SE Grand Rapids, MI 49503 ISBN 0-8028-2404-8.
   See also *Thayer's Greek-English Lexicon of the New Testament*
15 Hebrews 10:1–18
16 Hebrews 10:1
17 Hebrews 10:14 (NASB)

Chapter 40

1 Luke 24:38, my paraphrase
2 An expression coined by Michael Wells in *Sidetracked in the Wilderness*.
3 John 11:16
4 Hebrews 12:2

5   Luke 24:41

6   Romans 10:9

7   Sahih International Surah 4:157

> And [for] their saying, "Indeed, we have killed the Messiah, Jesus, the son of Mary, the messenger of Allah." And they did not kill him, nor did they crucify him; but [another] was made to resemble him to them. And indeed, those who differ over it are in doubt about it. They have no knowledge of it except the following of assumption. And they did not kill him, for certain. And [for] their saying, "Indeed, we have killed the Messiah, Jesus, the son of Mary, the messenger of Allah."

8   1 Corinthians 15:3–8

9   Luke 24:44 pretty well says it. Those hungry to go further can begin with Josh McDowell's *More Than A Carpenter*, a former skeptic's search to consider who Jesus claims to be and the reliability of Scripture. His *Evidence That Demands A Verdict* is decidedly deeper water providing a wealth of documented insight for the not so faint of heart. Lee Strobel's *The Case for Christ* documents another one-time skeptic's search.

10 The most robust of critics who vehemently debate any and all supernatural claims of Scripture admit to the historical accuracy of Jesus's death on a Roman cross. Historians as well.

11 Refer to endnote 39.

12 Short answer: Days and nights are measured as any portion qualify as the whole instead of full twenty-four hours.

13 *Bogus* meaning not true, fake. It's a word that goes back to the early 1800s to make and speak of counterfeit coins.

14 Colossians 2:14

15 Colossians 2:12

16 Romans 6:3

17 Romans 6:6

18 Again Romans 6:3

19 Do yourself a favor and take in Christian singer Danny Gokey's "I Will Not Say Goodbye," who wrote this song after his young wife's passing. His sentiments are raw and extremely honest. The YouTube video is worth looking into.

20 Luke 24:44–47

Chapter 41

1 John 20:21
2 Matthew 28:19
3 Jeremiah 18 and 19
4 *Problems, God's Presence & Prayer*, by Michael Wells, p. 49 copyright 1993, published by Abiding Life Press, a division of Abiding Life Ministries International P.O. Box 620998, Littleton, Colorado 80162. ISBN 0-9670843-1-8
5 1 Corinthians 4:15
6 1 Corinthians 3:2
7 1 Corinthians 9:26
8 Romans 11:36
9 Revelation 3:20
10 Ephesians 2:12
11 "Never say never," suggests God will send us where we don't want to go simply because we don't want to go there! Don't believe it. And for those calling on Jonah as a proof text for support, you better look elsewhere. It's true. Jonah despised the Ninevites for their heavy-handed corruption, and he wanted to see them fry. He didn't want people he deemed despicable dirtbags to repent and taste God's mercy—but that's not the reason Yahweh chose him. Why Jonah then? My best guess is God wanted to expose the bankruptcy of the prophet's heart in order to draw Jonah closer to His own. Convey mercy to folks who deserved only judgement.
12 Exodus 3:11
13 Matthew 5:3

Chapter 42

1 John 1:1–3
2 2 Corinthians 5:17
3 John 19:30 and 2 Corinthians 5:21
4 Genesis 2:7
5 John 20:19–22
6 John 20:22

7 I remember hearing Mike Wells, founder of Abiding Life Ministries International, share this in a message.

8 1 Corinthians 15:21

9 You remember, asking what if Adam hadn't eaten from the forbidden tree?

10 1 Corinthians 15:45

11 1 Corinthians 15:47

Chapter 43

1 Luke 15:13

2 Friends, acquaintances, and family

3 Genesis 25:25, Isaac's firstborn

4 Hebrews 12:17

5 Luke 15:13 (KJV)

6 Ecclesiastes 2:1

7 Genesis 6:5

8 Track number 6 on BS&T's second album, *Blood, Sweat and Tears* on Columbia Records

9 Luke 15:17, my freeform paraphrase, but I believe it fits.

10 Matthew 13:44

11 Luke 15:18

12 Isaiah 6:9, Matthew 13:11, 16

13 Give mes, an unreasonable and irrational sense of entitlement.

14 Job 42:6, Isaiah 6:5

15 Romans 1:18

16 Gomorrah, as I'm sure you know, is connected with Sodom. See Genesis 6:5 to better understand a preflood, or antediluvian earth, and Exodus where bricks without straw gets uglier still.

17 Thanks again, Bill Gillham!

18 Larry Crabb, *Shattered Dreams*, p. 86 published by Waterbrook Press 2375 Telstar Drive, Suite 160, Colorado Springs CO 80920 A division of Random House ISBN 1-57856-506-5.

Chapter 44

1 Albatross—an outsized sea bird—meaning, in this case, an impossible burden weighing us down. See it as a throwback to Samuel Taylor Coleridge's poem, "The Rime of the Ancient Mariner."

2 Romans 7:18

3 Matthew 23:27 (KJV)

4 My loose but accurate (I believe) paraphrase of Matthew 23:28

5 Matthew 5:16 (KJV)

6 1 Corinthians 3:12

7 Ephesians 4:17–18

8 I immediately think of Matthew 28:11 but can't help but remember the Beatles' "Carry That Weight" and their White Album. Humor me, will you?

9 The tree of the knowledge of good and evil

10 John 15:5, Colossians 1:17

11 Acts 17:28

12 Matthew 3:13–17, Mark 1:9–13, Luke 3:21–22 and John 1:29–34

13 Luke 1:35

14 Try John 1:9, 18, and 10:30 for starters. The oneness Jesus speaks of is oneness in essence. Also John 14:9.

15 1 Timothy 2:5

16 We're back to Philippians 2:6–8

17 George Harrison's "My Sweet Lord," his ode to Krishna

18 A repeated cycle of lifetimes to work out the kinks in hopes of gaining paradise, or Nirvana

19 Your good is weighed over against the bad to determine eternity in paradise or damnation.

20 Think motive and means.

21 1 Corinthians 2:14

22 1 Corinthians 2:9–10

23 Hebrews in Egypt get more than a bird's eye view of YHWH's deliverance (Exodus 19:4).

24 I'm referring to Cecil B. DeMille's *Ten Commandments* with Charleton Heston.

25 Exodus 6:7 N(ASB)

[26] Genesis 1:1

[27] 1 Corinthians 15:47

[28] Philippians 2:6–7 is the Son's surrender in eternity, His incarnation

[29] Preference over truth, wording I only just heard from Ravi Zacharias associate Abdu Murray in a lecture at Michigan State I took in online, "A Post Mortem on a Post Truth Culture."

[30] Matthew 4:3 and 27:40

[31] John 4:34, my paraphrase

[32] 1 Corinthians 15:45

Chapter 45

[1] That's prodigal from Oxford Dictionaries online

[2] Irish novelist, playwright, essayist, and poet living in the late 1800s, a self-indulgent gay hedonist and pedophile whose excesses and imprisonment made for a short life with a very ugly end.

[3] An abbreviated young life brought with it an awareness of sin only God could cleanse resulting in an obsession for repeated baptisms as he drew near the end.

[4] Cain's gift was rejected, why? He didn't believe God, his brother did (Hebrews 11:4). "So I'm not good enough?" as though a man is capable of impressing God.

[5] Psalm 14:3, Romans 3:12

[6] Mark 10:18 and Romans 3:23

[7] Psalm 51:4 (NASB)

[8] Romans 8:7, James 4:4 This gets personal. (See Galatians 4:16 for context.) Who's surprised? Satan, our adversary, is first out to assault God and does so by attacking us. What better way than the seduction of those created to bear His divine image and likeness? Get them to opt for unbelief and independence making God our personal enemy.

[9] Revelation 3:15–16

[10] The transcendent nature of God and the Scriptures are up for grabs among those who would see truth through the eyes of relativism—that is, that truth and morality can be different things to different people in different cultures at different times who insist there are no unchanging, or unchangeable, absolutes!

11 Acts 20:21

12 Luke 15:20—How else would he have recognized his son while the boy was still a long way off?

13 Matthew 9:36

14 John 14:9

15 King James has it right…literally.

16 Luke 15:24

Chapter 46

1 John 21:5

2 Acts 4:13

3 John 15:5

4 Matthew 8:27

5 Hebrews 12:2

6 For those who may not get my "fattened calf" reference, an image laid out in the prodigal's return, we're talking honor acceptance, affirmation, and security. The father's robe and signet speak immediately to his bond, that "you're my son" in a way he wishes to include everyone in the house—reminiscent of a covenant meal.

7 Matthew 10:37 (NASB)

8 Luke 14:26 (NASB)

9 Matthew 19:27, Mark 10:28, and Luke 18:28

10 John 21:17

11 John 21:15

12 That is, "Do you love me more than these?" Opinions as to who "these" are vary. A few contemporary renderings of the text have "these" as the "other disciples," suggesting, "Do you love Me more than they do?" Many see it that way, and for years, I was one of them. Another possible construct is, "Do you love Me more than you love these guys?" The *Aramaic Bible in Plain English* says "these things."

Deciding to investigate further, I came across a brilliant piece written by Greek exegetical scholar and consultant, Dr. Harold Greenlee, who sees (based on the original Greek grammar) Jesus confronting Peter on his loyalties. Everything had fallen apart to a degree this fisherman would never have wanted or imagined, so he falls back on what he knows. The problem lies now in his calling, fishing for men. "What are you gonna do, Pete? Follow through with what I've appointed you for, or play it safe with what you've known?" That works. See web page: http://www-01.sil.org/siljot/2005/2/46693/siljot2005-2-02.pdf

13 Luke 24:49

14 1 John 4:19

15 1 John 4:9 (NASB), marginal note included

16 1 John 3:1

17 See Matthew 25:40 for the overall gist.

18 1 John 4:12

19 Romans 5:5 and 2 Corinthians 5:14–21

20 John 21:16

21 "No holds barred" is a wrestling term meaning no restrictions. I use it to indicate in-the-trenches shepherding where real compassion and gut-level love minister hope and truth that makes a difference.

22 Ephesians 2:6

Chapter 47

1 Luke 10:1

2 Matthew 5:1 and John 6:2 point to numbers, not necessarily disciples.

3 1 Corinthians 13:12

4 Isaiah 6:9–10 and Matthew 13:11

5 Read all of Matthew 16

6 Matthew 16:24, Mark 8:34, and Luke 9:23

7 Matthew 26:41–46

8 Matthew 26:38

9 John 11:35—Two words that speak volumes.

10 Luke 19:41–44

11 1 Peter 1:12

12 Genesis 3:21

13 Remember Noah and Levitical offerings? Work through Joshua, Judges, Samuel, Kings, and Chronicles, but don't stop there. I'm hoping you get where I'm going with all of this. Read with eyes and heart wide open!

14 Matthew 26:37–38

15 Matthew 19:26

16 John 10:3, and while you're at it, how about Matthew 22:14?

17 Luke 18:18–30

18 Some may take issue with my use of "perverse" to describe the culture Jesus invaded. I take my cue from Peter on Pentecost with his exhortation, pleading with the people to, "Escape! Be delivered from this perverse generation" (Acts 2:40). So no exaggerations. This fits.

19 Matthew 16:21, Mark 8:31, Luke 9:22

20 Romans 6:3—Baptism speaks first to our union with Jesus, a supernatural work of the Holy Spirit we celebrate in coming to the water. There's no inherent value, no regenerative power attached to water baptism in and of itself. As believers we come to the water as an obedient faith response affirming our "Amen!" to what grace alone has bought, paid for and secured. See also 1 Corinthians 6:17.

21 Romans 6:7 (NASB)

22 John 8:36

23 No Kool-Aid, no stand-downs with the FBI. Jim Jones, sociopathic pastor of the People's Temple, led more than nine hundred followers, including children, in mass suicide by having them drink cyanide-laced Kool-Aid to avoid human rights abuse charges. David Koresh assumed leadership of a fractured offshoot of Davidian Seventh Day Adventists calling themselves Branch Davidians. A fifty-one-day siege on their Mount Carmel Center for multiple firearms violations ended in the deaths of Koresh and seventy-nine others.

24 Luke 14:26 (NASB)

25 Genesis 3:4

26 The serpent, if you recall, presented himself as an altruistic benefactor with their well-being in mind.

27 The serpent nudges this first couple to embrace self-sufficiency. It's how they became "like God."

28 Romans 6:23—Self-sufficiency is sin's birth mother, folks.

29 Luke 14:27

30 John 14:6

31 2 Corinthians 13:8

32 "Whole ball of wax" means "everything."

33 We're back to Luke 14:26 now.

Chapter 48

1 That's Hebrews 2:14–15, my own loose paraphrase that I pray communicates.

2 Romans 5:6

3 Romans 5:9

4 Romans 5:10a

5 Recognize Psalm 23:2, anyone?

6 The power of sin is who Paul so powerfully references in Romans chapter seven. I say "who" because of the way he speaks of this seductive and ruthless taskmaster. See p. 576 of W.E. Vine's *Complete Expository Dictionary of Old and New Testament Words* for clarification ISBN 0-8407-7559-8.

7 Romans 5:10b

8 Major Ian Thomas, *Christ in You, the Hope of Glory*, YouTube, https://www.youtube.com/watch?v=mVyJj993YsU.

9 John 15:5, my paraphrase

10 Romans 1:5

11 Read Galatians 5.

12 John 15:4

13 Remember chapter 7?

Chapter 49

1 Under the Old Covenant Law, animal sacrifices pointed to Jesus's offering of Himself in His blood. There is a difference. The blood of bulls and goats cannot take away sins or cleanse us and our

consciences of all unrighteousness (Hebrews 10:1–4, realities that tie into 1 John 1:9). The blood of Jesus pays our sin debt in full (John 19:30), and the Father is completely satisfied while we are thoroughly cleansed.

2 Isaiah 53:11a, notes inserted mine

3 Ephesians 1:8

4 John 10:10

5 See *My Utmost for His Highest,* December 11.

6 Galatians 2:20a

7 Romans 6:6

8 Colossians 1:27

9 Galatians 2:20 (NEB)

10 Online dictionary for *mumbo jumbo*: Language or ritual causing or intended to cause confusion or bewilderment.

11 It's the Major again.

Chapter 50

1 Luke 7:37

2 See Esther 4:16—*Spunk* is the word, a willingness to put her neck on the line—a faith choice to be sure.

3 From "Beautiful to Me," written and sung by Don Francisco Beautiful To Me lyrics © Universal Music Publishing Group, Capitol Christian Music Group

4 Psalm 42:1 (NKJV)

5 Psalm 42:2a (NKJV)

6 Matthew 6:21, my paraphrase

7 From "Maggie" by Redbone Songwriters: Matteo Di Franco / Sergio Moschetto / Andrea Zuppini / N Writer Unknown Maggie lyrics © Sony/ATV Music Publishing LLC, Ultra Tunes

8 Matthew 13:44

9 Luke 7:48

10 Colossians 2:13–14

11 See Matthew 9:36. The word used here for compassion has to do with entrails, as in bowels, kidneys, heart, etc., a penetrating of the deepest places that could possibly be. Hence my use of "gut-level."

[12] Acts 20:21

[13] *Theological Dictionary of the New Testament Abridged in One Volume*, Gerhard Kittel and Gerhard Friedrich editors, by Geoffrey W. Bromiley p. 88 William B. Eerdmans Publishing Company ISBN 0-85364-322-9.

[14] Matthew 18:21–35

[15] From Luke 7:47

[16] Matthew 18:2–35

[17] Luke 7:36–50

[18] Luke 15:25–32

[19] Isaiah 59:2a

[20] Postscript, an add-on to the main theme, if you will

[21] 1 Corinthians 6:17

[22] Acts 1:8

Chapter 51

[1] Isaiah 64:6

[2] *Birthright: Christian, Do You Know Who You Are?* by David Needham, p. 48 1979 Multnomah Press Portland, OR 97266 ISBN 0-930014-75-8.

[3] 1 Corinthians 1:23, 1 Peter 2:8

[4] Thank you again, David Needham, Multnomah Bible School teacher and author, whose book *Alive For The First Time* brought much-needed insight into my part of the world.

[5] Matthew 25:14–30

Chapter 52

[1] 2 Timothy 4:7 (NASB)

[2] 2 Timothy 4:2

[3] 1 Corinthians 2:3 (NASB)

[4] Self-aggrandizement is all about self-promotion through achieving power, influence, and possibly wealth.

[5] Philippians 3:8. Your King James has it right in calling such fleshly values "dung."

6   Philippians 3:5, my paraphrase
7   Acts 9:18. Referring to our brother's baptism.
8   No exaggeration here in calling Galatian distortions damnable. Paul did. "Anathema" is the Greek word he used for cursed, meaning to be eternally damned. It doesn't get any stronger than this (Galatians 1:8–9).
9   1 Corinthians 2:14
10 Romans 7:4, 6, 8
11 Galatians 2:20
12 ibid.
13 Romans 6:10
14 1 Peter 3:18
15 Hebrews 7:27, 9:24–28, 10:10, 12, 14

Chapter 53

1   A hammerlock is a wrestling hold designed to incapacitate one's opponent.
2   Watchman Nee, *The Normal Christian Life*, p. 22 online PDF http://www.thewichitafoundry.com/wp-content/uploads/2008/08/watchman-normal-christian-life2.pdf.
3   Mark 1:15
4   Hebrews 3:15, 2 Corinthians 6:2
5   Literally what repentance means.
6   Acts 20:21
7   Not to be taken lightly. Genuine repentance is a necessary precursor to new life in Christ. Seeker sensitive types may, in fact, be sincere as they unknowingly lead folks down a primrose path to damnation.
8   John 6:26, my paraphrase, which I believe gets to the people's gut-level motives.
9   Revelation 3:20
10 Matthew 11:28
11 2 Peter 1:10
12 Ephesians 2:8 (KJV)

Chapter 54

1 Referencing Philippians 3:8 and 10
2 Psalm 27:4 (KJV)
3 A. W. Tozer anyone?
4 Hosea 6:3 (NASB)
5 See Exodus 19:21–23 and 24:1–2
6 Hebrews 10:19–22
7 Philippians 3:10, my amplified notes
8 Acts 16:16–40
9 2 Corinthians 11:25
10 Philippians 3:7–8 my loose, yet poignant paraphrase
11 Isaiah 40:31
12 Depth of field is photography talk. It speaks of the front-to-back range (close-up or far away) of an image that's either in focus or blurred.
13 2 Corinthians 5:14–15
14 English translation of words from Gustav Mahler's 3rd symphony
15 Via Dolorosa, the street in ancient Jerusalem Jesus is said to have walked carrying His cross to Golgotha.
16 https://www.youtube.com/watch?v=eL8T5R-jwj0
http://www1.cbn.com/jim-caviezel-talks-about-playing-christ-passion
17 2 Corinthians 5:14
18 Don't forget Nicodemus who first came to Jesus by night (John 3:1) and many of the rulers who kept a low profile for fear of the unbelieving Pharisees (John 12:42).
19 Again 2 Corinthians 5:14
20 NASB
21 ESV
22 KJV
23 Philippians 3:8
24 By glitter and glitz, I mean rank and prestige, not specifically glamorous high life.
25 Back at you with Philippians 3:8

Chapter 55

1 Jeremiah 31:34 and Hebrews 8:11
2 Chapter 5
3 John 15:1–11
4 Revelation 2:4. Abandon is correct.
5 Revelation 2:5
6 Acts 2:42–47
7 Revelation 3:15–20
8 Revelation 2:5
9 Romans 6:1–2 lead in to the foundation and substance of grace.
10 1 Corinthians 2:2
11 John 4:10
12 John 1:17
13 Romans 3:19 and 13:10
14 Philippians 3:6
15 Some suggest the Paul we see and hear in Romans 7 is the unregenerate Pharisee. I respectfully disagree. Paul BC is the man described in Philippians 3:6 who measured himself against the Law with a nod of approval, as did his phylactery-laden cohorts. "O wretched man that I am" (v. 24) sums this one-time Pharisee up after Jesus steps to cast a decidedly different light on Paul's own self-effort.
16 Read Matthew 5–7 then shoot over to 11:25–30' although, it wouldn't hurt to read straight through.
17 "I Could Never Promise You" by Don Francisco on his album *Forgiven*
18 ibid.

Chapter 56

1 1 Corinthians 11:23–24
2 1 Corinthians 11:23, my paraphrase
3 Acts 2:23 and 4:27–28
4 Luke 22:2
5 Psalm 41:9

6 Figuratively speaking, Eden was a place where life was presented in terms of trust and obedience. Jesus, as the last Adam, found Himself fixed in the serpent's crosshairs by one of His own disciples who stood in such close proximity to a new humanity.

7 2 Samuel 15:12 and Psalm 55:12–15

8 Psalm 109:2b NASB)

9 Psalm 109:8b and Acts 1:20

10 From *A Treasury of David*

11 Matthew 26:24

12 Mark 8:37

13 Hebrews 12:16

14 Exodus 19:8

15 Exodus 32:1–6

16 John 1:11 in conjunction with Matthew 27:18

17 Matthew 21:12–13

18 Exodus 21:32

19 Zechariah 11:13

20 Matthew 9:36

21 John 15:13

22 Romans 5:5

23 Matthew 26:24, my paraphrase

24 Luke 22:3

25 Luke 22:22, Acts 2:23

Chapter 57

1 Luke 22:15 (KJV)

2 John 15:5

3 John 15:4 and 9

4 Luke 22:19 and Matthew 26:38 (NLT)

5 1 Corinthians 11:25

6 In his classic, *The Screwtape Letters*, Mr. Lewis lays out a fictional correspondence between two demons—uncle Screwtape and nephew Wormwood, the older mentoring the younger. Scripture never alludes to generations of angels or demons, as in younger

and older, but that's not the point. The interplay between two satanic minions provides more insight and understanding on the subject of spiritual warfare and demonology than many lectures on systematic theology. And it's enjoyable reading.

7   John 12:6

8   John 13:27

9   1 Samuel 18:1–4 and 20:8–17

10 Joshua 9:3–15

11 Again chapter 15, endnote 20

12 Romans 5:12

13 1 Corinthians 15:45 speaks to distinctly different humanities—one in Adam, the other in Christ.

14 Allow me a little humor in drawing from Sir Arthur Conan Doyle's fictional Sherlock Holmes and his oft puzzled sidekick, Dr. Watson, who were forever tagged in question-answer games.

15 Mark 8:27, my paraphrase

16 Matthew 16:16

17 Matthew 13:14–15 and the overarching principle in Revelation 2:7, 11, 17, 29 and 3:6, 13, 22

18 Matthew 16:17 and 1 Corinthians 2:9–14

19 Matthew 15:14

Chapter 58

1   Which is exactly how the elite of Jesus's day would have seen it.

2   Acts 7:54–60 and 8:1–4

3   John 3:3–5

4   John 17:3

5   Hebrews 8:8–9 and Jeremiah 31:32

6   Isaiah 54:13 and Hebrews 8:11

7   ibid.

8   Philippians 3:12 (NASB)

9   Ephesians 4:13 (NASB)

Chapter 59

1. John 12:24
2. 1 Timothy 1:15
3. Philippians 3:10
4. Galatians 2:20
5. ibid.
6. Ephesians 2:8
7. Romans 7:15, the latter part—my paraphrase
8. Romans 7:18 again, my paraphrase
9. Matthew 11:25
10. Matthew 18:3
11. 2 Corinthians 12:9, my paraphrase
12. Faith "in," as opposed to faith "of" the Son of God are equally appropriate renderings of Galatians 2:20. Most contemporary translations use "in" while the KJV and Young's Literal Translation use "of."

Chapter 60

1. Matthew 26:39
2. Genesis 22:2 (KJV)
3. Mt. Moriah being the place God instructed Abraham to sacrifice his son, Isaac.
4. Matthew 11:30
5. Matthew 7:14 (KJV)
6. Matthew 6:21
7. 1 Peter 1:8
8. 2 Peter 1:4
9. From the mid 1800s hymn "I Love to Tell the Story," the old, old story of Jesus and His love.
10. Galatians 2:20
11. Galatians 2:20 again
12. John 19:30. The term translated "It is finished" in English was used by accountants of the day to communicate the concept of a debt being completely paid up.

[13] Jeremiah 17:5 (NLT)

[14] 1 Corinthians 15:45b

[15] In this sense, I'm speaking of heady academic types who pontificate from on high in white lofty towers.

[16] See Colossians 1:24

Chapter 61

[1] Genesis 3:15

[2] Read Romans 4 and 9 then go to Galatians 3:16.

[3] Hence their choosenness

[4] Romans 11:26

[5] 1 Peter 2:8

[6] Acts 1:8

[7] 1 Peter 4:12, my paraphrase

[8] T. Austin-Sparks—transcribed from a spoken message given in February 1959

[9] 1 Corinthians 15:31

[10] 2 Corinthians 11:23–28

[11] My paraphrase based on *The Normal Christian Life* by Watchman Nee, pp. 64-65 Copyright © Angus I. Kinnear 1957 by Gospel Literature Service, Bombay, India American edition 1977 by Tyndale House Publishers, Inc., Wheaton, Illinois 60187 ISBN 0-8423-4710-0

[12] As popular as it has become, I've not been able to find the expression 'dying to self' in Scripture. Jesus speaks of denying one's self (Matthew 16:23–25, Luke 9:23) as it pertains to any and all who would "come after Me," and there are any number of references to a believer's co-crucifixion with Christ but not dying to self. Coming to Christ is the call to self-denial and taking up one's cross, as Dietrich Bonhoeffer so aptly noted. "When Christ calls a man, he bids him come and die." Paul's assertion, "I die daily" expresses his own very real conviction that each and every day his life was on the line. Each dawn might be his last. Each day then becomes a reckoning on our co-crucifixion, a believer's affirming one's true position in Him.

[13] Romans 6:11

Chapter 62

1. John 10:10, my paraphrase
2. Galatians 3:16
3. John 5:46 and Luke 24:44
4. 1 Peter 1:10–11
5. Hebrews 3:19
6. Exodus 20:3
7. Exodus 24:3
8. ibid., my paraphrase
9. Hebrews 8:8a
10. Hebrews 12:20–21
11. Meaning Abraham, Isaac, and Jacob
12. Exodus 6:4–5
13. Hebrews 8:8a
14. Matthew 26:41
15. Hebrews 12:29
16. A consideration we covered in chapter 12.
17. Exodus 1:6–8
18. 1 Kings 8:23
19. Exodus 19:4, my paraphrase
20. Isaiah 44:6–8

Chapter 63

1. Romans 5:20
2. Jeremiah 17:9
3. DOC is the department of corrections.
4. Jeremiah 29:1–10
5. 2 Timothy 4:3
6. Proverbs 3:5, my paraphrase
7. Deuteronomy 12:8 and Judges 21:25
8. Jeremiah 29:12
9. Jeremiah 29:13

10 Larry Crabb, *Shattered Dreams*, p.1 WaterBrook Press 2375 Telstar Drive, Colorado Springs, CO 80920 Copyright 2001 ISBN 1-57856-506-5.
11 Romans 6:16
12 John 8: 32–36
13 Romans 6:7
14 Galatians 2:20, Romans 6:7, and Ephesians 2:8–9

Chapter 64

1 Luke 15:11–32
2 Psalm 137:2
3 A summary of thoughts from Ezekiel 36, verses 18 and 19
4 Genesis 17:8
5 Ezekiel 36:17 (NASB)
6 ibid.
7 Romans 11:29
8 Ezekiel 36:22, my paraphrase
9 Taken from Shakespeare's Hamlet "To be, or not to be" soliloquy.
10 Psalm 24:1
11 John 3:16 generally speaking and Revelation 5:9 specifically
12 Try 2 Kings 19:19 and Malachi 1:11 for starters
13 Romeo and Juliet
14 Matthew 7:15–23

Chapter 65

1 Luke 9:57–62
2 See Isaiah 1:10–17
3 Matthew 21:13, but reflect back on Isaiah 1:10–17
4 "Fish" are new arrivals in prison.
5 The LORD's people speak directly to Him who is effectively tied to the Hebrew nation, as I Am (the LORD) has chosen to identify Himself with them.
6 Ezekiel 36:20b
7 Deuteronomy 6:5 (NASB)

[8] Proverbs 3:5

[9] Acts 17:28. A pagan said that!

[10] Colossians 1:17

[11] Galatians 5:7

[12] 2 Corinthians 5:14 and 1 John 4:19

[13] Matthew 6:21, my paraphrase

[14] Ezekiel 36:20, my paraphrase

[15] An Adamic twist on things that puts man in the center.

[16] In 1 Corinthians 10:20, Paul shoots straight. Sacrifices offered to pagan idols is demon worship.

[17] A. W. Tozer, *The Knowledge of the Holy*, p.1 Harper San Francisco, HarperCollins Publishers, 10 East 53rd Street, New York, NY 10022 ISBN 0-06-068412-7.

[18] Isaiah 6:3

[19] Genesis 15:6 and Romans 4:3

[20] Isaiah 6:5b

[21] 1 Corinthians 2:14

[22] Exodus 20:18–19, Hebrews 12:18–19, and Exodus 33:18

[23] American writer Max Ehrmann's "Desiderata," or desired things, was written in 1927 and published in a variety of venues over the years. The copyright, I believe, is forfeit, making the poem public domain.

[24] Exodus 33:18–20

[25] John 1:18

Chapter 66

[1] Ezekiel 36:23

[2] Isaiah 6:3

[3] Louis Berkhof, *Systematic Theology*, section 2 p. 44 WM B Eerdmans Publishing Company, Grand Rapids, MI 1932, 1938, 1996 ISBN 978-0-8028-3820-9.

[4] Exodus 33:20

[5] Matthew 12:34

About the Author

Dan's focus is a gut-level, in the trenches approach to discipleship, engaging folks in hopes of discovering the reality of "This is eternal life, that they might know You the only true God and Jesus Christ whom You have sent" (John 17:3, NASB). Genuine intimacy, through the finished work of the cross. It's with this in mind that Dan and his wife, Bonnie, started Hook Ministries in January of 2002, pouring into those having hearts to pour into others. Who would have guessed that God would see this worked out in housing units and on the yards in many of Colorado's state prisons?

Contact at:
P.O. Box 25265
Colorado Springs, CO 80936-5265
Email: dan.hookmin@gmail.com